THE MYTH OF THE GOOD CORPORATE CITIZEN

DEMOCRACY UNDER THE RULE OF BIG BUSINESS

Murray Dobbin

D1473817

Stoddart

Published in Fall 1998 by Stoddart Publishing Co. Limited
34 Lesmill Road, Toronto, Canada M3B 2T6
Tel. (416) 445-3333   Fax (416) 445-5967
Email customer.service@ccmailgw.genpub.com

Hardcover edition published by Stoddart Publishing in Spring 1998

Distributed in Canada by:
General Distribution Services Ltd.
325 Humber College Boulevard, Toronto, Canada M9W 7C3
Tel. (416) 213-1919   Fax (416) 213-1917
Email customer.service@ccmailgw.genpub.com

Distributed in the United States by:
General Distribution Services Inc.
85 River Rock Drive, Suite 202, Buffalo, New York 14207
Toll-free Tel. 1-800-805-1083   Toll-free Fax 1-800-481-6207
Email gdsinc@genpub.com

02   01   00   99   2   3   4   5

Canadian Cataloguing in Publication Data

Dobbin, Murray, 1945–
The myth of the good corporate citizen: democracy under the rule of big business

Includes bibliographical references and index.
ISBN 0-7737-3087-7 (bound)   ISBN 0-7737-6036-9 (pbk.)

1. Business and politics — Canada.
2. International business enterprises — Political aspects — Canada.
3. Democracy — Canada. I. Title.

HD3616.C32D62 1998   322'.3'0971   C98-930280-6

Research Associate: Ellen Gould

Cover Design: Bill Douglas @ The Bang
Text Design: Tannice Goddard

Printed and bound in Canada

We acknowledge for their financial support of our publishing program the Government of Canada through the Book Publishing Industry Development Program (BPIDP), the Canada Council, and the Ontario Arts Council.

CONTENTS

ACKNOWLEDGEMENTS

As with other books I have written, this is work of political intervention, as much a part of my involvement in social justice politics as of my work as an activist. In this sense, there are too many people to acknowledge for their contributions, intended or otherwise. However, I will mention a few.

The conclusion that this book needed to be written was the result of many years fighting the initiatives of provincial and federal governments, fights involving many thousands of Canadians. As we struggled against free trade and NAFTA, the GST, cuts to social programs, and privatization, a number of activists began to focus predominately on the fact that while government was implementing these policies, it was corporations that initiated them. Working this realization through to an evolving analysis with Maude Barlow, Ed Finn, Tony Clarke, David Robinson, David Langille, Jim Turk, and others has led to this book and, as well, I hope, to the beginnings of a new democratic politics. I thank these friends and colleagues for their insights and their commitment to anti-corporate work.

ACKNOWLEDGEMENTS

I am also indebted to others who helped in a variety of ways, from reading chapters, providing information, to helping with particular points of analysis. These include Jim Grieschaber-Otto, Jack Warnock, John Dillon, Duncan Cameron, Seth Klein, and Gil Yaron. I have leaned heavily on the work of others in the writing of this book. I am deeply indebted, for their contributions in exposing corporate power, to David Korten, Richard Barnet, John Cavanagh, William Greider, and Allan Engler.

Living with someone writing a book is like caring for someone with a chronic illness. I thank Ellen Gould, my partner, for her excellent advice, her assistance on the book — and her forbearance.

I dedicate this book to the memory of my parents: to my father, whose "downsizing" by Eaton's after twenty-five years as a dedicated employee was the seed of my activism, and to my mother, whose unfailing sense of right and wrong have helped to guide it.

MURRAY DOBBIN
Vancouver, B.C.

INTRODUCTION:
HOW DID THINGS
GET THIS BAD?

As Canadians approach the millennium we find ourselves in a world dominated at every turn by large corporations — banks, trust companies, transnationals, corporations involved in currency speculation, corporations that buy and sell government bonds, corporate agencies like bond rating companies that pronounce on government policies. Virtually every aspect of our lives is dominated by these huge corporations: what we buy and who we work for (or whether we work at all), the information we receive, the entertainment we "consume," and the physical environment that surrounds us. And as corporate control increases, the control we used to exercise over those areas of our lives, collectively or individually, diminishes. Corporate domination, brazen, ruthless, ever more powerful, is evident everywhere as civilization seems to devolve in its path.

The values of what we normally understand as civilization are swept aside by the new corporate imperative and its accompanying ideology. Thousands of years of human development and progress are reduced to the pursuit of "efficiency," our collective will is declared meaningless compared to the values of the marketplace, and communitarian values are rejected in favour of the survival of the fittest. A thinly disguised barbarism now passes for, is in fact promoted as, a global human objective. It is not only the best we can expect; it is the goal we should be seeking.

We are increasingly dependent, directly and indirectly, on large corporations for our jobs, for the kinds of jobs we have, and for how well they pay even if we do not work for them. Governments are (or say they are) prevented from passing progressive public policy because of corporate power; we watch, seemingly helpless, as corporations downsize, move jobs off-shore, and in general do whatever they please. And do it with virtual impunity because, well, business is their business. But more particularly because corporations have the status, rights, and protection of super-citizens.

Increasingly, we experience corporate power through the actions of the so-called global corporate citizen. With its awesome rights and powers, this artificial citizen can ignore national borders, national citizenship, and the rights and obligations of real flesh-and-blood citizens. This is a true ruling elite, a few hundred corporate citizens with more power than most nations, who rule the world and accumulate riches and power like the wealthiest of families run amok.

Real citizens are asked to sacrifice everything because corporations say we must. We must sit by as mere observers, wringing our hands while our most precious communitarian creations — medicare, public education, a protected environment — are eroded because collecting sufficient taxes to pay for these things will make us (in the lexicon, we become indistinguishable from corporations) "uncompetitive." These erosions are inevitable, we are told, and the destruction of the nation is somehow akin to an act of God: terrible in its consequences but irresistible. Indeed, we are told by the pundits that to resist is not only irresponsible, not only futile, but just as irrational as trying to command the skies to produce rain.

Not only do corporations want more — more cuts to their taxes, more cuts to UI and pension premiums, ever greater cuts to social programs, more repeals of environmental laws and protections for workers' health and safety, and more and better ways to squeeze more from their employees. They revel in their power and reward themselves obscenely for their success in bullying their employees, citizens, and governments into letting them have their way with our country or any other they choose. It is as if this abuse of power was a reflection of ability, even genius. Indeed, inside the corporate culture the more ruthless a CEO is in dealing with expendable employees, the higher the esteem in which he is held and the more he is paid.

Corporate spokesmen are the loudest voices for cutting deficits by cutting social spending, a brazen demand given that billions in revenue that would help pay for social programs are lost every year through corporate tax evasion, avoidance, outright fraud, and tax breaks. CEOs of 63,000 corporations making $13 billion in profits and paying no taxes clamour for ever greater cuts to welfare and medicare.

These corporate chiefs can afford to be brazen because through their media conglomerates, the free-market political parties, and think-tanks they fund, they have come to dominate the political debate in Canada and even the language with which we conduct that debate. So complicit is the media in popularizing this dominant ideology that anyone who describes a different take on reality is dismissed as a crank, out of touch, or, even worse, a "special interest." Only corporations whose lobbying is for one thing and one thing only — more and more money for shareholders, CEOs, and assorted courtiers — are not a vested interest.

Much of the increased power of corporations in Canada has developed with the advent of the Free Trade Agreement and NAFTA, deals with the United States and Mexico that had little to do with trade but are in reality corporate bills of rights. These deals give rights to corporate "citizens," rights to profit from investment with ever decreasing obligations to employees, community, environment, and consumers. These deals give corporations political rights by making it possible for them to stop governments from acting in ways that might affect their profits or growth. In vast areas of public policy, conflict between the interests of citizens and corporations is decided in favour of corporations by laws that are unchangeable by Parliament, unchallengeable in court. And there is more on the way.

We watch as many of our governments (those institutions that supposedly speak for us) grovel at the feet of corporations, passing and repealing laws to suit their new masters, or begging them to come to this or that province, gleefully offering up as sacrifices the communities they represent: low-waged workers, low or no taxes, interest-free loans, free land, cheap water and energy. Our governments have not yet offered our first-born but it might take such an offer to surprise anyone, given how subservient many of our elected representatives have become and how passive most citizens seem to be.

Thus we saw then New Brunswick premier Frank McKenna giddily grinning out at us from the pages of the *Globe and Mail* like some second-string used-car salesman desperate for a sale: "Act now! Give me a call." Why invest in New Brunswick? "Reduced workers' compensation costs: one more reason New Brunswick is Canada's best place to do business . . . and the best place for your bottom line." Phone 1-800-McKenna and, the ad implied, Brian would answer. "Open for business. Always." As if this wasn't enough, McKenna established a special zone where corporations have even fewer obligations. A kind of northern *maquiladoras*.

Who is responsible for this sorry state of affairs? As this book documents, the huge transnational corporations, the corporate super-citizens, have redesigned the planet and its economic system. The political elites of the developed world and the institutions they control have been complicit in this transformation. They have implemented an enormous transfer of power from government — that is, from citizens — to corporations. The media, corporate think-tanks, political parties, universities, and other institutions that we created to serve and even define civil society have instead betrayed it.

Ultimately, in a democracy the people who are responsible are its citizens. If their institutions fail them it is the responsibility of citizens to reform those institutions or create new ones that will do the job. Ironically, in the past fifty years we have collectively gone through a process of first creating such institutions and then watching them fail us. The other side of the seizure of power by corporate citizens is the ceding of that power by flesh-and-blood citizens. Comfortable in the thought that we had made progress, and believing or hoping that progress was assured, too many Canadians became observers instead of citizens. We forgot our history.

We are so accustomed to corporations and their power that we forget that they are our creation. Governments passed and continue to pass laws that give corporations their legal right to exist and behave the way they do. They are not aliens amongst us, created by forces beyond our control. To be sure, they behave as virtual aliens, demanding the rights of citizenship while refusing the responsibilities. But it is citizens, through governments, who created them and allowed them, bit by bit, to become what they are. And it is citizens who can, if they choose, change the laws to remake corporations and remove the citizen rights they enjoy.

We have also forgotten how we first achieved the things we are now losing. None of these community institutions was simply given to us by benign governments and good corporate citizens. The struggles of hundreds of thousands of men and women — citizens — in labour movements, farm movements, and social organizations made democracy real at a time when many of them did not know where their next meal was coming from. For them democracy was a process to be engaged in, not an institution to revere in the abstract and then blame for its failures.

Because the practice of democracy in Canada has become so truncated, and the language of participation so impoverished, the notion that the things we cherish are the result of citizen participation has largely been lost. The social and psychological distance between citizen and government has become so great that the notion of government as an expression of community is weaker now than at any time in the post-war period.

For too many people political citizenship is an afterthought or, at best, is reduced to brief and alienated participation in electoral rituals. Maybe we got into this habit because we believed medicare, public education, a full-time job, and a future for our children would always be secure. These things are our right. But as corporations prove every day, rights, like democracy, are a process, not an institution. As a community, as citizens, we haven't caught up with the new reality.

At its root democracy is a constant struggle for rule by the majority. Just saying those words implies what we instinctively know: most of the time it is a minority that rules. The increasing domination of huge corporations, the advent of so-called globalization, is just the current expression of the historic contest between social classes over the distribution of wealth and power.

We can't know where we are going if we don't know where we

came from. That is the thought that motivated the writing of this book. As citizens we are faced with a crisis greater than any since the Great Depression, and there are good reasons to believe this one is far greater. The consequences of not accepting the challenge of this crisis will be catastrophic. We have no choice. Either we change the world by becoming active citizens or we watch our world descend into a barbarism that is inherent in the amoral nature of the transnational corporations and their manic drive for wealth at any cost.

In the first part of this book I look at what has happened and what is likely to happen to the world as transnational corporations gain ever more power over our lives. In the second part of the book I examine just how the corporations, and those who benefit from their power and wealth, accomplished the neo-conservative counter-revolution that is now evident all around us.

The assault on democracy and equality by corporations and those who benefit from their power is couched in such terms as *globalization* for good reason. It creates an atmosphere of inevitability. We can, by this definition of reality, do nothing but attempt to adapt to the predetermined course of history. Globalization is like the Borg. We will be assimilated. Resistance is futile. But of course history teaches us that the only thing that is inevitable is change. What kind of change depends on the kind of people making it.

The social madness inherent in the drive for ever greater growth and profits, and its parallel creation of crushing poverty worldwide, will have a fearsome backlash. It could be chaotic, violent, and self-destructive or it could be enormously creative, rebuilding towards a truly egalitarian and ecologically sustainable world. The former is a virtual certainty if real citizens don't consciously direct the response to the corporate destruction of civil society. For this to happen there will have to be a revolution in citizen consciousness and a massive increase in participation in democratic politics.

This self-conscious citizenship has to include an explicit rejection of the logic of modern mass consumerism, the exchange of our rights and obligations as citizens for rights as consumers of global products. Democracy in the new millennium will be either the democracy of the customer — one dollar, one vote — or the democracy of the conscious, deliberate, self-aware citizen.

1

GLOBALIZATION AND THE RISE OF THE TRANSNATIONAL CORPORATION

Since trade ignores national boundaries and the
manufacturers insist on having the world as a market . . .
the doors of the nations which are closed against him must be
battered down. Concessions obtained by financiers must
be safeguarded by ministers of state, even if the sovereignty
of unwilling nations be outraged in the process.
— WOODROW WILSON, 1907

Globalization is one those words (like *deficit*) so loaded with ambiguous meaning, so packed with propaganda value, and so symbolic of modern-day angst that it carries with it the whole story of our current social and economic life. So much of what causes our anxiety about the economy, social programs, and the future of our children is encompassed by it. The dictates of the "global economy" imply that we simply have to accept all the misery, as if there was some uncontrollable source of the decline of the civil society in which we are all a part of, regardless of social class.

Globalization has a will-of-God dimension to it. It is presented to us as at once all-powerful, incomprehensible, impossibly complex, seemingly unchallengeable, and, on top of that, unprecedented. It is

as if globalization is a new phenomenon and not just the latest muta-
tion of capitalism. Nothing like this has ever happened before. It is
unique. None of what we knew before, none of the solutions, none
of the understanding, is of any use to us. Before this juggernaut, even
our values are swept aside as impractical, unachievable, naive, archaic.
Those who resist this vision of the future are dismissed as children.
All of this conveniently lends itself to a portrayal of the new world
order as inevitable.

Globalization is also conveniently class-neutral and effectively
obscures the fact that what we are really talking about is the power
of capital that is increasingly concentrated in the hands of transnational corporations. That globalization happens to benefit the top 15
to 20 percent of the world's population, that it has produced thousands of millionaires and hundreds of billionaires is rarely referred to.
Like the deficit, which is now being paid back by those who can least
afford it rather than by those who created it, globalization as an idea
serves the most powerful extremely well. With virtually the entire
political elite saying we simply must adapt, those who benefit from
globalization hope they can enjoy the spoils of unrestrained capitalism without worrying about a revolt of the dispossessed.

But of course nothing is inevitable in the rich and complex universe
of human relations, except change itself. Globalization is no more a
"natural" phenomenon than electronic banking. Dissect it and you
find that it has a history consisting of thousands of decisions, some
unconsciously contributing to the whole and others explicitly creating
the conditions for the advance of the global economy and the transnational corporations that direct it.

The deceptive neutrality of globalization and its effective use as an
ideological tool mask the powerful reality of the domination of the
world by a few hundred enormously powerful transnational corporations, or TNCs. It is these corporations, many American and backed
by American might, which are global in character and reach, and the
part of the world economy they dominate is likewise enormous. But
it is also true that billions of people are completely excluded from this
TNC economy even though, precisely because they are excluded,
their lives are profoundly affected by it.

While transnational corporations have benefited enormously from the ideology of inevitability that the notion of globalization provides, governments, too, have profited. Far from being helpless and outmoded entities facing a threat from without, the nation-states of the developed world are directly responsible for creating the agencies and institutions that have permitted TNCs to accumulate their unprecedented global power. To be sure, governments often find themselves working at cross purposes, responding to the needs of citizens (to the extent that they must to get re-elected) and of corporations. But the "global economy" could not have developed and TNCs could not have accumulated their power without the cooperation and complicity of governments. The so-called downsizing of governments is restricted to ordinary citizens. For the largest corporations in the world, the most powerful corporate citizens, governments are becoming more active, more interventionist, not smaller but much larger.

TRANSNATIONAL CORPORATIONS: SEEKING "FREEDOM"

The imperative of globalization and its principal agents, the TNCs, is the gradual elimination of all restrictions on capital investment and claims on the profits from that investment. Corporations have been seeking such freedom from the time they were conceived. Restrictions on the investment of capital from environmental regulation and labour law to taxation and requirements to create jobs are for corporations the costs of doing business and as such are to be eliminated. The more restrictions you eliminate, the bigger your profits.

Although the popularization of the idea of the global corporation is recent, corporations and their political servants have been fantasizing about total corporate freedom for decades. George Ball, the U.S. undersecretary of state for economic affairs, stated in 1967: "The political boundaries of nation-states are too narrow and constricted to define the scope and activities of the modern business . . . By and large, those companies that have achieved a global vision of their operations tend to opt for a world in which not only goods but all factors of production can shift with maximum freedom."[1]

Thirty years later, that global "vision," the dream of corporate domination, is close to being a reality for the largest corporations. The sheer power of the TNC today is breathtaking. American researchers

Sarah Anderson and John Cavanagh in their book *The Top 200: The Rise of Global Corporate Power* give graphic evidence of the economic power of TNCs. Of the one hundred largest economies in the world, fifty-one are now corporations. Wal-Mart, number twelve on the list, is larger than 161 countries; in other words, its gross revenue is greater than the total wealth, or gross domestic product, of any of these countries. General Motors is larger than Denmark, Ford is bigger than South Africa, and Toyota surpasses Norway. Canada ranks number eight. The largest ten corporations had revenues in 1991 exceeding the combined GDPs of the hundred smallest countries. Put another way, the two hundred largest corporations have more economic clout than the poorest four-fifths of humanity.[2]

Although we have been accustomed over the years to identify multinational and transnational corporations with the U.S., it turns out that the largest TNCs are no longer U.S.-based. Only three of the top ten corporations are American, while six are Japanese. All but fourteen of the Top 200 are headquartered in just six countries: the U.S., Japan, Germany, France, the U.K., the Netherlands. Of the Global Fortune 500 corporations, the U.S. is home to 153, Japan to 141. Canada counts six amongst the 500.[3]

And while the Top 200 have sales that account for 28.3 percent of the world's GDP, the percentage of the jobs they account for is minuscule in comparison. Out of a worldwide paid workforce of approximately 2.6 billion, the Top 200 TNCs employ 18.8 million, less than three-quarters of 1 percent of the world's workforce.[4]

When just five firms control more than half of the global market, economists consider that market to be highly monopolistic. The *Economist* recently listed twelve industrial sectors that demonstrate this highly monopolistic pattern. In consumer durables, the top five corporations control 70 percent of the global market; in the automotive, airline, aerospace, electronic components, electrical/electronics, and steel sector, the top five control more than 50 percent. Other sectors show equally strong monopolistic tendencies, including oil, personal computers, and media, where control of more than 40 percent of the respective world markets rests with five or fewer corporations.[5]

Monopolistic markets are nothing new; they have existed in developed countries since the 1970s. In the U.S. in that decade, one to four firms controlled 75 percent or more of the market in more than a dozen product areas. In Canada in 1991, according to Allan Engler in *Apostles of Greed*, "ten non-financial corporations accounted for more than one-fifth of the GDP. These were Bell Canada, G.M., Ford Canada, Canadian Pacific, Imperial Oil, Alcan, Chrysler, George Weston, Noranda and Thomson Corporation."[6]

In food retailing, the independent operator is a relic. The corner grocer has been replaced by 7-Elevens and Mac's and the local drug store by huge chains. George Weston owns Loblaws, Super Valu, and Real Canadian Superstores and the largest bakery chain in the country. The Weston empire shares the domination of the retail food business with U.S.-owned Safeway Corporation.

The monopolization of retail business is not always so obvious. How many shoppers have heard of Dylex? Not many unless they are also investors. Yet any given mall in Canada and other countries might have as many as ten outlets owned by this transnational giant, shops such as Tip Top, Harry Rosen, Big Steel, Fairweather, Suzy Shier, Town and Country, Club Monaco, Alfred Sung, Biway and Thriftys.[7]

This illusion of choice and competition is repeated in supermarkets. Although the aisles are full of hundreds of brand names, the truth is that a mere handful of companies produce the vast majority. In Canada these are Weston, Labatt, and McCain, and internationally, Nestlé and Unilever. And it is going to get much worse. Corporations are still merging at an incredible rate, and it was predicted in 1990 that the largest six hundred would become the world's largest three hundred by 2000, the same year that the international banks will merge into ten banking giants to form an elite cabal that will control the banking industry worldwide.[8]

THE MYTH OF THE FREE MARKET

Surveying this incredible concentration of economic power, and control of markets nationally and globally, exposes the sheer nonsense of any talk about competitive markets, the free market, the free enterprise system, and the critical economic role of the entrepreneurial spirit. The notion that the attraction of real investors and businesspeople to market ideology leads them to enjoy the excitement of competition flies in the face of everyday business practice. For flesh-and-blood owners, their worst enemy is uncertainty. And competition embodies uncertainty.

Corporations, particularly large ones, expend enormous effort to eliminate competition and avoid risk and uncertainty. David Korten writes in *When Corporations Rule the World*: "In a globalizing market, the widespread image is one of the corporate titans of Japan, North America, and Europe battling it out toe-to-toe in international markets. This image is increasingly a fiction that obscures the extent to which a few core corporations are strengthening their collective monopoly market power through joint ventures and strategic alliances with their major rivals."[9]

These TNCs, Korten says, share "access to special expertise, technology, production facilities, and markets; spread the costs and risks of research and new product development; and manage the competitive relationships with their major rivals."[10] The auto industry is a prime example, with Chrysler owning parts of Mitsubishi, Maserati, and Fiat; Ford owning 25 percent of Mazda; and GM having a 37.5 percent stake in Isuzu. The same alliances, joint ventures, and cooperation prevail in computer hardware and software, aerospace, pharmaceuticals, telecommunications, defence, electronics, and many others. The 1997 collaboration between Apple Computers and Bill Gates's Microsoft didn't surprise investment gurus at all.

Risk avoidance at the level of the global corporation absorbs a huge amount of effort because it pays off. And only huge corporations can successfully engage in such activity. When we hear corporate CEOs talk about the need to be ever larger in order to be globally competitive, what they really mean is they need to be gigantic in order to ensure monopoly control of their markets and gain enough clout to engage in the modern-day version of collusion.

What most TNCs are now doing is not new. It was pioneered at the turn of the century by what Allan Engler calls the technological monopolies. Westinghouse, GE, and Bell realized that they could not take full advantage of their innovations so long as they were competing in court over hundreds of patent suits. As a result, Engler writes, GE and Westinghouse "decided to pool their patents and divide the growing electrical business among themselves: 62.5 percent was assigned to GE and 37.5 percent to Westinghouse. In 1920 Bell joined the cartel."[11]

The widespread operation of free markets received its death notice with industrialization. With mechanized production came socialized labour. Since that time capital has been in the process of increasingly collectivizing itself in giant national and transnational corporations. The allocation of capital, labour, technology, and raw materials, theoretically accomplished by the invisible hand of the market, is ideology at its grandest. The market has long since been replaced by the administrative coordination of corporate managers. The transnational corporation is simply taking that administrative process to its logical conclusion. As Korten describes it:

> Central management buys, sells, dismantles, or closes component units as it chooses, moves production units around the world at will, decides what revenues will be given up by subordinate units to the parent corporation, appoints and fires managers of subsidiaries, sets transfer prices and other terms governing transactions among the firm's component organizations, and decides whether individual units can make purchases on the open market or must do business with other units of the firm.[12]

The propensity of corporate spokesmen, business columnists, and free-market think-tanks to engage in ideological hyperbole in favour of free markets and rail against state planning is amusing given the extent to which country-size corporations plan their "economies." Indeed, no country, short of the former Soviet Union with its command economy, comes even close to the command structures and decision-making power of the modern TNC.

Management guru Peter Drucker argues: "There is a remarkably close parallel between General Motors' scheme of organization and those of the two institutions most renowned for administrative efficiency: that of the Catholic Church and that of the modern army." Drucker says that the industrial corporations of the nineteenth century adopted the structure of the U.S. Armory at Springfield, Massachusetts. "CEOs played the role of general; below them senior managers commanded corporate divisions; junior managers commanded departments.

Foremen and supervisors were non-commissioned officers."[13] The top-down hierarchies that resulted from the collectivization of capital are as bureaucratic as any government department. The main difference with large corporations is that they are not accountable to the millions of people whose lives they affect. They are equally hierarchical and far more authoritarian.

The modern transnational corporation has taken the historic efforts to control markets, technology, and capital to heights never before imagined. One of the strategies of the super-corporation is to rid itself of as much risk as possible by contracting it out to smaller firms. Instead of internalizing the costs of doing business, the sign of a genuinely free-market economy, the global corporation does its best to externalize them.

U.S. agribusiness is a good example. Rather than have huge production facilities themselves, like the plantations of the past, the large corporations download the risk to smaller producers. The large firms have almost complete control of the market and therefore can dictate conditions to individual producers, no matter how large. Even as early as 1980 the percentage of U.S. farm production controlled by marketing contracts to huge buyers was 95 percent in milk, 89 percent of chickens, 85 percent of processed vegetables, and 80 percent of all seed crops.[14]

Under true competition thousands of buyers and sellers determined the price of each good. Today, as a result of corporately administered markets, the producer gets less and the consumer pays more than the free market would have dictated. This is true as well in developing countries, where the huge banana plantations of the past have been largely replaced by dozens of "independent" producers who are in fact dependent on one large buyer that has externalized the risks of production and restricts its activity to processing and marketing.

The *Economist* magazine, one of the most prominent cheerleaders for globalization, has actually suggested that the TNCs, already creating semifeudal relationships worldwide, go the last step in risk avoidance: don't produce anything, just rent out the "right" to produce. Those who have exclusive control over patented technologies would set a price for renting the patent to producers at a price equal to what they would have made if they had done the work themselves.[15]

But the ultimate transnational will look quite different, and the connections already developing between the corporate giants are the likely harbinger of the future. According to management consultant Cyrus Friedheim the world economy will become dominated by what he calls the relationship-enterprise. Rather than a single corporate entity the relationship-enterprise would be a continuously adapting network of strategic and tactical alliances. These alliances could be geographic, technological, or within sectors.

Friedheim gives as an example talks between the largest aerospace companies — Boeing, McDonnell Douglas, and Airbus, and Mitsubishi, Kawasaki, and Fuji — about a joint project to build a new super-jumbo jet. Such relationship-enterprises would dwarf anything seen today and could easily have revenues exceeding a trillion dollars. The Apple/Microsoft alliance fits this relationship-enterprise model as well. This is the model for the largest corporation in history.

MULTINATIONALS VERSUS TRANSNATIONALS

Today's TNCs are described as being separate from nation-states, in conflict with them and operating independently of state actions. As will be shown throughout this book, this is a convenient fiction. The TNCs are largely the creations of dominant nation-states and the agencies these dominant states establish. Not only is there no contradiction between the administrators of the nation-states and those who run the TNCs, but there is a coincidence of interests in the overlapping of memberships in the national economic and political elites, an interest reinforced by an almost universal acceptance of neo-liberal ideology.

It wasn't always thus. The phenomenon of the multinational corporation, the precursor of the transnational, was born out of competition between Europe and the United States. In the late 1960s the domination of U.S. multinationals was beginning to attract the attention of European policy makers. The alarm was raised by Jean-Jacques Shreiber in his book *The American Challenge*. He warned that American-based corporations were becoming the third-greatest economic power on Earth after the U.S. itself and the Soviet Union and would soon dominate Europe if not stopped.

The European counter-attack was the catalyst for the growth of the global-reach corporation. Led by Britain and France and followed by Germany, Austria, and Italy, state governments promoted the mergers of their own large corporations to counter the power of the U.S. giants. They also passed laws preventing further consolidation of American corporations. "France concentrated its steel, electronic, chemical and computer industries as preparation for the counter-offensive of the 1970s . . . In each [country] the ties between government and big corporations grew closer."[16] As government-sponsored mergers changed the economic landscape of Europe, Japan was already merging state and corporate interests with its integration of public and private institutions.

It became commonplace to talk about the growth of the multinational corporations and their influence in the world economy. While European states were promoting their corporate giants, U.S. corporations spent a decade dumping many ill-conceived subsidiaries and concentrating investment in those corporations best positioned to plan on a global scale and most able to integrate local operations into a worldwide enterprise. One lasting result was the merging of corporate and state interests and the increasing emergence of a single political and economic elite in all the developed countries.

The evolution from multinational corporation to transnational corporation, however, is a change of the past twenty years, and has its roots in complex changes in geopolitics (specifically the decline in American power) and in long-term corporate growth strategies. The old multinational corporation was characterized by its multiple national identities. It established complete operations in the countries it chose to do business in; that is, the operations were relatively autonomous and included production, marketing, financing, distribution, and sales, all developed largely with local labour and locally recruited management. Such practices meant that the corporation inevitably established roots in the communities where it chose to set up. While much of the profits were funnelled out of the country to the head office, some financed expansion and development.

Thus the multinational corporation was portrayed as a good local "citizen" because its local incarnation was genuinely integrated into the community. Even though owned and controlled beyond the borders, the managers and even the CEO were a part of the community. This reality was particularly significant in Canada, where so many sectors of the economy were dominated by American corporations. That domination, however, was not as visible precisely because the companies operated in ways that were not obviously different from those of Canadian-owned corporations.

Much of the economic and social integration of multinationals was determined by government policy. The more conditional investment regulations were, the more integrated the corporation had to be. When investment was contingent on providing jobs, transferring technology, hiring locally, doing research, and paying the statutory tax rate, corporations were not volunteering for good corporate citizenship. They were obligated by the rules of civil society. The more protected individual national markets were, the more obligated a corporation was to behave in the multinational mode. The initially gradual and now rapid removal of barriers to local markets freed up the corporate giants to take advantage of varying conditions in the countries they did business in.

The transnational corporation, according to David Korten, exists when a corporation's operations are integrated "around vertically integrated supplier networks." Korten gives the example of Otis Elevator when it set about to create an advanced elevator system. "It contracted out the design of the motor drives to Japan, the door systems to France, the electronics to Germany and small geared components to Spain. System integration was handled from the United States."[17]

Whereas the multinational corporation made efforts to create a local identity, the transnational is motivated to do just the opposite, to eliminate as much as possible any consideration of national identity or local corporate "citizenship." As the TNC is continuously calculating the advantages of producing here, financing there, and coordinating somewhere else, flexibility of movement is a priority and the location of any aspect of its operation is seen as contingent.

With such a motivation, the last thing a TNC wants is any kind of real integration into the local community or economy. The more ties there are, the less flexible it is; the more commitments it has made — everything from where it gets its supplies to who it has on its local board of directors — the messier it is to pack up and leave. The fewer the organic connections with the nation and the local community the better. Put another way, the fewer rules and regulations there are to cement and formalize those connections, the better it is for the TNC. As we will see, the free-trade deal with the U.S. created the conditions for multinationals to become transnationals virtually overnight.

The trend towards TNCs is so pronounced that their CEOs brag about their lack of any connection with a nation-state, as if such a disconnection indicates success in itself, as indeed it often does. Charles Exley, of National Cash Register, boasted to the *New York Times*, "National Cash Register is not a U.S. corporation. It is a world corporation that happens to be headquartered in the United States." Another example is IBM, once the quintessentially American corporation, which now employs eighteen thousand Japanese workers as one of that country's largest computer exporters. General Motors has an agreement with Toyota whereby GM produces twenty thousand Toyota cars in the U.S. for export to Japan.[18]

The TNC plots its global operations by identifying where it is cheapest (labour costs, taxes, and environmental regulation, for example) to produce its goods, where it is cheapest to arrange financing, in which jurisdiction it is most convenient to declare profits and expenses, where research subsidies and tax breaks are most generous, and what markets are the most lucrative and the easiest to penetrate. And it is not difficult to understand why. As the international trade and investment rules by which corporations operate are swept away, the need to establish full-blown operations in each country where there may be a viable market simply vanishes. The purpose of the corporation has always been to enhance the bottom line. Liberalization of corporate regulations has been both a cause and an effect of the power of TNCs and has made it easy to split corporate operations into many divisions, each contributing to the maximization of profits on the basis of geographic advantage, with each discrete aspect of the operation acting almost as an autonomous unit.

That describes the mechanics of the transnational corporation, but how would one describe the ethos of the development of TNCs? David Korten sees globalization as the most sweeping transformation in human history: "It is a conscious and intentional transformation in search of a new world economic order in which business has no nationality and knows no border. It is driven by global dreams of vast corporate empires, compliant governments, a globalized consumer monoculture, and a universal ideological commitment to corporate libertarianism."[19]

He goes on to list the key objectives of those carrying out the global corporate agenda:

- The world's money, technology, and markets are controlled and managed by gigantic global corporations;
- A common consumer culture unifies all people in a shared quest for material gratification;
- There is a perfect global competition among workers and localities to offer their services to investors at the most advantageous terms;
- Corporations are free to act solely on the basis of profitability without regard to national or local consequences;
- There are no loyalties to place and community.[20]

I suggested earlier that governments have been instrumental in establishing the conditions for the rise of transnationals. But it is not just individual governments that play this role. The International Monetary Fund, the World Bank, the World Trade Organization (formerly the General Agreement on Tariffs and Trade), Asia Pacific Economic Co-operation (APEC), and the secretive Multilateral Agreement on Investment (MAI) being brokered by the OECD are run by, funded by, and responsible to governments. And every one of them has, at different times and in different ways, aided and abetted the growth of transnationals and the internationalization of capital. More than that, they have been absolutely key in the design and development of transnationals. Without these institutions and the role they have played, it is fair to say that the current shape of the world's economy and the nature and role of corporations would be totally different.

TRANSNATIONALS IN CANADA

Canada features just six of the top 500 global corporations, and none of the world's two hundred largest transnational corporations are based here, though of course many operate here as if they are Canadian, accorded, under free-trade agreements and other international accords, virtually the same rights as Canadian corporations. But there are homegrown corporations that typify the TNC in their behaviour and lack of any commitment to their home country, its communities, or the workforce that built their company.

One of the most prominent Canadian transnationals is Northern Telecom, the crown jewel of the high-tech sector in Canada. It has demonstrated at one time or another in its recent history all of the characteristics of the TNC: the transfer of domestic jobs to low-wage countries, its efforts to undermine unions, the concerted attempts to arrange its activities to take maximum advantage of tax, environmental, labour, and other laws in the various countries in which it operates.

Nortel began in 1882 as a Canadian subsidiary of AT&T, and its later relations with Bell Canada gave it a large and secure base that facilitated the early development of its technological capabilities. It benefited considerably from defence department spending in the Second World War and from research conducted by the National Research Council. By the late seventies it was selling into the American market; by 1986 half its market was there, as were half its jobs. By 1991 Nortel had operations in eight countries.[21]

As early as 1975 Northern Telecom had identified the importance of low-wage facilities in the U.S. to its manufacturing strategy. The firm shut down a unionized plant it had purchased in Michigan, and shifted the production to a non-union facility in Nashville. Throughout the latter stages of its U.S. expansion Nortel increasingly chose Southern right-to-work states for its facilities, simultaneously closing down those in the northern U.S. where its employees were unionized. Between 1984 and 1989, Nortel campaigns decertified five of the seven unionized plants.[22]

If the company's North American workers were denied the benefits of Nortel's tremendous success, its workers in the cheap labour locations fared even worse. In Turkey, Northern Telecom fired sixteen hundred union members after they won a three-month strike. In

1992 the company decertified a union in Britain months after it acquired the company the union bargained with. Over an eighteen-year period, Nortel worked hand-in-hand with the Malaysian government to thwart five attempts by its employees to unionize.

Nortel's labour relations improved somewhat by 1993, but its restructuring did not stop. In the early 1990s serious restructuring in the new global mode saw the loss of three thousand jobs in Canada. The company, which is itself controlled by huge conglomerate BCE Inc., now has 68,000 employees in fifteen countries; only 22,000 of those are in Canada. As is the pattern worldwide, it is the shareholder who benefits and the employees and communities who pay the price.[23] In 1993 when Nortel closed or sold plants in Montreal, London, Winnipeg, and Saskatoon, it increased its dividend; it increased it again the next year after announcing the closing or selling of four more plants. During those same two years, Nortel opened plants in two of the most notoriously low-wage, politically repressive, and environmentally unregulated countries in the world: China and Mexico.[24]

In 1997 the company announced that it was adding six thousand jobs in Canada as part of a boom riding the electronics revolution and massive deregulation of telecommunications.[25] But consistent with another Nortel pattern, these jobs were in marketing and development, not the most valuable production jobs. Partly as a result of Nortel, Canada has a large electronics trade deficit, and it has grown by over 300 percent in the past decade, reaching $12 billion in 1994.[26]

Yet the principal objective of government R&D tax incentives is to build Canada's high-tech productive capacity. Nortel has been a huge beneficiary of those credits, yet uses the research to export jobs abroad. Nortel has received at least $880 million in federal research and development tax credits. The Canadian taxpayer has subsidized each job remaining at Nortel's Canadian operations (as of 1995) to the tune of $140,000.[27]

Lest it be assumed that Nortel pays back the Canadian taxpayer for the largesse it receives, its worldwide income tax bill in 1994 totalled $35 million, just 0.4 percent of total revenue.[28] As of 1996, the company owes $213 million in deferred taxes.[29] Even its expansion plans in Montreal in 1997 saw it get a two-year property tax holiday and reduced taxes for three more years.

Without laws and regulations, Canadians might well be working sixty-hour weeks and be subject to extremely dangerous work conditions in order to make a living. The proof seems close at hand. The same chief executives and board members who run our large corporations in Canada also run corporations in Mexico, the Philippines, Indonesia, Thailand, and a host of other underdeveloped countries.

Canadian-based Placer Dome consists of four regional business units, in Vancouver; Santiago, Chile; Sydney, Australia; and San Francisco. It also has an international exploration office in Miami and a joint-venture office in London, England.[30] The company is infamous for an environmental disaster at the Marcopper Mine in the Philippines. On March 24, 1996, a tunnel from a containment pit collapsed and sent four million tonnes of tailings into the Boac River. A U.N. report cited negligence on the part of the mine's management. The spill was so serious and the culpability of Placer Dome so obvious that the Philippine government charged Marcopper president John Loney and mine manager Steve Reid with criminal gross negligence.

It now appears that all charges will be dropped, however, as Placer Dome has succeeded in persuading the government to quash the prosecution. Charges were "indefinitely" postponed and President Fidel Ramos pointedly "welcomed" Placer Dome to "continue its investment in the Philippine mineral industry."[31]

It wasn't the first time that Placer Dome had the president directly intervene to save its skin. Since it began its operations, Marcopper has intentionally dumped the overburden from the mine directly into the waters off Santa Cruz on the island of Marinduque. By 1992 there was a 4.7-kilometre causeway into Calancan Bay, and the overburden covered 71 square kilometres of the coral-rich bottom of the bay. This kind of dumping is outlawed in all developed countries.

As early as 1974, residents had tried to stop the practice. In 1981 and 1988, they succeeded in having Philippine government agencies order Marcopper to cease its dumping, and twice Marcopper executives intervened to have the Office of the President overturn both orders. Placer has refused to compensate villagers for the loss of their livelihood, denying that the mine has had any environmental impact.[32]

The same year as the Boac River disaster, the company was being condemned for its environmental record at its joint-venture Porgera mine in Papua New Guinea. That mine discharges 40,000 cubic metres of tailings a day directly into the Maiapam-Strickland River. The waste rock includes heavy metal sulphides, hydroxides, and cyanide compounds up to three thousand times the country's legal limits. The Mineral Policy Institute of Australia has documented 133 unusual deaths of villagers along the river between 1991 and 1993.[33]

Placer Dome's operations elsewhere provide little promise of any better treatment of local populations or the environment. In a Mineral Policy Institute news release, Placer Dome is cited for its operations at the Misima gold mine at Milne Bay in Papua New Guinea, whose processing plant dumps tonnes of softrock into the oceanic trench next to the island. The institute warns that "the effects of unrecovered cyanide in the Misima's tailings are potentially disastrous." At the proposed Placer Dome mine at Namosi in Fiji, one of the largest open-pit mines in the world, the intention is to engage in "submarine dumping of 98,000 tonnes of tailings daily."[34]

A gold mine planned for Costa Rica is being opposed by environmentalists and residents. According to a report in the newspaper *La Nacion*, the area where the mining exploitation would take place runs along a border area with Nicaragua of enormous ecological value.

In Venezuela, Placer Dome managed to get the currency control laws changed, allowing it to repatriate all of its profits, a condition for its developing its Las Christinas gold property. Placer Dome's plan to mine this property is now the subject of a lawsuit brought by several environmental organizations. Las Christinas is smack in the middle of the Imataca Reserve of the Amazon rain forest, a spread as big as Holland. Placer Dome's plan is for a 2-square-kilometre open-pit mine, 300 metres deep. In the judgement of the World Conservation Union, "The potential destruction here is much larger than in other parts of the world" because of the reserve's ecological richness.[35]

Placer Dome's conduct and its public image building inhabit different worlds. In its 1994 corporate profile, the company goes on at length about its international record with such phrases as "living the ethic of environmental responsibility in our business practices"; "working towards high standards of environmental protection and safety at all our operations worldwide"; "sensitive to cultural differences . . . [striving] for harmonious relationships in different cultural environments."[36]

What the examples of Northern Telecom and Placer Dome demonstrate is not just that corporations flout ethics and morality when they operate in less developed countries. Their behaviour extends to participating and cooperating with local authorities to undermine democracy and suppress political dissent. Placer Dome's intervention with President Fidel Ramos, and Northern Telecom's enlisting the Malaysian government to thwart its workers' legal attempts to unionize, reveals a willingness of Canadian corporations to align themselves with reactionary and repressive governments in order to enhance their bottom line.

As corporations become ever larger and the regulations governing them increasingly weaker, we get to see the raw power of capital in ways not observed since the last century. It is an instructive, if frightening, revelation. As transnational corporations use their unprecedented power and global reach to expand their freedom, all large corporations take advantage of that power and that freedom.

As we observe the steady erosion of communities, social programs, the power of workers, and environmental and other regulations we are observing the true nature of the corporation. As it strips away the features of civil society, the corporate citizen reveals itself as a dangerous fraud. Without the state's strict enforcement of the obligations of citizenship, the corporation is exposed for what it is. It is not a citizen, or anything even vaguely resembling such a multifaceted and complex entity. The corporation is strictly one-dimensional, demonstrating only the narrowest of characteristics: greed.

2

DEMOCRACY, THE STATE, AND THE CORPORATE CITIZEN

*We are calling upon [those who wield corporate] power and property,
as mankind once called upon the kings of their day, to be good and kind,
wise and sweet, and we are calling in vain. We are asking them not to
be what we have made them to be. We have put power into their hands
and ask them not to use it as power."*

— HENRY DEMAREST LLOYD, AMERICAN WRITER AND
POPULIST ORGANIZER AGAINST CORPORATIONS, 1894

*When approaching these issues [of financial regulation] our obligation is
to our constituents but also our obligations [are] to you . . . . You recognize
that as members of Parliament our first duty is to our electors . . . but you
are also our electors because you provide jobs. We will go about that
difficult task in working with you in the future and if we don't get it right
this time we'll work with you to make sure we will get it right.*
— LIBERAL MP JIM PETERSON, CHAIR OF THE COMMONS STANDING COMMITTEE ON
FINANCE, TO GORDON FEENEY, CHAIR OF THE CANADIAN BANKERS' ASSOCIATION, 1996

Corporations are to all intents and purposes — and certainly their own — legal citizens. They communicate their views directly to other real citizens through advertising, they assume the status of citizen in dozens of public forums, they have the standing of citizens in court, are sought out for their opinions on public policy, take part in elections by contributing to political parties. Indeed, corporations enjoy many of the same "freedoms" that flesh-and-blood citizens enjoy, although the power and influence of the corporate citizen far outweighs that of the flesh-and-blood variety.

An obviously artificial person, the corporate citizen in the era of the TNC is now a kind of super-citizen, with overwhelming power on the one hand and ever decreasing responsibilities on the other. The TNC is a special case, with the status of global corporate citizen whose "rights" are transnational, in effect superseding the cultural and social basis of the citizenship enjoyed by you and me. Of course, it is precisely these features — the excessive power, the refusal to accept responsibility, the distinct international status — that should disqualify corporations from citizenship. What is so astonishing about their continued status is that almost no other entity on Earth is less qualified to be a citizen.

THE EVOLUTION OF THE CORPORATION IN CANADA

Somewhere along the line, we seem to have simply accepted the notion that corporations have a far superior status to a real citizen, more power, more influence — access to power that no ordinary citizen, or group of citizens, could possibly imagine. If this super-citizen had super-abilities and superior ethics and yet was benign, it might be argued that giving corporations this status made sense. But in fact corporations have gained this status by stealth and accident over centuries of organizational and political evolution.

When the Charter of Rights and Freedoms was passed in 1982 many Canadians felt that their rights as citizens had just taken a major leap forward. Having watched American crime dramas on TV in which people were read their rights, we felt that we too would now be protected from the abuses of the state. Like the Americans, we would now have constitutional rights. Democracy, the right of ordinary people to determine their own future, would be enhanced. Our fundamental freedoms — of expression, of association, of religion, against false arrest — would be protected by the power of a constitution, not just by the legislature, the common law, or by our demanding those rights in the streets.

Thirteen years later, in the fall of 1995, Canadians received a powerful signal that their initial assessments of the Charter may have been mistaken. The Supreme Court of Canada, building on a number of lower-profile, precedent-setting cases over the years, ruled that the right of citizens not to become addicted as children to cigarette smoking was subordinate to the right of the powerful tobacco companies to freedom of expression. Specifically, the highest court of the land said: "Freedom of expression, even commercial expression, is an important and fundamental tenet of a free and democratic society. If Parliament wishes to infringe this freedom, it must be prepared to offer good and sufficient justification for the infringement."[1] (Apparently, the deaths of forty thousand Canadians annually and the targeting of children with sophisticated marketing did not provide sufficient justification.)

The ruling was just the latest instance of the rights of corporate citizens being enhanced and written in stone in Canadian law. Sometimes the rulings bordered on the farcical, such as the one declaring the right of a margarine company to "express" itself by colouring its margarine to look like butter. And other times they were so far-reaching that they changed the course of the country's history.

In 1984, for example, an Alberta judge threw out a law limiting third-party spending in elections. Had this law been in place, it would have prevented the most powerful corporations in the country from engaging in an unprecedented $19-million propaganda campaign to subvert the 1988 election, in which free trade was the central issue. Corporations, said Mr. Justice Donald Medhurst, had to be free to express themselves as citizens. He dismissed the argument that corporations' overwhelming financial resources represented a threat to democracy; he said there had to be "actual demonstration of harm or a real likelihood of harm to a society value" before any government could impose limits on the freedom of expression guarantee in the Charter.[2] The challenge to the law was brought by the National Citizens' Coalition, a right-wing lobby group funded in large part by corporations.

The Charter of Rights and Freedoms, though it has narrowly advanced the rights of some groups in Canada, has, according to Osgoode Hall law professor Michael Mandel, done far more to damage democracy than it has to enhance it. Mandel believes all such charters have been designed precisely to counter the effects of majoritarian democracy. He argues that the Charter is "an antidote to democracy that appears throughout the world when you have universal suffrage, or when representative institutions start to cause problems. Then the powerful people — the property owners, the wealthy — in society start to get scared. They look for means to control them . . . judicial review, charters of rights, as an antidote to really representative government."[3]

The property Mandel refers to is not personal property but capital. Under representative democracy the rights of capital — that is, corporations — to do as they please in their pursuit of profits, such as targeting children in tobacco advertising, or clear-cutting forests, or building a factory on a riverbank, can be challenged by citizens. Charters, argues Mandel, give corporations a whole new arsenal in their fight to be free of restrictions.

Explicit property rights are not included in the Charter, and so Canadian courts have looked south for guidance in giving citizens' rights to corporations. The U.S. has long experience with efforts to protect property from the sovereign people. According to Mandel, "the American constitution and its Bill of Rights put interference with property beyond state and congressional reach." That is, in his view, precisely what the Canadian Charter does in placing the unelected court above the authority of parliamentary sovereignty. Not only can corporations challenge governments on whether they are obeying the laws but they are given "the unlimited right to veto those laws, indeed the right to final approval of the legitimacy of all government action."[4]

While the Charter gives new, substantive citizen rights to corporations, it simultaneously puts explicit restrictions on governments. In effect, it puts forward the notion that we have more to fear from our governments, our elected representatives, than we do from corporations. Allan Blakeney had grave reservations about the Charter, which came into being while he was premier of Saskatchewan. He has said: "Charters of rights are predicated on the belief that . . . the only people who interfere with rights are governments, and therefore the charter will restrict governments and no one else; and that government action always curtails freedom and . . . never enhances freedom. I think that many government actions, including minimum wage laws . . . expand freedom."[5] (It all depends on what you mean by freedom.

For corporate libertarians it is freedom to do what you want; for Blakeney, governments provide freedom from want, insecurity, freedom based on the protection of citizens from powerful interests.)

And Canada ended up with a very different form of government with the Charter of Rights and Freedoms, one that greatly weakened the principle of representative democracy through parliamentary sovereignty. In so doing it handed over some of that sovereignty to that fictitious citizen, the corporation. It is powerfully reminiscent of the time when Canada was a sovereign corporation.

CANADA AS A CORPORATION

Canada's intimate relationship with the corporation may well be unique. The country's character and beginnings were established within the bounds of a single corporation, the Hudson's Bay Company. In addition to organizing the fur trade, "the Company" carried out the activities of government, including making laws and regulations governing the lives of its employees and the aboriginal population within its jurisdiction. It maintained its own policing and arrested, tried, and jailed people. It was, of course, completely undemocratic, with no accountability to those it governed.

Similar to trends we can recognize with the transnationals of today, the Hudson's Bay Company (HBC) was an amalgam of state and corporation. The charter for the HBC and similar companies did establish obligations as well as money-making privileges for them. The Royal Proclamation of 1763, one of Canada's founding documents, granted to the governor the power to incorporate but cautioned: "It is our express will that you do not, upon pain of Our highest displeasure, give your assent to any Law or Laws setting up any Manufactures and carrying on any Trades, which are hurtful and prejudicial to this Kingdom."[6]

But by the end of the eighteenth century, a new colonial economic elite wanted freedom from any obligation and insisted that governments serve them. According to historian Donald Creighton, the colonial business elite demanded changes to the way the colony would be governed: "The state should make the way smooth for the commercial concerns, the banks and the land companies. The state should provide harbours, ship channels and canals. The state, in fact, must become the super-corporation of the new economy, dominated like any other corporation by commercial interests and used to its full capacity as a credit instrument in a grand programme of public works."[7]

According to legal researcher Gil Yaron, by the mid-1880s the act of incorporation was changed to the simple one of registration rather than royal charter, and from then on incorporation was a right, not a privilege. In contrast to the limited life of the chartered corporation, the registered version opened the door to "perpetual succession" or, in effect, a corporation that never went out of existence.[8]

Corporations so dominated colonial life in Canada that our nation's key constitutional document, the British North America Act, is completely void of any mention of human happiness or other lofty goal. Unlike its American counterpart it was strictly a business proposition, reflecting the business objective of creating a separate market for the Canadian business class. According to Gerry Van Houten, writing on the history of corporate Canada, "Canada's ruling class was able to determine the main content and characteristics of the new constitution . . . The constitution had nothing to say about the rights of Canada's farmers and workers. It also had nothing to say about the First Nations or Quebec's unique position in the Canadian state."[9]

THE AMERICAN EXPERIENCE WITH CORPORATIONS

The United States is now home to most of the world's most powerful transnational corporations. The U.S., which we now see as almost synonymous with the transnational corporation, developed that character only after a dynamic and popular struggle against corporate domination. While Canada was established almost as a corporate project, the U.S. began as a revolutionary democracy, founded on the principles of the sovereignty of the citizen and the subordinate status of all other entities, including corporations. Corporations existed only with the explicit permission of citizens. Early citizen-imposed constraints on what corporations could do help remind us just how artificial a being the corporation is and may help point the way to re-establishing sovereign authority over corporations in the future.

Richard Grossman in his booklet "Taking Care of Business: Citizenship and Charter of Incorporation" tells many stories of how corporations were held to account. In an 1809 judgment, the Supreme Court of Virginia decreed that if an applicant's purpose in seeking a corporate charter "is merely private or selfish; if it is detrimental to, or not promotive of, the public good, they have no adequate claim upon the legislature for the privileges."[10] Corporate charters were routinely denied because the corporation failed to prove it would serve a clear public purpose.

The principle for challenging a corporation's charter was *quo warranto* — by what authority? — underlining the fact that in most states the corporation was allowed to engage only in those activities explicitly allowed in the charter legislation. The revocation of corporate charters was commonplace. President Andrew Jackson, to great popular acclaim, in 1832 vetoed a law that would have extended the charter of the Second Bank of the United States. Pennsylvania revoked the charters of ten banks in that same year and in 1857 passed a constitutional amendment instructing its legislators to "alter, annul or revoke any charter of a corporation . . . whenever in their opinion it may be injurious to citizens of the community."[11]

The tide began to turn in favour of American corporations in the latter part of the nineteenth century, when they began to successfully use the courts to challenge or get around the chartering powers of the states. The Civil War had made many corporations fabulously rich. According to Grossman, "Following the Civil War and well into the twentieth century, appointed judges gave privilege after privilege to corporations. They freely reinterpreted the U.S. constitution and transformed common law."[12]

The biggest victory of the corporations came in 1886, when the Supreme Court ruled that a private corporation was in fact a "natural person" under the U.S. constitution. In a fundamental reversal of practice, and reflecting their new "person" status, corporations were given the right to operate in any fashion not explicitly prohibited by law. By the turn of the century the judiciary had led the way in positioning the corporation to become, in the words of a Ford executive, "America's representative social institution, an institutional expression of our way of life."[13]

By the early part of the twentieth century the battles were over. In 1941 a congressional committee concluded, "The principal instrument of the concentration of power and wealth has been the corporate charter with unlimited power." Indeed, that power was used in the Supreme Court to block the New Deal of President Roosevelt. Although Roosevelt eventually forced the court to back down, the legal power of the corporation was not changed. Says Grossman, "Many U.S. corporations are transnational. No matter how piratical or where they roam, the corrupted charter remains the legal basis of their existence."[14]

THE ORIGINS OF THE WELFARE STATE

The Ford executive's proud declaration that the corporation had become the institutional expression of the American way of life was an accurate description of the reality for ordinary Americans and Canadians. Once corporations were accorded the right to exist forever and operate with limited liability, under legislation that made no mention of any responsibility to society, they were by far the most important organizing institution in society. With government so conspicuous today, it is hard to imagine just how dominant corporations were in the early part of the twentieth century.

Hardly any area of life wasn't affected by the power of corporations. The romantic view of western grain farmers challenging the elements in a heroic struggle to improve their lot masks the monopolistic stranglehold that banks, grain companies, and railways had on their lives. The same was true for workers. Factories and mines employed only the most minimal safety standards, and there were virtually no legal mechanisms to protect workers' rights during industrial disputes.

Almost every important decision affecting ordinary citizens was either made by corporations or made in their interests. There was no social safety net, no medicare, no unemployment insurance. Economic life was completely in the hands of private capital. The corporate way of life was one in which the corporate leaders, at least when it came to all important governance questions, were indistinguishable from the political leaders.

This was particularly the case in Canada. The extreme suffering experienced during the depression of the 1930s turned Canadian politics into a cauldron of conflict, which shook the confidence of corporate elites. The respective roles of the state and corporations had to be reconceived. With the goals of social control and infrastructure support for business, the Canadian state undertook a broad series of social reforms.

Programs such as government mortgage lending, unemployment insurance, a federal manpower agency, and a variety of marketing boards were proposed, and some were implemented by the Conservative government of R. B. Bennett. Bennett himself was a multimillionaire, and his cabinet was dominated by men with ties to large corporations, and the senior civil service was made up of former businessmen. Their apparent change of heart was explained by A. E. Grauer, writing for the Royal Commission on Dominion-Provincial Relations in 1939: "The note sounded has not been so much the ideal of social justice as political and economic expediency."[15]

In fact many businessmen supported a workers' compensation scheme because it was ultimately cheaper than paying private insurance companies for protection against workers' lawsuits; a shorter work week was popular because it "spread work around"; unemployment insurance was supported, said Grauer, because of "the appalling cost of relief" and the hope that UI would "give some protection to public treasuries in future depressions."[16]

The Bennett government was the same one that was utterly ruthless when it came to suppressing workers' demands for rights of any kind and union rights in particular. The state directly assisted corporations' efforts to stop organizing drives. It jailed communists, deported non-British immigrants who were seen as the source of communist ideas, forced the unemployed into camps, and ended a trek to Ottawa by the unemployed with a violent assault in Regina. Reforms were one thing; rights, another.

Liberal prime minister William Lyon Mackenzie King was not convinced of the necessity of social reforms and spent his early years in power doing everything possible to block them, claiming that governments could do nothing about unemployment and should not run up debts to deal with crises. It was an argument that the war years rendered obsolete. Canadians daily had the evidence before them that if a situation was considered serious enough (like the threat of Nazism that affected more than just the poor and the unemployed), their government was willing to undertake an extraordinary amount of intervention in the market, creating full employment, controlling trade, taxing wealth, providing incentives for industry — and going into massive debt.

In addition, during the war years the union movement doubled in size and increased in militancy. Still King resisted, until he felt he was in a position to run on a platform of social reform without alienating the more reactionary wing of the business elite. Both the Progressive Conservatives and the Co-operative Commonwealth Federation, or CCF, which was now calling for reforms rather than fundamental change, had policy platforms calling for state intervention, and were thus serious threats to Liberal dominance. King's program included a family allowance scheme and spending to help in converting the war economy back to its domestic version. It also included historic legislation that legalized unions and collective bargaining. The debate about social legislation continued to focus on tactical questions about what was necessary for preserving the relations between business and labour.

Alvin Finkel documents how intimately the corporate chieftains of the day were involved in determining what combination of repression and social reform was best to preserve labour peace. Fully integrated into both the Liberal and Conservative parties, corporate executives embodied corporate rule in its quintessential Canadian mode, with the political and corporate elite deciding what was best for corporations.

The historic state-mediated compromise between corporations and working people was also based on a major weakness of corporations at that time. Corporate investment was relatively hard to move right through the 1960s, which meant that foreign and domestic corporations that established in Canada had to respond to conditions as they were, including a militant labour movement. It wasn't until the 1970s, when investment became more mobile, that the practical basis for the social contract and corporations' willingness to compromise would begin to disappear.

The rising expectations of workers and farmers following the war became a part of the political culture. The notion of citizenship was greatly enhanced as a result of the victories Canadians had achieved. In Alvin Finkel's view, "Canadian citizenship came to mean more than simply having a formal set of 'negative' constitutional rights such as 'life, liberty and the security of the person,' it meant you were entitled to an assortment of more 'positive' social welfare rights that 'you are entitled to simply because you are a Canadian.'"[17]

Canadian citizenship in a sense came of age. The notion of a collectivity based on the values of mutual responsibility and social solidarity became a theme in our political culture. The individualism of the early part of the century, enforced as a cultural value by the power of corporations, was fundamentally altered in the post-war period. The corporate elite had allowed the development of a political culture hostile to its interests, one that it would have to confront eventually. The ideological attacks on the notions of rights and entitlement, and the explicit promotion of the values of individualism, that we are witnessing today are no accident but a calculated effort to reinvent the notion of citizenship.

Another key factor in the development of the welfare state in Canada was the crucial role of the civil service. Mackenzie King had become extremely indecisive as a leader in the post-war period. As Robert Chodos argues in his book *The Unmaking of Canada*, "It was into this vacuum that the civil service stepped, overflowing with policy ideas acquired from [John Maynard] Keynes in Cambridge and brought to Canada by way of the New Deal Washington . . . The fledgling Canadian mandarinate was made up almost entirely of disciples of John Maynard Keynes."[18]

By the 1960s, the Canadian state was pursuing policy associated with the work of Keynes, objectives such as full employment, high economic growth, price stability, and an equitable distribution of income. New measures were aimed at establishing equity between regions through regional development programs and equalization payments. It also introduced nationwide medicare in 1966 and a greatly enhanced UI program in 1971. Payments to the provinces to share the costs of post-secondary education and social assistance programs completed the main features of the second wave of the egalitarian welfare state.

Two decades of virtually uninterrupted growth, and robust profitability, fostered in part by the Keynesian programs of Liberal governments, resulted in a de facto policy of benign political neglect on the part of corporations. The state had delivered to the corporations what it had promised: stability, the conditions for mass consumption, programs that smoothed out the economic cycles, and absorption of the costs of maintaining a healthy, educated, and contented workforce. And all of this was done with a fairly regressive tax system, one which taxed the better-paid workers and the middle class to pay for social programs for everybody. While corporations paid a much greater portion of the tax bill than they do today, that was partly a consequence of high profits, not high tax rates.

LIBERAL DEMOCRACY — AN OXYMORON?

The approach of Canadian governments both before and after the war was the classic expression of liberal democracy: an uneasy marriage between free-market individualism and democratic government policies that provided for a modicum of economic and social equality. But the question would be raised in the 1960s and early 1970s about just how democratic liberal democracy was. With the growth of the economy there were rising expectations not only with respect to the delivery of government programs and regulation of the economy but of substantive democracy. In short, there began to develop a strong sentiment for a more democratic process, not just state-sponsored equality.

Not only was the voice of corporations muted, there were New Democratic governments in place in three western provinces, the Parti Québécois was strongly social democratic, and even the national Conservative Party was dominated by Red Tories. Social movements had captured the imagination of thousands of young people across the country. The anti-Vietnam War movement, the radical student movement, the rebirth and rapid growth of feminism, anti-poverty groups, and a sometimes militant aboriginal movement grabbed headlines. Common to all of them was the demand for a more substantive democracy.

This was a demand for democracy of a different sort, a radical democracy in the sense of returning to the roots of the idea, based as it was in effective rule by the majority. Aboriginal people demanded self-determination, women demanded equality, and the anti-war movement focussed on the role of corporations in the Vietnam War. The student movement insisted on an end to privilege, demanding that universities serve the community, and publicly denounced professors for their failure to teach anything relevant about the world around them.

A powerful moral and ethical spirit was at the centre of much of the new politics, and young people targeted both corporations and governments. The latter were seen as complacent and ossified, the former as self-serving and immoral. Alongside high levels of poverty, estimated at 27 percent, were corporations that received all sorts of tax breaks. NDP leader David Lewis effectively played to this audience with his "corporate welfare bums" campaign in 1972. Even Prime Minister Pierre Trudeau acknowledged, in the debate over tax reform in 1971, "It's likely that we heard more from the vested interests than we did from the little taxpayer who didn't . . . have high-paid lawyers to speak for him."[19]

In addition, the labour movement, awakening after years of complacency, was increasingly aggressive at the bargaining table and much of it was adopting social unionism, a broader involvement of all the social issues of the day, as part of its revival.

It was the first time since the conflicts of the 1930s and 1940s that liberal democracy was seriously exposed to a radical critique. And liberal democracy was very vulnerable to those who wanted the real thing. The renewed passion for democracy, and the critique of the existing model, was perhaps best captured by C. B. Macpherson in a 1965 CBC lecture series called *The Real World of Democracy*, to this day one of the most compelling essays on democracy written in Canada.

Until the latter part of the last century, wrote Macpherson, democracy was considered a "bad thing . . . feared and rejected by all men of learning, men of substance, men who valued civilization."[20] It was a "levelling" doctrine, and giving the franchise to those who were "dependent" on others would level it downward. In Western societies the democratic franchise was established only after the liberal capitalist society was firmly established.

In liberal democracies, liberalism, understood as the freedom of the individual, came first. Macpherson explained that before democracy "there came the society and politics of choice, the society and politics of competition, the society and politics of the market. This was the liberal society and state . . . Both society as a whole and the system of government were organized on a principle of freedom of choice."[21] The impact of the market on society had been profound, changing relationships between people into market relations. Democracy, said Macpherson, was an "add-on."

It was inevitable that the principle of freedom of choice would be taken up by those without property who were denied any say in the governing of the state. But the very nature of the liberal state and society, governed by market relationships, was such that the demand for democracy was not a radical demand. "By the time democracy came . . . it was no longer opposed to the liberal society and state. It was, by then, not an attempt by the lower class to overthrow the liberal state or the competitive market economy; it was an attempt by the lower class to take their fully and fairly competitive place within these societies. Democracy had been transformed. From a threat to the liberal state it had become a fulfilment of the liberal state."[22]

With democracy transformed by, and absorbed into, the competitive political culture of market society, the substance of democracy was reduced to the welfare state and the regulatory state. In fact, argued Macpherson, these two elements would have been introduced even without the extension of the franchise because the capitalist economy could not have flourished without them. It was often the most conservative, pro-business governments, like R. B. Bennett's, that introduced the welfare state. Not only had democracy not fundamentally altered market society but for the most part people's understanding and expectations of democracy were as much transformed as the actual fruits of democracy were.

The flowering of democratic movements in the 1960s and early 1970s was briefly accommodated and even promoted by the government of Pierre Trudeau. Perhaps uniquely amongst Western developed countries, the Trudeau Liberals institutionalized the political movements of previously marginalized groups through a program of participatory democracy. At least part of the motivation of this funding was a genuine attempt to give access to policy making to those who had so far been excluded. But, unfortunately, the era of participatory democracy turned out be extremely short-lived.

Just when social movements seemed to have hit their peak, corporations faced their biggest crisis since the Great Depression. Both profitability and growth were in decline. The crisis was brought to a head by the 1973 Arab oil embargo and the enormous price rises that followed. Suddenly everything changed in the world of the corporation and capital investment. The oil crisis led to a severe decline in profitability (except, of course, for the oil companies), a flight of capital out of North America looking for cheaper manufacturing locations, and a resulting deindustrialization. In addition, the drive to reduce production costs and increase productivity prompted a technological revolution that between 1971 and 1979 would see the loss of 630,000 jobs in Canada.[23]

Classic liberalism, with its emphasis on individual (and, by extension, corporate) freedom, was back; majoritarian democracy was once again seen as a threat to profitability, at least in the corporate circles that ultimately determined what the liberal democratic state did. In the mid-seventies the state was scrambling to fix the system, but nothing seemed to work. A new phenomenon, "stagflation," caused by the sudden and rapid jump in oil price, put Keynesians inside the government on the defensive. The country was facing growing unemployment and rising inflation, something that wasn't supposed to happen. In a desperate effort to appease business and stimulate growth, a new finance minister, John Turner, introduced dozens of tax breaks aimed at creating a quarter-million jobs by 1979. Instead, the number of jobs decreased. As a result of all of these factors, the federal government began accumulating the debt that would become the issue of the decade fifteen years later.

Corporations were eager to get out from under the regulatory welfare state, not cooperate in its expansion. The relationship had soured as the state had failed to maintain the conditions for continued profitability. According to Duncan Cameron, chair of the Canadian Centre for Policy Alternatives, corporations rejected the other option, more regulation of investment. The solution to inflation would be the crude instrument of monetarism, the control of the money supply. Keynesian theory on investment allowed for creating the conditions for private investment. The Keynesian theory on inflation required wage and price controls. Cameron says: "It really required the social-ization of the investment process. It meant that investors had to agree that if we're going to, as a society, give you lower wages through wage controls you are going to make more money and in return we want you to invest that money in more jobs and more income."

But private property was sacrosanct. The government went instead to monetarism. Curb the growth of the money supply; if interest rates go sky-high, so be it; if the economy crashes, so be it. "The business community preferred to see the economy crash, as it did in 1981–82 and again in 1990–91, rather than go into a tripartite negotiating process, which the logic of Keynesian economics would have led to."[24]

It was the answer that corporations gave in virtually every Western country. They were strongly assisted by the Organization for Eco-nomic Co-operation and Development, made up of all the indus-trialized nations, which was hugely influential in promoting tight control of the money supply as the solution to the crisis, arguing against both corporate cooperation with labour and government and wage and price controls. The larger corporations in particular were receptive to the idea of breaking from the welfare state and the social contract implied in the historic compromise with labour. The state had provided stability and subsidized the "reproduction" of labour through provision of a healthy, educated, and reliable workforce. But it had also shifted the balance of power in favour of labour, and in a time of continuing falling profits, the welfare state was seen as a liability.

When the corporate elite in Canada and elsewhere decided to break its historic compromise with labour and the welfare state, it freed itself from the restrictions of national boundaries, already severely weakened between 1974 and 1979 by the increased mobility of capital. That political decision changed everything, and effectively accelerated the globalization of the economy. Growth based on healthy and stable domestic economies in the developed world was abandoned, in large part out of necessity. Preferred now was growth through global expansion, and the drive for "efficiency" that interna-tional competitiveness demanded.

The abandonment of the social contract, and with it Keynesian economics, was explicitly an abandonment of a compromise between social classes and a tacit recognition that class tensions would increase and political debates would polarize along class lines. But in Canada, situated as it is next door to the American superpower, it meant much more. No other nation in the developed world has relied so much and for so long on the state for its existence. As Steven McBride and John Shields argue in *Dismantling a Nation*, in Canada "an active role for the state has been an instrument of nation-building and national identity . . . The attack on the state's role and the promotion of unrestricted market relations involve a challenge to the definition of the country rather than merely to established social relations within it."[25]

The Liberal government's efforts at regional development, from its unique UI program to equalization payments and regional development strategies, were strategic devices that helped resist the powerful north-south pull created by the huge American economy. That north-south pull was already powerful because of the continentalist policies of previous Liberal governments. The freeing up of market forces inevitably meant a return to that continentalist strategy. It also inevitably jettisoned the moral imperative that was implied in Keynesianism. Nation building necessarily contained the moral element of equality and fairness as well as the principle of democracy, which were much more difficult to impose on international capital.

The new imperatives of international trade and competitiveness were the perfect context for ideas about freeing the market from interference by government. Arguments in support of the new global economy, and those who stood to benefit, poured through the cracks in the consensus underpinning the welfare state. They soon amounted to the equivalent of an ideological holy war against the old forces of Keynesian economics, state social intervention, collective rights, and egalitarian values.

The sweeping changes that have taken place in Canada since 1980, accelerating since the election of the Mulroney Tories in 1984, are referred to as neo-liberal because they represent a new version of the old liberal free-market values of the nineteenth century. Neo-liberal prescriptions have a profound effect on building up the power of corporations at the expense of citizens. These prescriptions, which include eliminating public-sector jobs, privatizing government corporations, and cutting the social safety net, all make citizens more dependent on corporations for their livelihoods.

Dependence on corporations reflects the new balance of power between capital and labour or, put another way, the erosion of the enhanced citizenship that arose out of the struggles of the 1930s and 1940s. It is, then, a decline of the more substantive democracy that citizens in those struggles took from the corporate state. Indeed, the new economic order, with its roots in the crisis of the 1970s, pits a weakened real citizen against a new breed of corporate citizen goliath whose power and capacity to influence political events dwarfs that of the corporations of the past.

The abandonment of Keynesianism and as a consequence domestic economies as the strategy for growth unleashed the forces that would create the transnational corporation. The strategy of international investment and trade was a catalyst to the growth in size and reach of the corporation. At the same time, it freed the corporation from the state-enforced "good citizenship" that seemed to characterize developed nations for the two decades after the war. However meagre the benefits of that level of corporate responsibility, it had always been expedient for both the state and the corporations. After the mid-1970s that expedient was gone.

This did not mean that the corporations wanted the state to leave the playing field. Far from it. As we will see, corporations have since used their power to enlist the state in implementing their new global strategy. The power they now wield, individually and collectively, as global corporate citizens is formidable. Yet their transnational character does not free them from acting at the national level where state power is exercised.

In the history of transnational corporations, some governments are obviously more important than others. The U.S. is now the only superpower and what it does both domestically and internationally has enormous influence on how the world works. This superpower status makes it important to know how American-based TNCs operate to influence the U.S. government and, by extension, the world. The gradual merging of corporate and state governance is easily illustrated in the U.S. The most "free market" of any of the developed countries, it still has the power to set trends if not dictate the behaviour of other nation-states. And how corporations dictate to the U.S. government is important to our understanding of the development of global corporate rule.

CITIZEN GE

Some corporations take their political role more seriously than others, but it is fair to say that none works harder at governing than General Electric, rated the fifty-fifth largest "economy" in the world in 1995 (ahead of the Philippines, Iran, Venezuela, Pakistan, and New Zealand). William Greider in his book *Who Will Tell the People?* talks at length about "Citizen GE."

Greider begins his tale with an account of how the corporation built up its team of political operatives by hiring people who were among the smartest political figures in government, often those whose job it had been to develop policies regulating GE and other corporations. Benjamin Heineman Jr. (Harvard, Yale, Oxford) had been assistant secretary for planning at the department of health, education and welfare under President Carter. He went to GE because the corporation offered him more opportunities to make public policy than any government job could have — "from the tax code to defense spending, from broadcasting to environmental regulation, from banking law to international trade, from Head Start to Star Wars."[26]

William Lacovara, a former Watergate prosecutor, went to GE because "GE recognizes that as a major economic entity it has the stature and responsibility to form opinions."[27] One of his first efforts was to derail new corporate-sentencing guidelines being drawn up for the federal courts. Stephen D. Ramsey had been assistant attorney general for environmental enforcement under Reagan. GE hired him to produce a "play book" on how to "confound the government's efforts to collect billions owed by polluters." GE has one of the worst pollution records in the U.S., with the highest number (47) of priority clean-up sites of any U.S. company.

GE hired a former legislative counsel for the treasury department to head its tax-planning policy and a former counsel for the energy department as its chief lawyer for its appliance division. The list goes on, and while GE is not typical because it is so large, its behaviour demonstrates a growing reality: for corporations like GE the politics of governing is as natural as producing light bulbs. Indeed, it is an integral part of all that it does. GE's breadth of activity has been almost as broad as the government's. The products it makes and the corporate interests they reflect have converged with nearly every aspect of Washington's decision making.

Its very size and the breadth of its economic activities, from making hydrogen bombs to owning media conglomerates, from banking and stock brokerage to jet engines, determined that GE would begin to act, in Greider's words, "like a mediating institution." In other words, like an instrument of government. It begins to behave as if it actually speaks for whole groups of people, but people to whom it has no accountability and with whom it never consults: workers, consumers, shareholders, communities, other corporations, and the country at large.

GE has the resources to develop and promote new political ideas and to organize public opinion around its political agenda. "It has the capacity to advise and intervene and sometimes to veto. It has the power to punish political opponents." And its political opponents are usually Democrats, because like most large U.S. corporations GE has consistently supported the party of business. It sponsored Ronald Reagan's TV career in the 1950s and "launched him on the lecture circuit as a crusader against big government."[28]

The job of governance is important enough at GE that it is directed by a senior vice-president. He is backed by a sophisticated program and a staff to match, a whole infrastructure of different elements including twenty-four full-time lobbyists in Washington, and strategic financial investments in charities, politics, propaganda, and education.

GE nurtures its good corporate citizen image with an $18.8-million fund for its foundations (less than half of 1 percent of its net earnings). But even here much of the money is directly self-serving, going to business think-tanks, business associations, and coalitions fighting government regulation. So the Institute for International Economics lobbies for the corporate line on trade, and the Americans for Generational Equity campaigns for cuts to entitlement programs like social security. GE was a key funder of the Committee on the Present Danger, which propagandized for the massive military buildup of the 1980s, and of the Center for Economic Progress and Employment, which, despite its name, is a front group of industry giants determined to gut product-liability laws. GE is also prominent on the Business Roundtable, the prototype corporate governance lobby group copied in Canada by the Business Council on National Issues.

Like most mega-corporations in the U.S., GE combines a soft image created by tens of millions of dollars in yearly image advertising with a ruthless hardball politics on Capitol Hill. As the congressional vote on a corporate tax cut approached in 1981, Congress members were flooded with telegrams and lobbied personally by CEOs (organized by the Carlton Group of corporate tax lobbyists, headed by a GE executive) warning them that lack of support would mean a loss of jobs in their districts.

GE was one of the biggest winners in the tax cut bill, getting a $283-million tax rebate for the period 1981–83 despite making profits of $6.5 billion. The tax windfall allowed GE to go on a buying spree of other companies, including RCA and NBC. This was a pattern for all the corporate giants as capital investment increased dramatically, with almost all of it going to other countries. In effect, the billions in tax dollars sacrificed by the American people were used to further deindustrialize their own heartland and boost the growth of super-corporations.

GE is the quintessential corporate citizen of the global era — with virtually unlimited resources, which it uses to intervene at every level of government from the White House down. Indeed, its political branch operates almost as a parallel government, with policy-making capacity and its own propaganda arm capable of selling its policies to the public at the same time that it persuades or blackmails elected representatives into carrying out those policies. Whenever the nominal government veers off the desired course, GE intervenes to bring it back.

CORPORATE DEMOCRACY IN CANADA

There are no parallels to "Citizen GE" in Canada, largely because Canada does not host any of the truly huge transnational corporations with the breadth and depth of a GE. As well, the stakes in changing Canadian policy are not normally as high as they are for American TNCs. There was one instance, though, in which the stakes were extremely high and when Canadian corporations, in partnership with their American branch plants, intervened as forcefully as a U.S. corporation: the corporate campaign to buy the 1988 federal election and ensure that the free-trade deal would become law.

Corporations intervene politically everywhere in the world wherever they have interests. It is part of doing business. In Canada, every industry has had its methods and key issues. But what if they could all intervene just once, in order to secure a law that could render them super-citizens, that would make interventions on hundreds of separate issues virtually unnecessary?

That is essentially what the Canada-U.S. Free Trade Agreement (FTA) promised. It has been called a bill of rights for corporations, but even this description underestimates its eventual impact. In effect, the FTA allowed corporations to begin the final stage of opting out of the social contract altogether. It established the principle that corporations had no inherent obligations to the nation-states in which they did business. They had all the legal rights of citizens but had the obligations waived. It was a kind of unilateral declaration of transnational corporate citizenship.

The Mulroney government's reversal on free trade was the direct result of the intervention of the Business Council on National Issues (BCNI), the voice of the 150 largest corporations in Canada. The BCNI, which will be examined in detail in chapter 7, had already developed a consensus amongst the dominant corporations and simply delivered that message to Brian Mulroney.

According to writer Nick Fillmore, analysing the corporate role in the election for *This Magazine*, in the two years leading up to the 1988 "free trade" election, the Tory government spent an estimated $32 million promoting free trade, most of it through the International Trade Communications Group in external affairs.[29] But when the time came to put on a serious push, the group, headed by Philippe Beaubien, CEO of the giant Telemedia Corp. and a BCNI executive member, decided that a public advocacy campaign was needed to sell the deal. That campaign would be headed up by the Canadian Alliance for Trade and Job Opportunities.

The alliance, a creature of BCNI behind-the-scenes organizing, was announced on March 19, 1987. It consisted of thirty-five business organizations, including the big four: the BCNI, the Canadian Manufacturers' Association (CMA), the Canadian Federation of Independent Business (most CFIB members would eventually suffer under free trade), and the Canadian Chamber of Commerce. It had as its figurehead co-chairs Alberta's former Tory premier Peter Lougheed and Liberal Donald Macdonald, who had chaired the royal commission on Canada's future economic prospects and had called for a "leap of faith" in free trade. But it was David Culver, Alcan's CEO and the chair of the BCNI, who ran the alliance.

The alliance would end up spending $6 million in the months leading up to the election. Although that was the single largest amount spent by a single organization, big business altogether would spend more than $19 million promoting their deal of the century.[30] In addition to the alliance, other member organizations spent heavily, with the BCNI putting up $900,000, the Chamber of Commerce $400,000, and the CFIB $750,000. Seventy-five of the largest corporations came up with $3.75 million, with Alcan, the Royal Bank, and Noranda each pledging $400,000.[31]

The alliance spent $1.5 million on a four-page insert that went into thirty-five English-language daily newspapers across the country and $75,000 on a five-page insert in *Maclean's* magazine that arrived at the homes of 600,000 subscribers the week before the election. The Alberta government, eager to permanently end federal "interference" in the oil patch, spent $600,000 in advertising.[32]

In addition, corporations made a major propaganda assault on their own employees. Stelco and Loblaws, among others, put pro-FTA leaflets in pay packets; others, such as Crown Life Insurance, gathered their employees together for dire warnings about plant closures or layoffs if they didn't vote for free trade; Enfield Corp., a finance and management company, sent out ten thousand pro-FTA pamphlets to employees and clients.

Last but not least, corporate Canada united beyond one of the pro-business parties in a way that had not been witnessed at any time in the post-war period. Making its new consensus very clear, and in an explicit expression of displeasure with the Turner Liberals, big business filled the Tory coffers to overflowing. The Conservatives were able to spend to the maximum in the 1988 election, in excess of $14 million. The Liberals went into the election $5 million in debt.[33]

The free-trade initiative was the most concerted and massive corporate intervention in an election in the history of the country and probably unprecedented in any other developed country except the

U.S. It made a mockery of election rules that restricted what political parties could spend but said nothing about powerful corporations. The grassroots opposition to free trade, organizations representing several million citizens, raised an extraordinary budget to fight the deal but were still outspent by almost fifteen-to-one by a relative handful of corporate "citizens."

There is more than a little irony in the growth and development of the corporate super-citizen. For while corporations have spent millions of dollars and enormous effort to increase their influence, their strategies, and their effectiveness as citizens, they and the think-tanks they fund promote the notion that government and nations are virtually obsolete. In fact, the power of the state has never been more important to the success and power of the corporation. And because of this, the role of the corporate citizen is increasingly important.

The flip side of the enhanced status and activity of the corporate citizen is the reduced power, influence, and effectiveness of the real citizen. As governments withdraw from regulating the economy and providing programs and services, the ordinary citizen faces a world with less and less public space, less collective expression. In a world dominated by corporations selling goods and services, people are more and more defined by what they buy and less by their participation in the community. We are being reduced to little more than customers in the world marketplace, our citizenship increasingly reduced to a set of negative constitutional freedoms.

3

From Citizen
to Customer

I shop, therefore I am.
— Bumper sticker

The advent of the transnational corporation is just one way in which the world economic order has changed. The TNC is both the agent of that change and a product of it. But the driving force of that change and the resulting strategy of the transnationals, the governments that serve them, and the agencies designed to facilitate their growth have as great an influence on daily life and democracy as the structure of the global economy.

That strategy focusses on the world's middle-class consumers, the "global shoppers," those individuals with discretionary income, a (manufactured) desire to immerse themselves in mass consumerism, who increasingly have no separate cultural identity or loyalty and who, willingly or otherwise, begin seeing themselves less as citizens and more as consumers. Even Prime Minister Jean Chrétien has absorbed this ideology of the global economy. In a speech to the National Press Club in Washington, explaining his conversion to free trade, Chrétien expressed the confidence in the transnational corporate future: "I'm not pessimistic about the twenty-first century because you have 1,200,000,000 people in China and they will develop a middle class; they will need to buy all sorts of products and both you and I will be there selling."

It is this consumerism that produces the social base for the globalization revolution. Cause and effect begin to blend into an indecipherable amalgam as citizens, under a barrage of business propaganda, expect less from their governments and identify less with their countries, in exchange for increased access to more and more consumer goods. As communities fracture and disintegrate under the withering assault of corporate power, the things that once held people together are giving way to a new paradigm of common identity and connectedness: the products we consume. The transnational consumer, jettisoning citizenship and local culture, is the key to the growth of the transnational corporation.

The consumer culture is hardly new. The whole counter-culture of the 1960s was preoccupied with opposing it, ridiculing it, and opting out of it. But the counter-culture was no match for the consumer culture's capacity for adapting and co-opting its icons and the corporate/government alliance promoting it. The hippies lost the battles and the war. And new factors have strengthened consumer culture (and weakened communitarian, citizen-based culture) beyond anything imagined by the flower children or the targets of their movement of thirty years ago.

Given that so much of Canadian history has unfolded within a developing consumer culture, it is easy to forget just how artificial this culture really is. Living next door to the country where the alliance between mass production and mass consumption was pioneered, we could be forgiven for thinking it is a natural phenomenon. But William Leach, in *Land of Desire: Merchants, Power and the Rise of a New American Culture*, reminds us just how artificial and manipulative consumerism is. He argues that "the culture of consumer capitalism may have been among the most nonconsensual public cultures ever created."[1] It is manipulative in two ways, first because it was created not by ordinary people but by organized commercial interests, and second, because it was promoted so forcefully it took on the characteristic of being the only path to personal fulfilment.

The current push to create a global consumer culture is simply the final stage in the transformation of citizen into consumer, and of what remains of civil society into a society based almost exclusively on the consumption of private goods. The overwhelming message of the last ten years of corporate assault on the egalitarian state is that we shall have more choices in the marketplace (if we have the money) but less choice about what kind of society we have. By weakening our environmental laws, we might get cheaper goods but we cannot "buy" breathable air, and only the privileged few will be able to buy drinkable water. Few consumers are aware that the price of an automobile is subsidized by billions of dollars in infrastructure, health care, and more expensive food as arable land is used up for highway construction. In comparison, the cost of a mass-transit system is an obvious public expenditure, made more obvious by those who attack such spending.

The most recent phase in the promotion of the consumer culture includes every individual, worldwide, with enough income to take part. It began in the early 1980s with the realization by American (and other) banks that the possibilities for profits to be made from lending to underdeveloped countries was virtually exhausted. That recognition coincided with the presidency of Ronald Reagan, arguably the most unabashedly pro-business president in fifty years.

With banks desperate to find new sources of profitability, Reagan was only too willing to comply. That new source was vastly increased consumer spending at home, and the door to that new wealth was easy credit. And it was just a matter of time before that easy credit in the U.S. market was extended to the wealthy and middle classes of every country in the world. That combination of stateless production and a stateless (and increasingly cultureless) class of consumers to purchase global products represents the essential character of the global economy. The application of easy credit opened the door to the growth of transnational corporations.

The role of credit was a key factor in the formative stages of the global economy because it created the conditions for the rapid expansion of the consumer economy. The stimulation of mass consumerism by mass credit is well documented by Richard Barnet and John Cavanagh in their book *Global Dreams*. The authors feature the story of Citicorp, the American bank that in effect pioneered credit as just another consumer product. Citi figured out that credit could be sold like any other product using the tried and tested tools of smart packaging and aggressive promotion. Millions of people who rarely used a bank could be enticed into buying on credit.

Citicorp sent out tens of millions of application forms and, after only cursory checks to identify current bankrupts, sent out tens of thousands of new credit cards without further credit checks. Since the business depended on volume, defaults were factored in as a normal business cost. Based on Citi's criteria for creditworthiness, all but 20 to 30 million of the 150 million American adults would qualify for credit.

The newly stimulated consumer culture kept American banking happy and profitable through most of the 1980s, but declining real incomes rang alarm bells. In 1991 Citi lost $1 billion. Yet the power of consumer credit was borderless, and Citi had anticipated the decline. Even as it took that large loss at home, its European operations were already more important than its U.S. base, and it was spending millions expanding its credit reach. It already had 13.8 million cardholders in thirty-seven countries.

Citi believed it had discovered the secret to its continued success: "People's attitudes about their finances are a function of how they're raised, their education, and their values, not their nationalities. What works in New York also works in Brussels, Hong Kong, and Tokyo," claimed Citi chairman John Reed.[2] The notion that financial services could be marketed with little or no reference to local cultural differences helped create the notion of the global middle class. The bank's strategy — and the world's transnational providers of goods and services would not be far behind — was to focus exclusively on the wealthiest 10 percent of the developing world's population.

Examining the Indian market, Pei-yuan Chia, Citi's head of global consumer operations, said: "Forget about 90 percent of the people and focus on the top 10 percent. That's 80 million people, larger than West Germany, and if you look at their standard of living, it's higher than the average German's."[3] How do you identify this top 10 percent? Simple. Look them up in the phone book. If they could afford a telephone, Citi could afford to offer them credit.

The idea of the global customer with identical desires unmediated by local culture had tremendous appeal for all global corporations. It was the perfect concept and marketing strategy for corporations wishing to end their multinational character, which required complete operations in each country. Marketing to the global customer further eliminated the need for a local, corporate citizen, presence. Providing the top 10 percent of the world's population with credit and then bombarding them with advertising for truly global products and services was enough to make any corporate strategic planner giddy with fantasies of unlimited growth.

No corporation presents a stronger image of the global corporation and global product than Disney. Its success at peddling its relentless cheer, as Barnet and Cavanagh call it, is well known. As if to deliberately take on the most formidable cultural challenge in the world, Disney, after a huge success in Japan, decided to set up a Disney World outside Paris. The initial visitor count was disappointing and it was universally attacked by the country's cultural and political elites as a cultural Chernobyl.

But millions now pay high ticket prices to see Disney's version of the American Dream. Disney remains confident that its "universal themes of love and adventure as seen through unmistakably American eyes . . . is exactly the experience large numbers of non-Americans want." As Barnet and Cavanagh explain, Disney World and other theme parks have much in common with early American expositions, which, with government participation, were used to impart explicit political and ideological messages — "views of empire, views of science, views of racial superiority and views of what constituted progress."[4]

As well as selling consumerism itself, Disney is marketing something quite different. Disney theme parks are, say Barnet and Cavanagh, "mood enhancers" designed to give people a few days of diversion, offering "illusions of connectedness while providing protected private space and canned dreams."[5]

Of course Disney World is just one example amongst hundreds of heavily marketed American pop culture products. The U.S. movie, music, TV, and video industries have for decades been penetrating the markets of virtually every country. And it wasn't just relentless cheer that the American culture exporters were selling. It was the American brand of personal freedom, reflected in every cultural product offered, which was so compelling that even efforts to slow it down seemed to have the opposite effect. It was as if by trying to suppress American culture, governments were trying to suppress the very freedom promoted by the songs, films, and videos. It was a marketing result that could not have been more effective if it had been planned.

Of all the products that have been most successful at becoming global, none surpasses Coca-Cola, which now sells 560 million cans and bottles every day in 160 countries. The marketing of Coke reflects the view of global marketing guru Theodore Levitt, who argued that "the products and methods of the industrial world play a single tune for all the world and all the world eagerly dances to it." The global marketing strategy was the advertising world's contribution to the shift from multinational corporations to transnational. Multinationals, according to Levitt, paid too much attention to local customs, tastes, quirks, and religions, adjusting their practices accordingly. The global corporation, on the other hand, "sells the same things the same way everywhere."[6]

THE THREAT OF CULTURE TO CORPORATE DOMINATION

The sophisticated psychological manipulation by the world's advertising agencies has had as much to do with the evolution of the transnational corporation as the changes in communications technology. Armed with the proposition that diverse cultures were not the obstacle they were thought to be, the advertising industry itself globalized and grew exponentially. It portrayed the notion that culture was a barrier as a lie. "The lie is that people are different. Yes, there are differences among cultures, but a headache is a headache," claimed Norman Vale, international area director for Grey Advertising Agency.[7]

While the idea of the global product was a boon to international sales, creating and marketing its appeal didn't come cheap. Corporations in 1989 were putting $240 billion into advertising and $380 billion into creative design and packaging, an amount exceeding $120 for every man, woman, and child on the planet.[8] The need to spend huge sums to get people to engage in mass consumption underlines the fact that the actual cost of producing a product is becoming a smaller part of the end price.

In other words, manufacturing the desire for the product is more costly than manufacturing the product itself, and indeed drives the efforts to reduce production costs. Japanese industrialist Kenichi Ohmae states, "Production costs are typically only about 25 percent of the end-user price; the major contribution to a product's price comes increasingly from marketing and support functions such as financing, systems integration and distribution."[9] Ohmae fails to mention the costs that we all pay in increased pollution, social costs, crime, and stress and other health problems that result from creating "cheap" products.

While not every product has the potential to be easily transformed into a global item pitched the same in every country, the efforts are still being made. And the advertising for Western products, global or otherwise, has a reach and depth that is the cultural equivalent of saturation bombing. Television now penetrates nearly every village in the world, and where it doesn't other forms of advertising, including door-to-door cosmetics sales in African villages, almost certainly do.

Amway, the American-based direct seller of shampoo, detergent, and other household products, now has a worldwide sales force of 2.5 million in forty-three countries. The Philippines is especially vulnerable to American pop culture and products. At just one of dozens of such Amway events, fifteen hundred eager salespeople snapped up starter kits for $77. The company trained expatriate Filipinos from the U.S., Australia, and New Zealand to return to their country to recruit thousands of new salespeople.

In the developed world, dozens of TV channels bombard consumers, increasing the number of commercial "hits" on each American from sixteen hundred a day in 1980 to three thousand a day ten years later. Increasingly, no matter where you turn, the efforts to commercialize daily life and human consciousness are unavoidable. Ads appear everywhere there is a flat surface to put them on — above urinals, on parking meters, on vehicles of all kinds, and even projected onto clouds. In New Zealand cuts to medicare have resulted in huge billboards being placed atop hospitals and on the sides of ambulances as a new source of revenue.

Advertising executive Norman Vale's declaration that culture is not a barrier is, however, more a declaration of cultural war than a description of current reality. It is a reality nonetheless that Vale and other advertising giants are trying their best to bring about. It is the inherent barrier to global products presented by "culture" that explains the ferociousness of the TNCs' assault on national cultures. The attack on Canada's remaining cultural protections by the giant American entertainment companies is not simply a demand that they have a level playing field for investment. It is the Canadian front of a general corporate war against individual national cultures that act as a barrier to mass consumption of global products.

The identification of culture as a barrier to trade was stated clearly by Sony chairman Akio Morita in an influential article, "Toward a New World Economic Order," in the *Atlantic Monthly*. Calling for the complete elimination of every barrier to trade and investment world-wide, and lauding NAFTA as a good start, Morita stated: "A level playing field cannot be declared into existence . . . The history of each country and region generates political, social, economic, and cultural factors that result in a business environment unique to that nation or region. This in turn gives rise to a variety of competitive factors . . . which can be seen as non-tariff barriers."[10]

The comic bumper sticker "I shop, therefore I am" has become a serious description of modern life. And the message to those who cannot "shop" is just as real: if you don't consume, you don't exist. For the new transnational corporations that is a brutally exact description of how they view humanity. The focus of all their attention on people able to afford consumer goods, like those in India defined by telephone ownership, excludes most of humanity. At first glance that might seem a blessing in disguise, but being excluded from the global economy does not mean you are not affected by it. For all but a few who have managed to create community economic models, the alternative is dangerously close to no economy at all.

YOUTH: THE FIRST GENERATION OF GLOBAL CUSTOMERS

While the world's middle-class adult population is still by far the largest consumer market, the American marketing juggernaut is aimed carefully and deliberately at teenagers everywhere. The long-term advantages of hooking a whole generation into the consumer culture are difficult to exaggerate. As civil society, and the connectedness it provides, steadily erodes, this generation and the one to follow will identify by default with whatever does provide that feeling of connectedness. And about the only thing left, given the erosion of citizenship and the decline of religion in most countries, is the global product.

The global teenager already exists in the developed world. Says William Roedy, director of MTV Europe: "Eighteen-year-olds in Paris have more in common with eighteen-year-olds in New York than they do with their parents . . . They go to the same movies, they buy the same music, sip the same colas. Global advertising merely works on that premise."[11] More important, they have more connection with other Coke drinkers than they have with their own communities and their own history.

The enormous industry picking apart the entrails of the consumer leaves no subculture unexamined. There are companies that compete with each other to tell producers what nine-year-olds like. Others specialize in age groups from twelve to fifteen, or from six to fifteen. Teenage Research Unlimited claims that 13.4 million Americans aged twelve to fifteen spend $10.5 billion a year of their own money and much more when they shop with their parents' money. Children start to become the focus of corporate attention when they reach the age of nine because that is when they start to take on part-time jobs.[12]

Business Week magazine ran a major feature article in 1997 titled "Hey, Kid, Buy This!" and subtitled "Is Madison Avenue Taking 'Get 'Em While They're Young' Too Far?" It also carried an editorial calling for a return to the days when marketers pitched to parents, who acted as gate-keepers. The enlightened scepticism of the editors aside, there is no sign that the trend to hooking kids will end any time soon.

Youth are now subjected to a dizzying array of advertising formats, from logos on underwear to dozens of magazines and Web sites aimed at them. Advertising targeted to kids in the U.S. increased by 50 percent from 1993 to 1996, to $1.5 billion. It starts, writes *Business Week*'s David Leonhardt, about three days after the newborn gets home. "As an infant, Alyssa may wear Sesame Street diapers and miniature pro-basketball jerseys. By . . . 20 months she will start to recognize some of the thousands of brands flashed in front of her every day."[13] By seven she will be seeing twenty thousand TV commercials a year.

The systematic targeting of ever younger children reveals the desperation of mass consumerism to pump up the North American market where the adult market is largely flat. The effect on these children as future citizens is potentially enormous. Says Leonhardt: "As kids drink in the world around them their cultural encounters . . . have become little more than sales pitches, devoid of any moral beyond a plea for a purchase. Even their classrooms are filled with corporate logos . . . Instead of transmitting a sense of who we are and what we hold important, today's market-driven culture is instilling in them a sense that little exists without a sales pitch attached and that self-worth is something you buy at a shopping mall."[14]

The consumer-profile industry is not only huge, it operates largely without the knowledge of the people being manipulated. How many citizens know that they and their children are regularly divided up into dozens of categories and subcategories of "belongers, outer directeds, inner directeds, need drivens (poor people), emulators and achievers," to name just a few, by psychologists, market experts, and product designers?[15]

Choices: Public versus Private

That the sinister manipulation of children, teenagers, and adults is not even considered an important social and political issue is itself a sign of the times. Ordinary citizens are being subjected to the most sophisticated and well-financed manipulation in human history. And the impact is not trivial. Having these forces manoeuvring and micromanaging what people buy and how much, not to mention what they watch and listen to, goes a long way towards determining what kind of society we end up with. Imagine if the world's societies spent even one-tenth of the world's advertising budget on providing information designed to nurture self-aware citizens.

Money spent on artificially induced needs and desires in the consumer world is money not spent on other things: books, magazines, travel to heritage sites, cultural pursuits. Immersing oneself in the cornucopia of consumer products also takes time, time otherwise spent (in the past, at least) with family, community, friends. And the more money people feel they need to engage in this consumer world, the less they are able and willing to "spend" in taxes for public services.

The industry argues that people still have the choice to buy or not buy, yet this is true only at the most abstract level. It is the same argument used by the tobacco industry when it claims that its advertising of sports and cultural events has no effect on whether young people start smoking. If that were true, the billions they spend would be completely wasted. That they keep spending is proof enough that they believe the money well spent.

The impact of the global consumer revolution is felt everywhere. Countries now define their national purpose almost exclusively in terms of how well they will fare in the global competition for investment. History, culture, equality, civil society are all swept aside as nonconsumables and therefore incapable of being factored into the new order of things. Some countries have little choice in the matter; other states do so willingly as their elites eagerly surrender sovereignty to the TNCs.

The irony is that global competition is not focussed as much on consumption at home in developed countries where real incomes are steadily dropping, but on developing world consumption. And as governments deregulate investment and labour so we can compete with the lowest-paid, lowest-taxed, and least regulated developing countries, corporations depend more and more on the spending of other nations' elites just as they depend on the labour of other nations' workers. The result is a global levelling involving two classes, those who can earn enough to consume the global products and those who can't, including working people in the developed world.

The new world of the devolving citizen/evolving customer is not a parallel world to civil society, it is a replacement world. Freedom is no longer freedom from want, freedom from insecurity. It, too, has devolved. Now freedom means consumer choice. The success of the TNC in creating global consumerism is at the same time the gradual destruction of civil society. The cause becomes the effect; as more people acquiesce to the lure of the marketplace, they abandon their status as self-conscious citizens and with it the ability to resist the slow destruction of their community.

The key to the global marketplace is the global customer whose identity is found in the stuff they buy. This is precisely why Sony's Akio Morita declared that not only culture but all the particularities of civil society are a barrier to commerce. What he was talking about was connectedness. The more connected we are to community, neighbourhood, tradition, family, and history, the more likely we are to resist the lure of consumerism.

The gulf between the evolving and increasingly powerful corporate citizen and the devolving citizen/customer has been growing greater. Real citizens have abandoned the field, voluntarily or because they can no longer find ways of engaging civil society; corporate citizens rule the world, and liberated from even the minimal social responsibility once imposed by civil society, reveal themselves for what they are.

4

THE TRANSNATIONAL CORPORATE CITIZEN

The foundation of Chile's strong economic position today . . .
was courageously laid by [former Chilean military dictator Augusto]
Pinochet. [The coup was justified] because it brought wealth to an
enormous number of people, I mean in my terms. If you ask somebody
in jail, he'll say no. But that's the wonderful thing about our world:
we can have the freedom to disagree.
— PETER MUNK, CEO OF BARRICK GOLD, WHOSE COMPANY IS ACTIVE IN CHILE

[The large corporations] are latter-day versions of colonial empires.
They defend their positions not with machine guns or cruise missiles
but with trademarks, copyrights and huge marketing budgets that
dwarf the resources of many governments.
— ANGUS REID, *SHAKEDOWN: HOW THE NEW ECONOMY IS CHANGING OUR LIVES*

If, for the sake of argument, we accept the notion that corporations can be citizens, then these particular citizens exhibit the behaviour of textbook sociopaths. Incapable of telling right from wrong, demonstrating severe antisocial behaviour, they are often a threat to the community, even a deadly threat. The men (they're almost exclusively men) who are the collective mind, heart, and soul of the corporate citizen are somehow capable of deciding, as Ford executives did in the 1970s, that it was not cost effective to fix the gas tank of its Pinto model, although they knew it could explode on rear impact. Ford calculated that the cost of fixing the defect in existing and future cars, $11 per car, was greater than the cost of court settlements arising from the predictable number of fatal accidents, estimated at 180 deaths per year at $200,000 each.[1]

We have to assume that the men who made this decision were not evil monsters capable of murdering people and then going home to their families as if nothing had happened. Indeed, what makes this story so horrendous is that these men, as individual citizens, were not evil monsters at all, and were very likely no less ethical and decent than average Americans. Walking through the doors of Ford Motor Company had transformed them into corporate citizens, mutated by corporate imperatives. This contrast between corporate and personal behaviour was identified by former General Motors vice-president John Delorean in the insider's profile he provided of his company: "It seemed to me . . . that the system of American business often produces wrong, immoral and irresponsible decisions, even though the personal morality of the people running the businesses is often above reproach. The system has a different morality as a group than the people do as individuals."[2]

The Pinto example is just one of many where corporations demonstrate that they do not operate as good citizens. Corporate Crime, a study, done in 1975–76, reported that 60 percent of large corporations in the U.S. had been charged with at least one form of criminal behaviour. And the largest corporations accounted for over 72 percent of the most serious crimes.[3]

In recent years, North Americans have witnessed the spectacle of tobacco executives declaring solemnly before government committees that they do not believe smoking is addictive. As it was soon revealed, these men knew that in the files of their corporations were stacks of documents disclosing the lie of what they were claiming. Not only did corporate records show nicotine is addictive, they also detailed efforts over two decades to increase a cigarette's effectiveness as a "nicotine delivery system" by adding ammonia.

Today, clearly, corporate culture does not allow executives to make moral choices. Publicly traded corporations that undermine their profitability by behaving as good corporate citizens would soon find their shareholders demanding a change in management.

There is a very short list of corporations in North America that try to behave like good corporate citizens. But these companies are so rare that they become newsworthy because they are such aberrations. The *Globe and Mail*'s *Report on Business* has featured a couple of Canadian companies whose treatment of its employees is exemplary. Husky Injection Molding Systems is a small transnational (seventeen hundred employees in sixteen countries) and, though not unionized, has a record for treating its employees with respect in a management structure that is almost democratic. Management consultant Jim Collins calls Husky one of the ten greatest firms he has ever seen. "They do not exist to maximize profits; they practice a set of unwavering core values; they embrace constant change; they set audacious goals; they instill unwavering devotion in their employees." Husky is also very profitable and growing, from sales of $72 million in 1985 to $609 million in 1995.[4]

A number of features of today's corporate environment make Husky the rare exception rather than the rule. In fact, in the ruthless world of corporate raiding it is precisely the features of a good corporate citizen that make a company a prime target for a takeover. A company that has large cash reserves, a well-funded pension fund, a large resource base, or a highly paid workforce is a plum waiting to be picked by those who make their money in the raiding business. The ferociousness of speculative finance to find ever greater levels of profitability and ever higher rates of return for investors does not permit many examples like Husky. Indeed, it is the speculative markets that are at the root of much of corporate pathology in the nineties.

MONEY FOR NOTHING

Every day the amount of money that changes hands in the world's foreign exchange markets amounts to nearly $2 trillion. Over just three days the trade in currencies equals the dollar value of the gross domestic product of the U.S. More important, 97.5 percent of that currency trading is devoted purely to speculation. Just 2.5 percent involves the financing of real economic activity — trading, buying, and selling goods, services, and capital assets. In the 1970s, only about 10 percent of the currency trading was speculative.[5]

Much of what we see in the daily business press that seems inexplicable and irrational — stock prices plummeting with news of decreasing unemployment rates, years of high interest rates despite near zero inflation — is explained by the financial markets, including currency speculation. The apparent abandonment of integrated domestic markets by corporations and government policy makers, corporate strategies of downsizing and decentralization, the almost maniacal focus on short-term corporate profits can all be traced in large measure to the power of the financial markets.

The influence of the international foreign exchange system has been nothing short of revolutionary. It has severely eroded the links between the productive economy — the real economy of creating and selling goods and services — and the money system. It is now more profitable to speculate in the money system than it is to invest in the production of goods and services.

In a healthy money system, creating and using money is directly linked to real things, to exchanges of goods and services that we use or productive capital such as machinery, land, technology, and labour. But as David Korten argues, ours is a sick money system in which money and productive activity become delinked and a class of "money manipulators," whose specialty is extracting money that is no longer linked to real wealth, develops. Yet while delinked from real wealth, this money still provides those who hold it with a demand on the real wealth that is being produced.

According to Bernard Lietaer, a former currency trader, "This new [currency] asset class has some tremendous advantages from an investor viewpoint. The first is the extraordinarily low transaction costs. Placing a few billion dollars in foreign exchange costs very little, for major currencies just a fraction of a percent. Compared to stock transactions this is 10 to 20 times cheaper."[6] It costs only eighteen cents and takes just a few seconds to complete a multimillion-dollar currency transaction across the ocean.

But perhaps the most critical aspect of the foreign exchange market is its dependence on volatility for its profitability. The more volatile a currency, the greater the potential profits from buying and selling. The worst thing that could happen to a currency trader is to buy a million French francs and then nothing happens; it just sits there. The longer you wait for a change in its value, the more money you lose.

As David Korten puts it, "The global financial system has become a parasitic predator that lives off the flesh of its host — the productive economy."[7] The domination of the financial sector has had profound effects on investment patterns. The wealth to be extracted from currency speculation has directly spurred other areas of speculation as well as indirectly affected other phenomena of the 1980s and 1990s such as the mergers and acquisitions mania that continues to this day.

The financial markets present a number of opportunities to make money, to extract wealth, without engaging in any productive activity. Besides currency speculation, there is the international bond market. Just as in the currency market, very small fluctuations in bond prices can yield large profits for institutional investors. A change of just three to ten cents per $100 is enough to persuade such investors to make trades, to get out of one country's bonds and into another's.

All of this speculation has huge repercussions for the global economy and for the ability of governments to create public policy in the interest of their citizens. It also affects what business does with its money. For example, Bernard Lietaer suggests, "for real international businesses that do mining, make cars, or electronics, the foreign exchange risk is the biggest single risk they face. If a chemical company wanted to set up a plant in India the business risk is minimal compared to the foreign exchange risk. Real investments are not being made because the foreign exchange risk is not manageable."[8]

Because of this new risk TNCs are obliged to develop strategies for dealing with the volatile currency markets, and it is here that the behaviour of large corporations is partly determined by speculative activity. According to Lietaer, corporations cope with currency markets in two ways: decentralization of production and marketing, and recentralization of financial and treasury functions. Both are aimed at increasing profitability to the level attained in the speculative financial markets. The decentralization strategy allows for externalizing the costs of production. For example, instead of costing in pollution control as part of the picture, a particularly polluting industry will set up a plant in Mexico or the Philippines, where it can pollute with impunity.

The centralization of the finance and treasury functions gives maximum control over exchange markets — if you can't beat 'em, join 'em. Most of the largest transnational corporations now have huge financial divisions, and many of them engage in speculation themselves. John Dillon reports that a survey of 530 U.S. nonfinancial corporations found that 75 percent used derivatives to hedge their financial exposure, and fully 40 percent were actively speculating.[9]

These are not minor parts of these businesses. British Petroleum's director of money transactions has stated, "Our currency trading is as important as our oil trading." This pattern, says Dillon, prevails for some of the world's largest corporations. "General Motors and General Electric both made more profits from their internal financial subsidiaries than they did manufacturing real automobiles or electronic products."[10] In fact, the largest financial institution in the U.S. today is General Electric.

The enormous amounts of money to be made in these sophisticated forms of gambling has created a new class of investor. Geared to the expectation of instant profits and fast turnarounds, they are impatient with the old world of buying shares in a company and waiting for the company to grow. As Magna Corporation owner Frank Stronach put it, "Why would you pour a foundation, buy machines, hire employees if you could make as much money buying bonds?"[11]

A NEW CLASS OF INVESTORS

The speculative markets not only create a whole new class of investors. Their impact — setting the standard for profit taking — has an enormous influence on the behaviour of nonfinancial corporations. It means such corporations are in a constant race to make profits as high as those in speculative markets and as fast. The behaviour of large corporations is driven by shareholders, and shareholders today have changed. The owners of corporate stocks are now dominated by huge institutional investors who "speak" for the millions of ordinary citizens in Canada and elsewhere who have money in pension funds or mutual funds.

In the U.S. one-third of all corporate shares, $4 trillion in assets, are held in workers' pension funds managed by the trust departments of the giant banks. And in 1996 mutual funds overtook pensions as the most important players on stock exchanges. In Canada, pension fund administrators manage $360 billion. In addition, more than $260 billion is invested in mutual funds. And although these funds are managed for ordinary citizens, including union members who often suffer from the lean and mean behaviour of their corporate employers, they are the most influential force in the market today.

The fund managers feel under tremendous pressure to perform well, and, says David Korten, in the hot-money atmosphere of the 1990s that means providing "nearly instant financial gains. The time frames involved are far too short for a productive investment to mature, the amount of money to be 'invested' far exceeds the number of productive investment opportunities available, and the returns the market has come to expect exceed what most productive investments are able to yield even over a period of years."[12]

If nonfinancial corporations are constrained by the heady atmosphere of the speculative markets, governments are even more affected. The power of money speculators to transfer massive amounts of money instantly between markets has given this handful of traders a weapon by which they hold public policy hostage to their own narrow pursuits. And corporate advocates aren't shy about using their power to threaten even the most powerful governments. The Cato Institute, a leading free-market think-tank, issued such a warning to President Bill Clinton and Congress in the pages of the *New York Times*, reminding them that "equity investors have developed a global perspective and they prefer markets where government is downsizing and the prospects for economic growth are good." The author suggested that the government get rid of "hundreds of ill-considered laws that benefit special interests" and "thousands of counter-productive rules in the Code of Federal Regulations."[13]

Walter Wriston, the former chair of Citicorp, made this boast about the government of François Mitterand of France: "The market took one look at his policies and within six months the capital flight had made him change course." The "decision," said Wriston, was made by those sitting at "200,000 monitors in trading rooms all around the world [who conduct] a kind of global plebiscite on the monetary and fiscal policies of governments issuing currencies."[14]

The most dramatic example of how a large-scale speculator can affect a country's currency involved the British pound. Currency speculator George Soros actually caused the British pound to fall 41% against the Japanese Yen, and in effect sabotaged the system of fixed exchange rates planned for the European Union, eliminating a major threat to speculators who depend on floating rates.

Speculators also wield enormous influence over government policy in the bond market. Political science professor James Laxer refers to the bond market as "the most powerful force in contemporary capitalism."[15] It is the floating-rate bonds that allow bondholders to sell government financial instruments, such as Treasury bills, in such quantity that buyers can successfully demand a discount to purchase them. Because financial markets are all linked together, the effect is an upward pressure on all that country's interest rates.

The collapse of the speculation house of cards that many had predicted finally happened in late 1997. The madness of unfettered currency speculation came home to roost — and right where global capital had been pinning most of its hopes, among the so-called Asian Tigers. First Thailand was obliged to devalue its currency, then Indonesia, followed by the Philippines, all second-string Asian economies. But then came Hong Kong and South Korea, the eleventh-largest economy in the world, humiliated by being forced to sign a bail-out from the IMF of $57 billion. Estimates of the total for all countries was well over $100 billion. It did not stop even there as the "Asian flu" spread to Japan, where the country's fourth-largest brokerage house collapsed.

The stock market followed the downward plunge as the ridiculous overvaluation of real world assets at last collapsed. The fully integrated, speed-of-light, twenty-four-hour-a-day world markets virtually guaranteed that a currency crisis in Thailand, a bit-player in the global scheme, would bring global chaos. The crisis spread to Latin America, where Brazil's stock market plunged in sympathy. In Southeast Asia, it was estimated that purchasing power dropped by $300 billion in just a few weeks.

While shareholders around the world lost big, middle-class Asians as well as workers and peasants suddenly found their money worth 30 to 50 percent less than it had been. Tens of billions were drained from central banks, much of it headed for numbered bank accounts. The crisis for individuals was paralleled by the crisis for nations as debts owed in dollars were suddenly 30 percent higher, tax revenues started dropping, and money for economic activity disappeared.

The response of the elite to this global catastrophe was in perfect synch with free-market ideology. Avoiding at all costs any call for bringing money traders and the speculative economy to heel, everyone in authority from President Clinton to the market pundits began with the mantras of "sound fundamentals" and "market corrections." They then tried to blame the "structurally weak economies" of Southeast Asia, the very same economies that just weeks before retained their status as Tigers. Just two months before the collapse, the director general of the IMF praised the economy of Malaysia as a model economy for the rest of the world to follow.

The crisis underlined the fatal contradiction of the global system. It must have stability of function, otherwise every mini-crisis has the potential to become a catastrophe. Yet the system itself is driven by and is inextricably meshed with a subsystem of uncontrolled speculation that depends on instability.

None of this broke through the armour of the true believers among the world "leaders." Only Malaysia's eccentric and largely discredited Prime Minister Mahathir Mohamed broke ranks. During the 1997 APEC summit, Mahathir, guilty in his own right of economic mismanagement, attacked the free market as the source of the problem. Demanding the imposition of strict regulations on currency traders, he stated, "Currencies don't fall on their own . . . We want to know how much money [currency traders] made and are they being taxed and who should tax them."[16] For his efforts at declaring that the emperor had no clothes, he was accused by Canada's trade minister, Sergio Marchi, of uttering conspiracy theories.

Instead of dealing with the issue of money speculation and re-regulation of international trade, Canada backed the U.S. in its call for even greater powers for the IMF to force countries to further liberalize their economies. The deal finally worked out between the IMF and South Korea will take a staggering human toll. The IMF demanded that the country cut its growth rate from 6 percent to 3 percent and its deficit by $10 billion. The result will be a rise in unemployment from 2.5 percent to 7 percent, throwing 1.5 million people out of work.[17]

VULTURES THAT TARGET THE HEALTHY

The search for super-profits and increased share prices has unleashed a ruthlessness in the business world that destroys not only individual lives but companies themselves. In his book *When Corporations Rule the World*, David Korten provides a number of compelling examples of corporations whose social responsibility made them vulnerable. One was the Pacific Lumber Company (PLC), acquired by corporate raider Charles Hurwitz. Before the acquisition, PLC was known as "one of the most economically and environmentally sound timber companies in the United States. It was exemplary in its . . . use of sustainable logging practices on its substantial holdings of redwood timber stands, was generous in the benefits it provided to its employees, overfunded its pension fund to ensure it could meet its commitments, and maintained a no-layoffs policy even during down-turns in the timber market. These practices made it a prime takeover target."[18]

After taking control Hurwitz doubled the cutting rate and described the mile-and-a-half-wide clear-cut into thousand-year-old forest as "our wildlife biologist study trail." His contempt for ecology was matched by his contempt for his employees as he raided the $93-million pension fund to the tune of $55 million and invested it in the insurance company that had financed the junk bonds he had used to underwrite the takeover. This insurance company eventually failed.

The attitude demonstrated by such corporate raiders and CEOs in general is vastly different from that of recent generations of corporate executives, although each decade has had its share of robber barons. Revelling in the mass destruction of thousand-year-old redwood trees and gleefully dismissing tens of thousands of employees seems to be a new form of ostentatiously antisocial behaviour. Indeed, these corporate takeover executives almost go out of their way to humiliate their new employees. According to Korten, "To justify the mass firings and wage cuts that followed the takeover of the Safeway supermarket chain, investor George Roberts told the *Wall Street Journal* that the supermarket chain's employees 'are now being held accountable . . . They have to produce up to plan, if they are going to be competitive with the rest of the world.'"[19]

At the top of this list of celebrity CEOs is "Chainsaw" Al Dunlap, who gained notoriety for his turnaround of Scott Paper. Self-cast as a saviour of badly run companies, Dunlap brags about being the superstar in the field of downsizing and restructuring, claiming to be "much like Michael Jordan in basketball and Bruce Springsteen in rock 'n' roll."[20] By laying off a third of Scott's employees, selling hundreds of millions in assets, slashing research and development, closing plants, and eliminating all charitable donations, Dunlap increased the value of the company's shares from $2.9 billion to $9.4 billion in less than two years.

Dunlap's book *Mean Business: How I Save Bad Companies and Make Good Companies Great* describes his business philosophy. "Executives who run their businesses to support social causes . . . would never get my investment dollars. They funnel money into things like saving the whales . . . That's not the essence of business. If you want to support social causes . . . join the Rotary International." His pleasure at bullying people is legendary: "If people balk at something and say 'We've tried that before,' that's the kiss of death. They're a disease; cut them out."[21]

But Dunlap's bragging conceals as much as it reveals. Scott Paper was not in nearly as bad shape as Dunlap claims (it was number one in the world in sales) and many of the reforms he implemented, other than the asset stripping and layoffs, had been in the planning stages for years. When he bragged about creating 107 new products, it turned out that 44 of them were the same two products packaged in twenty-two countries. His macho slashing of R&D has resulted in Scott losing market share in all three of its core businesses, paper towels, bathroom tissue, and facial tissue.[22] Following his devastation of Scott Paper (which Dunlap delivered into the merger arms of its long-time competitor, Kimberly-Clark), Dunlap went on to "save" Sunbeam by cutting its workforce of twelve thousand in half and closing 18 of its 26 factories and 37 of its 61 warehouses.

Corporate raiders spend much of their time poring over annual reports to identify companies that have not already downsized and stripped their assets in the name of quick returns. There are even investment funds that specialize in looking for opportunities in labour-intensive industries that have resisted the trend of moving to low-wage countries.

American and Mexican investors set up the AmeriMex Maquiladora Fund to target U.S. companies. AmeriMex's prospectus reads: "The fund will purchase established domestic United States companies suitable for maquiladora acquisitions, wherein a part or all of the manufacturing operations will be relocated to Mexico to take advantage of the cost of labor."[23]

AmeriMex goes on to describe how much money could be saved by companies that currently pay wages in the $7–$10-an-hour range by moving to Mexico, where they would pay $1.15 to $1.50 an hour: "It is estimated that this could translate into annual savings of $10,000–$17,000 per employee . . . It is anticipated that most investments will be retained for three to eight years." At maximum savings, a company with a thousand production employees could see the market value of its stock increase by $170 million over a very short period.

It is exactly these kind of super-returns that the rogue financial system demands of any publicly traded company. The problem, beyond the obvious moral and ethical questions, is that once the savings have been realized the company has to come up with another trick to keep its growth rate at such a peak. Having already externalized its greatest cost, it is unlikely to be able to do so, which accounts for the short period that ownership of the company is held by AmeriMex. The raiders are not builders and leave their targets crippled, decimated by asset stripping, or bankrupt.

As Korten points out, examples such as AmeriMex underline the ultimate futility of demanding that individual corporations act as good corporate citizens. The global financial system effectively renders such management a recipe for corporate suicide through raiding and asset stripping or shifting production off-shore. Says Korten, "Those who call on corporate managers to exercise greater social responsibility miss the basic point. Corporate managers live and work in a system that is virtually feeding on the socially responsible."[24] Simply to head off being a victim of a corporate raider, even responsible managers are forced to mimic those who would take them over. In the end, the result is much the same, often differing only in the degree of restructuring or the speed at which it takes place.

The irony is that in most cases downsizing doesn't accomplish what its promoters said it would. Michael Hammer, co-author of *Reengineering the Corporation*, essentially a handbook on cutting and slashing, is now scrambling to recast his advice. His examples of successful companies now include a joint venture between GE and Fanuc of Japan, "which boosted revenue by 18 percent during the past two years, while the number of employees has risen by just 3 percent."[25]

A 1993 study of Canadian firms that went through restructuring supports Hammer's about-face. The study, by Watson Wyatt Worldwide, concluded that "relatively few companies accomplished their goals." Of the 148 firms studied, 62 percent said they reduced costs but only 37 percent increased profits; just 17 percent improved their competitive advantage, and only 40 percent increased their productivity.[26]

Another study, by University of Saskatchewan commerce professor Marc Mentzer, found similar results. Mentzer studied 250 large Canadian companies over eight years and concluded: "There is no relationship between downsizing and profit," he found. In fact, there is no clear relationship even to share price. The trend is for a share to increase in the short run and then go into a long-term decline. Repeated waves of layoffs damage companies severely. Mentzer argues, "This water-torture style of downsizing kills morale and forces everyone to think about job hunting instead of doing their current job well."[27]

Instead of using layoffs as a last resort as companies should, they do it almost as a fad. Mentzer concluded that unsure managers downsize because big companies like GM and IBM do it. Downsizing becomes "a badge of honour because it shows other executives and the investment community how tough you are. It should be a badge of shame because it's a sign of bad management. Any idiot can go through a payroll and fire every fifth person."[28]

The downsizing mania has an enormous effect on economies where it is practised. A comparison of G7 countries by economist

Frank Lichtenberg showed that countries in which companies lay off employees in response to a downturn suffered the most prolonged recessions. The U.S. and Canada were the two least stable countries; Japan and Italy the most stable. In the U.S., "when output falls by $1 the income of workers tends to decline 48 cents and profits 52 cents. In Japan, by contrast, virtually 100 percent of output fluctuations was borne by shareholders." By laying off workers, companies take demand out of the economy in a way that doesn't happen when shareholders' dividends go down.[29]

Despite the evidence that downsizing doesn't accomplish what its practitioners say it does, and despite the decamping of some of its gurus, in late 1997 downsizing showed signs of increasing again. The return to the trend was signalled by Kodak, which announced a layoff of 10 percent of its workforce over two years — ten thousand employees worldwide. Five of the ten largest cuts in the U.S. in 1997 occurred in the fall. The reasons for the continued trend, according to the U.S. Conference Board, was "intense import competition . . . Businesses have to drive earnings up."[30] Sometimes it appears as though the layoffs are carried out in order to pay for outrageous CEO compensation packages. Such was the case at Levi Strauss. In 1996 it paid its retiring president $126 million; in 1997 it fired 6,395 employees and closed eleven plants.[31]

Robert Hare of the University of British Columbia is Canada's leading researcher in psychopathic behaviour. He describes the corporate downsizers like Al Dunlap as "sub-criminal psychopaths." These are the people who work amongst us but are incapable of forming genuine allegiances or loyalties even in their personal lives. They are equally incapable of feeling guilt or remorse and package all of this antisocial behaviour in a veneer of charm. In the end they are extremely destructive to the companies that hire them and, in Hare's words, "they manoeuvre to have detractors fired and ruin other people's careers without a hint of remorse."[32]

According to Canadian psychologist Paul Babiak, it is precisely in the atmosphere of restructuring that corporate psychopaths flourish. They do not do well in stable corporate bureaucracies, where there are well-established controls and operating systems. In companies undergoing massive change, Babiak says, "there is chaos, or breakdowns of norms and values in the culture, and in that chaotic milieu, the psychopath can move in and do very well."[33]

MILLION-DOLLAR CEOS: REWARDING GREED

The breakdown of societal constraints on corporate behaviour manifests itself in increasingly obscene CEO compensation packages, especially in Canada and the U.S., while employee incomes are held at the levels of the early 1980s. In 1996, eighty Canadian CEOs took home more than a million dollars in compensation — usually a combination of salary, bonuses, and the exercising of stock options.

Including stock options in compensation goes a long way to explain why asset stripping and massive layoffs happen: the rapid driving up of share prices means that the stock options of the CEO and other executives will be worth that much more. The CEO's incentive to drive up the stock price in the short term works against any ambition to build the company over the medium term or plan for its long-term future.

The constant hype around the market and its supremacy tells us that money is everything; in Al Dunlap's words, "Money is a CEO's report card." Apparently not in Canada. According to a *Globe and Mail* report of the one hundred top-paid executives in Canada in 1996, CEOs did very nicely whether or not their report cards were good. Twenty-two of the companies managed by these men saw their profits decline from the year before. But of the twenty-two CEOs responsible for those declining results, only four had their compensation reduced. The rest had increases.[34]

Some of the increases were spectacular, starting with number one on the list, Laurent Beaudoin at Bombardier, whose compensation increased by 1,335 percent (to $19,100,317) while profits dipped by 36 percent. Michael Brown of Thomson Corporation got a 166 percent increase for his accomplishment — decreasing profits by 28 percent. Nova's Edward Newall got a whopping 283 percent increase (up to $6,350,750) while presiding over a decline in profits of 39 percent. Gulf Resources chief James Bryan achieved a decline in profits of 232 percent but got a nice surprise in his pay packet with an increase of 65 percent to $1.75 million. Peter Munk, one of the most aggressively outspoken advocates of the free market, saw his pay increase for the two companies he runs when both had decreased profits, and in each case part of those increases were in fatter bonuses. Sixteen of the twenty-two CEOs presiding over declining profits earned increased bonuses, presumably a measure of their gall as well as a sign of the gross irresponsibility of their boards of directors respecting shareholders' interests.

How much can one man (all of the top 100 CEOs in 1996 were men) be worth? The notion that a CEO is worth millions a year suggests that there is real genius involved, that the increase in share price is the result of an extraordinary business talent. But in fact corporations don't work this way. No one person is that smart, nor can their presence be so pervasive in a huge organization that they can affect all its decisions and planning.

In his study of General Motors, Peter Drucker dismissed the idea that corporate organizations naturally bring executives with exceptional ability to the top. "No institution can possibly survive if it needs geniuses or supermen to manage it. It must be organized in such a way as to be able to get along under a leadership composed of average human beings. No institution has solved the problem of leadership . . . unless it gives the leader a sense of duty and a sense of mutual loyalty between him and his associates; for these enable the average human being . . . to function effectively in a position of trust and leadership."[35]

By this measure, the current crop of CEOs, whose expertise is increasingly in the area of finance and cost cutting, should be paid less, not more. Loyalty and duty have been so devalued in the current corporate culture that they have virtually disappeared. The drive for short-term share price increases in effect invites the selection of CEOs whose logic is disturbingly similar to the U.S. general in Vietnam who declared in all seriousness that he had to destroy a village to save it.

The notion that professional managers must be paid astronomical sums to motivate them to do their jobs seems absurd on the face of it, not least because these same men support government policies that take money away from the poor to motivate them to work. Former Harvard University president Derek Bok believes that CEOs are paid a bonus precisely because they are being asked to work against their better judgement as managers and human beings. The obsession with short-term returns means that managers must ignore the interests not only of their employees and the community but also of the long-term interests of the company they are working for. In short, their bonuses are paid because their jobs have become so distasteful.

There are no doubt some managers who are uncomfortable over their destructive roles, yet they are clearly in the minority of those who are receiving gargantuan pay packages. There may be a simpler explanation of why CEOs get paid so much. It has more to do with social class than with psychology or motivation. They pay themselves obscene amounts quite simply because they can get away with it. No matter how ridiculous the amounts, the other shoe never drops.

The comparison of what corporate executives pay themselves and what they pay their average employee reveals just how out of proportion their compensation is. In 1996, Bombardier's Beaudoin took home 627 times what his average Canadian employee earns; Francesco Bellini of BioChem Pharma got 328 times.[36] The CEOs of all the banks were paid at least a hundred times more than their average employee. It is worth noting that these ratios are unique to North American and other English-speaking developed countries. In Japan, executives by informal consensus take home on average about seventeen times what their average employee earns. There is no evidence that Japanese CEOs lack motivation or success.

CORPORATIONS AND DEMOCRACY, LIKE OIL AND WATER

When the political and economic elites of developed countries promote democracy in Third World countries, clearly it is that brand of democracy advocated by libertarians and not the sort fought for by the people themselves. Stability and the protection of property rights are what corporations are seeking from governments. Substantive democracy, in its original sense of rule by the majority, is a threat to the corporate bottom line. Corporations have a long history of ridding the world of that kind of democracy.

One of the favourite investment locations for Canadian companies is Chile, and for good reason. Following the military coup in 1973, the entire country was restructured in the exclusive interests of corporations and those with property. Every deregulation fantasy of corporate CEOs and finance capital was put in place. Labour has been largely silenced, taxes are low, environmental protection is minimal, nearly every public service has been privatized. And the corporations that operate there have their fellow corporate citizen, International Telephone and Telegraph (ITT), to thank for it all.

The military takeover of Chile was engineered by the U.S. government in close cooperation with three of the major multinational corporations with investments in that country, ITT and mining giants Anaconda and Kennecott. The 1970 election victory of Salvador Allende, a socialist who had campaigned on a platform of nationalization of Chilean resources, had taken the U.S. and the American corporations by surprise. As soon as the election results were known, an ITT official contacted Henry Kissinger's senior adviser on Latin America to indicate how determined ITT was to prevent Allende from becoming president and how much it was willing to spend in the effort: "I told [him] to tell Mr. Kissinger [ITT chairman] Mr. Geneen is willing to come to Washington to discuss ITT's interest and that we are prepared to assist financially in sums up to seven figures."[37]

In the wake of the Allende victory ITT established close contacts with the State Department, the National Security Council, the U.S. Information Agency, the CIA, the Inter-American Development Bank, the Senate Foreign Relations Committee, and other agencies with the purpose of pushing the U.S. to intervene covertly in Chile. Efforts were made to prevent Allende from taking power, which he could do only with the help of the centrist Christian Democrats. The CIA immediately implemented a program of economic destabilization to demonstrate to the Christian Democrats the folly of supporting the inauguration of Allende as president. When that failed, tactics changed. An ITT memo from field operatives in Chile read: "A more realistic hope . . . is that a swiftly deteriorating economy (bank runs, plant bankruptcies, etc.) will touch off a wave of violence resulting in a military coup."[38]

Once Allende was assured of the presidency, the CIA moved quickly to foment a military coup, and ITT with its many contacts and operatives in Chile was close at the CIA's side. ITT executive William Merriam gave the following description of a meeting at CIA headquarters: "Approaches continue to be made to select members of the Armed Forces in an attempt to have them lead some sort of uprising."[39] In fact, ITT was ahead of many transnationals in its capacity to respond to the actions of national governments. It was, as ITT chronicler Anthony Samson stated, effectively a sovereign state. In Chile it had a foreign policy, a foreign service, an information service, a clandestine service, and other operations more typical of governments than of corporations. The coup in Chile cost the lives of thirty thousand civilians and ensconced in power one of the most ruthless dictatorships in all of Latin America.

Equally important was the role that the dictatorship would play in the application of new-right economic theory after the coup. An entire package of Milton Friedman–inspired policies was implemented — deregulation, suppression of labour rights, and massive privatization of public services.

It is no wonder that corporate planners love Chile. What was done there is exactly what they would like to do in every country — and would were democratic freedoms not in place. The coup in Chile wiped clean the social, political, and cultural landscape of a nation and prepared the ground for a massive experiment in new-right social engineering. It was carried out at the behest of transnational corporations in their interests, and the subsequent "new society" was designed by the ideologues of the counter-revolution. Economists from Friedman's Chicago School of Economics applied their neoliberal tools to the defenceless people of Chile, creating social divisions and economic disparities unprecedented in the country's history.

That Chile is touted as a proud accomplishment of the forces of globalization reveals a great deal about where corporate rule would take us. Among the Canadian corporations eagerly taking advantage of the fruits of military-enforced restructuring of Chile are the Bank of Nova Scotia, the National Bank of Canada, Bata, Canadian Airlines, CanWest Global Communications, Shell Canada, and mining giants Falconbridge, Inco, Noranda, Placer Dome, Rio Algom, and Munk's Barrick Gold.

GLOBAL GREED AND PRIVATE ARMIES

The counter-revolution in Chile took place in the global context of the cold war. The United States spent hundreds of billions of dollars keeping the Soviet Union in check and suppressing movements for social and economic justice wherever they occurred and regardless of the size of the threat. As the invasion of Grenada demonstrated, no opposition was too small to crush.

In the post–cold war years everything has changed and everything has stayed the same. Authoritarian governments, dedicated primarily to protecting private property, are in place in most of the countries that the U.S. considers important sites for corporate investment.

Where governments are not powerful enough to enforce property rights on behalf of corporations, another strategy is adopted. The extent to which corporations now feel little compunction in challenging the sovereignty of governments and assuming their role was dramatically revealed in early 1997. Executive Outcomes, a private army for hire, was established by two Britons, a businessman and a former army officer. Antony Buckingham was the CEO of Heritage Oil and Gas, which had close links to a Canadian company, Ranger Oil. In 1993 the companies teamed up with Eeben Barlow, a former South African Defence Force officer who had served with some of the most ruthless units of the apartheid military, including its assassination network, which was organized along corporate lines.

Ranger Oil recruited Executive Outcomes to drive the rebel Unita army out of Soyo, a centre of the oil industry in Angola. For $30 million, Ranger, in cooperation with the Angolan government, purchased a force of five hundred former South African soldiers as well as sophisticated weaponry (including fuel-air bombs and helicopter gun ships). The intervention of this force virtually changed the course of the civil war. From Angola, Executive Outcomes moved on to Sierra Leone, where it shored up the corrupt regime of Valentine Stroesser against an armed rebellion that was on the verge of seizing the capital city.

Executive Outcomes is a complex network of some eighteen companies, the advance guard for major business interests engaged in a latter-day scramble for the mineral wealth of Africa. The corporation has worked with more than thirty countries, mostly African, and also has links with South Korea and Malaysia. And according to a British Intelligence report, it is growing rapidly. The *Guardian* predicts that "Executive Outcomes will become ever richer and more potent, capable of exercising real power even to the extent of keeping military regimes in being. If it continues to expand at the present rate, its influence in sub-Saharan Africa could become crucial."[40]

It seems more than a coincidence that Executive Outcomes, first identified in 1991, has developed into such a potent force at the same time that the cold war has come to an end. Until now, transnational corporations could count on the U.S. to either intervene or use its threat of military force to ensure compliant, pro-business governments no matter where they were. With the Soviet threat gone, such intervention is politically harder to sell to the American public. The major powers see Africa as a geopolitical morass and are happy to hand off its minor conflicts to corporations with their limited liability. In the absence of any efforts from major powers or the U.N. to stop them, corporations are now free to hire armies to enforce their interests. Corporate use of private armies represents the expropriation of one of the most fundamental roles of government, the sanctioned use of violence. The agreement by citizens not to resort to violence is rooted in this aspect of the state. We each agree to give up any "right" to use violence in defence of our individual interests on the understanding that everyone else will also give up that right or face the democratically sanctioned coercion of the state.

The very existence of Executive Outcomes raises the question of who will be next to decide that it is legitimate to create their own armed force. As we will see in chapter 6, that answer is not hard to come by. With private security forces outnumbering public police by three to one in the U.S. and Canada, wealthy individuals and corporations are blurring the lines between state-sanctioned violence and the private use of force.

SLAPPING DEMOCRACY

The use of private armies and the growth of private police services are not the only examples of the assault on democracy by corporations. They are also intervening through the courts to intimidate individuals and community organizations that speak up in the public interest. Corporate efforts to strategically target longstanding democratic rights have become known as SLAPP suits, for Strategic Lawsuits Against Public Participation.

SLAPP suits explicitly target the exercise of democratic rights, from citizens' submissions to government and published articles to public speaking or boycotts. In virtually every case the defendant in SLAPP cases has been successful in bringing public attention to the issue. SLAPP suits target individuals or community groups because they are the most vulnerable to intimidation and cannot afford the court costs.

American corporations are far ahead of their Canadian counterparts, although these suits are being used more frequently here. In the U.S., the strategy of tying up advocacy groups in the courts started in the 1970s. "Tens of thousands of Americans have been silenced by threats," say George Pring and Penelope Canan in "Slapps: Getting Sued for Speaking Out."[41] Nine states have passed legislation to stop SLAPP suits, seeing them as almost always frivolous and aimed only at silencing critics.

Several such corporate-sponsored suits in B.C. have targeted members of municipal councils who have spoken out against irresponsible practices. But perhaps the most notorious is the case of Daishowa, a huge Japanese conglomerate, against the Lubicon Indian Band of northern Alberta.

The Lubicon case pits one of the most desperately impoverished aboriginal bands in the country and their supporters against an enormously powerful transnational corporation. The suit is against Kevin Thomas and the Friends of the Lubicon, an Ontario-based group that organized an effective nationwide boycott of Daishowa paper products. The boycott was prompted by Daishowa's decision to log an area that is part of the Lubicon land claim. It was so effective that it was credited with shutting down Daishowa's operations in the area. Daishowa responded by going to court, arguing that the boycott had cost it $5 million. The court found in favour of Daishowa, granting it a temporary injunction against the boycott.[42]

It needn't be a huge corporation that brings a SLAPP suit. In Nova Scotia the Jacques Whitford Group, a consulting firm, sued a citizen in that province's Supreme Court for speaking at a Halifax City Council meeting as a member of one of council's committees. He had criticized a waste-incineration proposal put forward by the Whitford Group, referring to two previous projects in which the firm had been involved, both of which had gone over budget.[43] Clearly, the threat of a SLAPP suit delivers a strong message to anyone thinking of becoming an active citizen.

The use of SLAPP suits is not the only modern addition ot the corporate bag of tricks to subvert democracy. Corporations spend millions to support their interests. This practice is documented in *Masks of Deception: Corporate Front Groups in America*,[44] which identifies thirty-six industry-sponsored groups whose public interventions are regularly portrayed as those of citizens' groups. Thus the green-sounding National Wetlands Coalition is actually sponsored by industries fighting to ease government restrictions on the commercial conversion of wetlands. When the U.S. Senate was debating the new clean-air legislation in 1990, car companies hired Bonner and Associates, a sophisticated peddler of grassroots democracy. It convinced groups as diverse as Big Brothers, the Easter Seal Campaign, and the Paralyzed Veterans' Association to lobby against the legislation. They were persuaded by Bonner that the new rules would make it impossible to produce any cars larger than a Honda Civic.[45]

The critical development that makes corporations in the late twentieth century use such a threat is that their power is now applied on a global scale, increasingly immune to the authority of nation-states and citizens. The power of governments to moderate the behaviour of market forces, in place for almost three generations, has been ceded to a social organization second only to nation-states in power and without their moral or democratic imperative. The response of corporations has been anything but benign. They have not simply taken advantage of government deregulation and withdrawal from the field. Sensing their power and assuming that governments will not intervene, they have now become aggressive in further challenging democratic institutions and citizen rights.

The popular notion of the nation-state becoming obsolete in the face of the power of transnational corporations is more accurately described as the amalgamation of corporate and state rule. As consensus has developed between economic and political elites and resistance to corporate domination is undercut, the lines between corporate governance and national governance have blurred.

There is, of course, a new twist to the old theme of corporate efforts to end government meddling in their affairs. What transnational corporations bring to this new era of corporate control is precisely their global reach and aspirations. They don't want the state to disappear because they could not operate for a week without it. But they do want to put in place appropriate state institutions that serve their particular global agenda. That agenda is driven by fierce competition for trade and investment opportunities that can provide the greatest return on investment. And the key to success in this global struggle is total flexibility to move, change, merge, and otherwise manipulate every aspect of corporate operations on a worldwide scale.

The demands of transnational corporations have outgrown the services that the traditional nation-state can provide. In order to assist corporate profitability, it was necessary for those industrial states to create transnational institutions that would meet the requirements of the transnational corporation. These institutions, mechanisms, and agencies would superimpose on nation-states a regime of rules, regulations, governing bodies, and effective sanctions that would reflect the new era and its new paradigm. Such institutional mechanisms are now rapidly being put in place, and Canada and Canadians have played a special role in testing them out. That role was one of guinea pig in global corporate governance, and the tests were the free-trade agreements.

5

HOW CORPORATIONS RULE THE WORLD

We are writing the constitution of a single world economy.
— RENATO RUGGIERO, DIRECTOR-GENERAL, WORLD TRADE ORGANIZATION,
DESCRIBING THE MULTILATERAL INVESTMENT AGREEMENT

*The strategy [on the Free Trade Agreement] should rely less on
educating the general public than in getting across the message
that the trade initiative is a good idea. In other words a selling job.
It is likely that the higher the profile the issue attains, the lower the
degree of public approval will be. Benign neglect from a majority
of Canadians may be the realistic outcome of a well-executed
communications program.*
— FROM A MEMO LEAKED FROM THE OFFICE OF PRIME MINISTER
BRIAN MULRONEY, 1985

How do corporations "rule the world"? In many respects they do
so in the same ways that they always have. First, they rule the
world because they make many of the important decisions that affect
the lives of ordinary people and their communities, decisions about
where to establish a plant, what to produce, who will work and who
won't, how much pollution will go into the environment, and which
countries will get the next factory. But they also rule politically.

They rule country by country; they influence politicians and

political parties with huge amounts of cash; they threaten governments that dare to consider any laws that lessen their power or
privilege; they withdraw capital to punish governments that don't
take them seriously; they spend millions on lobbyists to persuade
legislators; they spend hundreds of millions on public relations experts
and advertising firms to convince the public that what's good for
corporations is good for them; they have phalanxes of lawyers to get
around regulations and more lawyers and tax accountants to avoid and
evade taxes.

And they own newspapers, TV networks, and radio stations whose
editorial policies and programming they control, directly or indirectly,
and thus can publicly punish politicians who defy their agenda, and
determine the information and analysis given to citizens to help them
decide who to vote for and, more generally, how to view the world.

They use their virtually unlimited resources in a relentless, continuous, and self-interested assault at every level of government, from
presidents and prime ministers down, from senior policy makers to
schoolboard members, town councillors and the lowest-level func-
tionaries of municipal governments. They have the resources to hire
the cream of the crop in any area of expertise, and they have the
ability to be everywhere at once promoting their bottom line.

Most large corporations have at one time or another intervened in
the political process to advance their own interests. Such activity is a
normal part of doing business. But in the era of the transnational
corporation the sheer size of some corporations means that there
has been not just a quantitative change in the way corporations "do"
the politics of business. There has been a qualitative change. That
change involves not only how and how much TNCs intervene in the
governing process but the scope of the demands they now make on
governments. They have enormous capacity to intervene, and they
now do so with global objectives in mind. They don't simply want
the local, provincial or national rules changed. They want international rules established so that they don't have to be bothered by local
or national rules or take the time to intervene. The future that the
corporations are seeking has no surprises.

Corporations now exercise the power not only to force governments to back off environmental legislation but to create international

treaties and agencies and regimes of punishment for countries that dare to enact environmental policies that might restrict their activities. The Canada-U.S. free-trade deal, the North American Free Trade Agreement (NAFTA), APEC (Asia Pacific Economic Co-operation forum), the World Trade Organization (replacing the General Agreement on Tariffs and Trade), and the OECD's Multilateral Agreement on Investment (MAI) are all examples of the international agreements and laws aimed at permanently changing the rules by which corporations, and by default people, are governed.

The old-fashioned interventions into government, the traditional ways of thwarting citizens' efforts to build humane communities, are being superseded by a level of corporate political intervention appropriate to the new era of TNCs. We have a transnational regime of world governance to match the transnational nature of corporations, and the "governing" institutions are as remote and unaccountable as the corporations that designed them. This is world government with only a few thousand "citizens" — the largest corporations in the world — and with laws that exclusively serve their interests.

Corporate rule in the 1990s does not entail destroying democratic institutions, halting elections, or jailing opposition politicians. What we are witnessing in Canada and elsewhere is not the classic political coup, not an illegal seizure of power, but what John Ralston Saul calls "a coup d'état in slow motion." It is as if the FTA and NAFTA deals, and other international agreements, are slowly dissolving the substance of democracy while leaving the institutional facade intact.

Long before the Free Trade Agreement, NAFTA, the WTO, MAI, and other such agreements were in place, the world's largest companies had extremely powerful agencies working on their behalf. The International Monetary Fund, the World Bank, and GATT were all institutions created as a result of the famous Bretton Woods meetings in July 1944. Forty-four nations gathered in the U.S. to create the foundation for a world economic system. The new multilateral institutions promised general prosperity and economic interdependence as a bulwark against further armed conflict.

John Maynard Keynes, the intellectual father of the modern egalitarian state, had prepared a set of principles for the design of a new financial system in preparation for the Bretton Woods conference. The basic features of the plan included a world central bank, which he intended as a "clearing union" to extend credit to countries suffering from balance-of-payments problems and which would hold deposits from nations with a surplus. There would also be an international currency, which would be used for international transactions. An international trade organization would work to stabilize commodity prices by establishing buffer stocks of commodities and setting up binding commodity agreements between states. Lastly, and directly through the U.N., there would be an aid program to provide unconditional below-market-rate loans and grants to less developed countries.[1]

Keynes had expressed serious doubts that freer trade would lead to a more equitable international division of labour. "Ideas, knowledge, science, hospitality, travel — these are the things which should of their nature be international. But let goods be homespun wherever . . . possible and above all let finance be primarily national."[2]

Yet it was power, not the strength of ideas promoting social and economic justice, that would prevail, and the U.S., with its large holdings of Britain's debt, had that power. In the discussions leading up to Bretton Woods the two key figures, Keynes of Britain and Harry Dexter White of the U.S., had agreed that it was essential to control the movement of international capital and to allow national governments to pursue full employment policies. White, in line with Keynes, had suggested in an early draft that deposits or investments from another country not be permitted without the approval of that country's government.

Keynes's vision would have both creditor and debtor nations share the burden of international adjustment, something White did not disagree with personally. A crucial issue at Bretton Woods centred around whether nations would have automatic access to the IMF. Keynes's position was that automatic access was crucial to the development of poorer nations. Whatever Harry White's personal conviction, U.S. corporations had their own thoughts. The deliberations, like those that created the United Nations, were dominated by the U.S., and there was another agenda at Bretton Woods — in the words of David Korten, "to create an open world economy unified under U.S. leadership that would ensure unchallenged U.S. access to the world's markets and raw materials."[3]

When New York bankers heard of White's proposal for currency controls, they intervened with the U.S. treasurer, and the country's position changed. During the negotiations White pressed for conditions to be attached to access to the new IMF. The U.S. position won out. The idea of an international currency was dropped and the new world currency system, the basis for world trade, would be the American dollar, with the U.S. given the right to print and spend the world's principal currency. The new international agencies would assist the world's largest corporations, at the time mostly American, in their efforts to accumulate capital and power.

THE WORLD BANK AND THE IMF

The World Bank was intended to assist European countries and Japan to rebuild in the post-war period. But within a couple of years of Bretton Woods, European countries did not need World Bank loans because they were getting billions from the American Marshall Plan. Third World countries were disinterested for another reason. Their elected officials and policy analysts were divided about lining up behind World Bank objectives. Economic nationalists wanted to follow a policy of protecting local markets and avoiding international financial alliances and dependencies.

Amongst the elites the debate turned around whether a country should follow an industrial policy of import-substitution or an export-led strategy of producing goods locally for export to the developed world. The import-substitution strategy ran counter to the World Bank's policy because it required fewer imports and therefore reduced the need for foreign exchange. The whole point of the World Bank was to provide financing for the purchase of corporate products from advanced industrial countries.

Like the corporations whose goods it was intended to help sell, the World Bank soon set out to create new customers in the Third World. In doing so it began circumventing and manipulating elected governments and accountable officials, actions that continue today with trade and investment treaties. The World Bank, as David Korten points out, "gave priority to 'institution-building' projects aimed at creating [in the developing nations] autonomous governmental agencies that would be regular World Bank customers . . . staffed primarily by transnational technocrats with strong ties to the bank."[4] As a result elected officials were increasingly subject to advice from their own bureaucrats that was crafted by the bank in the interests of transnational corporations eager to sell into their countries' markets.

The less developed countries descended into the vortex of World Bank loans and the contradictions they produced. The bank itself was so blinded by its free-market, comparative advantage ideology that each failure to help a country increase its wealth and pay down its debt was met with irresistible offers of more loans and a repeat of the cycle.

While the economic nationalists of the developing countries were prevented from effectively pursuing policies of self-sufficiency, their debt situation, already difficult, was about to take a turn for the worse. Basing the world economy on the U.S. dollar worked for about fifteen years. But by the late 1950s the U.S. was experiencing a continuing balance-of-payments problem, and in 1971 it arbitrarily ended the fixed exchange rate. What followed was a wave of currency speculation involving what were called Eurocurrencies, currencies deposited in other countries, such as French francs held in Germany or yen in Britain. The new floating exchange rate led to an enormous growth of Eurocurrencies, supplemented by OPEC dollars, from $150 billion in 1971 to $5.4 trillion by 1988.[5] By mid-1997 it was up to $13 trillion. That money had to go somewhere. Starting in the 1980s much of it went to the least developed countries.

These nations went on a borrowing spree promoted by the World Bank's extremely low interest rates and aggressive "selling" of loans by multinational banks. Larger loans, of course, meant even more loans were needed to pay the interest and the ever increasing principal. From 1970 to 1980 the long-term external debt of low-income countries increased from $21 billion to $110 billion. That of middle-income countries rose from $40 billion to $317 billion.

The crushing debt burden was a further boon for the international lenders and the transnationals, as the debt crisis opened the door to what would become known as structural adjustment. This began the period of the World Bank's and the IMF's policy of conditionality, a euphemism for the elimination of the sovereignty of indebted nations. The two agencies of corporate libertarianism dictated macro-economic and social policies to scores of countries. To get more loans to pay the interest on the old ones countries were obliged to alter their policies to channel more and more of their resources and productive capacity towards foreign trade and debt repayment.

The IMF was the debt collector for the system, while the World Bank was literally an institution of governance, as Jonathon Cahn described it in the *Harvard Human Rights Journal*, "exercising power . . . to legislate entire legal regimes and even to alter the constitutional structure of borrowing nations. Bank-approved consultants often rewrite a country's trade policy, fiscal policies, civil service require-ments, labor laws, health-care arrangements, environmental regula-tions, energy policy, resettlement requirements, procurement rules, and budgetary policy."[6]

FREER TRADE: THE MISSING THIRD LEG

When the major capitalist powers established the IMF and World Bank there was a third agency that the U.S. administration had wanted but didn't get. In place of the planned International Trade Organization, twenty-three countries, including Canada, signed in 1947 the General Agreement on Tariffs and Trade (GATT). Its oper-ating principle was that of "most-favoured nation," under which any member country reducing the tariff on a commodity for one of its trading partners would automatically reduce it to all other members.

By the late 1970s tariffs were no longer the major barrier to trade and certainly not the greatest threat to the world capitalist system. The crisis facing the industrialized nations was much deeper. In Europe corporate profitability fell from 11 percent to 5 percent between 1970 and 1975 and the American balance of trade worsened. In the early 1980s there was nearly a trade war between the U.S. and Europe over the latter's agricultural price support system, designed to maintain farmers' incomes. The GATT did not address this issue, and Europe was in no mood for free trade.[7]

At the same time, mass consumption in the U.S. seemed to have reached a saturation point. The new phenomenon of stagflation revealed both high inflation and stubbornly high unemployment at the same time. The golden age of capitalism was well and truly dead, and with the 1980–82 recession and its aftermath came the threat of cutthroat international competition and, for Canada, increased fears of American protectionism.

As for the Americans, barriers to trade, and more particularly to investment, were not coming down fast enough. The U.S. was prepared to pursue economic integration, the means to knock down investment barriers, one country at a time. So when free-trade negotiations began Canada wanted some firm guarantees against U.S. protectionist legislation, and the U.S. wanted greater access to Canadian resources and energy, and new investment rights. But it was also clear that for the U.S. the negotiations were, as Duncan Cameron argues in *Canada Under Free Trade*, integral to a long-term strategy designed to set precedents for future multilateral agreements.[8]

CORPORATIONS: REAPING THE BENEFITS OF FREE TRADE

The intractable problem of stagflation and the intervention of Milton Friedman's free-market ideology provided the basis of an assault on the historic compromise between capital and labour. The crisis of the welfare state allowed its opponents to attack the whole notion of using Keynesian economic policies to moderate the excesses of the marketplace. That foundering social contract demanded a new state/corporate equilibrium, one that would be dominated by corporations and their ideological allies. Its first major manifestation for Canada was the Free Trade Agreement, a constitutional charter of rights for transnational corporations that embodied the principles of corporate libertarianism. Its designation as a trade deal obscured its essential purpose: to economically integrate Canada with the U.S.

It was clear to the largest corporations in both countries what this deal meant, not just for what was in it but for what it presaged for multilateral agreements. If they won, it would be a huge step forward in their desire for a permanent counter-revolution against the egalitarian state. The deal reconstructed democracy and the state so that corporate interventions in the political process would require little more than minor adjustments.

Much of the attention on the FTA (and later NAFTA) focussed on how Canada "lost" to the Americans. But in effect what happened was that all workers and most citizens, Canadian, American, and Mexican, lost to corporations. In a myriad of ways average citizens lost human rights, lost citizen power, lost control over their communities, lost the ability to determine what kind of society they and their children would have. In one sense Canadians lost more because we had more to lose: the state was more active in redistributing wealth, ensuring public services, financing culture, and promoting regional equality. Americans never had the egalitarian state in the first place.

To the extent that it was nominally "nations" negotiating with each other, Canada clearly lost and the U.S. won. Yet even here it was U.S. trade laws working in the interests of U.S. corporations that defined the American victory. The FTA and NAFTA were not trade "deals" between sovereign nations so much as they were declarations by national governments of their willingness to give up sovereignty and political power to corporations.

The collaboration of Canadian and American corporations to get these deals passed proves the point. It did not matter to the very largest corporations which country they were based in because they were seeking a new charter of transnational corporate rights that would permit them to treat the two countries as one jurisdiction.

Between the end of 1988 and 1994, as many as 334,000 manufacturing jobs were lost in Canada, 17 percent of the pre–free trade total. Most of these were shed by the largest corporations, members of the Business Council on National Issues (BCNI) who spent millions promoting the deal. Between 1988 and 1996, thirty-three BCNI member corporations laid off 216,004 employees (eleven others increased employees but by just 28,073). The big losses were in labour-intensive industries. By the end of 1994 the clothing industry had lost 32.8 percent of its jobs, electronics 24 percent, paper 22.5 percent, food and primary metals both 16.5 percent. At the same time, those thirty-three corporations increased their combined revenues by more than $40 billion, to $158.2 billion.[9] During the free-trade debate the deal's proponents promised "more and better jobs" — 350,000 of them. The jobs that have been created have been in low-wage personal and commercial services.

A major feature of life under free trade is the development of a dual economy, one global and the other domestic. According to the

Canadian Centre for Policy Alternatives (CCPA), "We have a growing export-oriented manufacturing and resource sector, alongside a depressed domestic market. The export boom has failed to generate any jobs. The domestic economy is held down by high unemployment and stagnant demand for locally produced goods and services."[10] This is the "jobless" economy.

FTA opponents pointed out a hidden agenda: corporations' desire for a level playing field in social programs. It was always understood that this would mean lowering the field to the American level. The denials by the Mulroney government and its corporate allies came fast and heavy during the lengthy debate over free trade.

Corporate leaders were not so foolish as to make their intentions known during the debate but they weren't always so reticent. In 1980, Laurent Thibault, a corporate executive who later headed the Canadian Manufacturers' Association, told a Senate committee: "It is a simple fact that, as we ask our industries to compete toe to toe with American industry . . . we in Canada are obviously forced to create the same conditions in Canada that exist in the U.S. whether it is unemployment insurance, workmen's compensation, the cost of government, the level of taxation or whatever."[11]

As the CCPA analysis of the FTA shows, within a few weeks of the federal election, the Canadian Manufacturers' Association, the Canadian Chamber of Commerce, and the BCNI began campaigning for spending cuts, especially to UI, arguing that it was crucial to Canada's competitiveness — a self-fulfilling argument after the deal was signed. The chair of the powerful Canadian Manufacturers' Association demanded that every federal and provincial program be re-examined: "All Canadian governments must test all their policies to determine whether or not they reinforce or impede competitiveness. If a policy is anti-competitive, dump it."[12]

The Mulroney government's first free-trade budget, five months later, began the series of unprecedented cuts to UI, old age security, and transfers to the provinces for health and education that continued unabated for eight years. These cuts have taken us back to the level of community spending achieved in 1949. Of course these cuts were made without any reference to free trade. As we will see in chapter 9, the level playing field was accomplished by debt hysteria. Canada's

high debt, created almost exclusively by policies promoted by corporations, was a convenient weapon against our social programs, which
U.S. corporations saw as unfair subsidies to Canadian business.

One of the most oft-repeated assurances of corporate Canada and
the Mulroney government was that medicare would not be touched.
Yet the impact of the agreement was clear: medicare would be changed
to accommodate the increased involvement of private corporations.
According to the CCPA, "Chapter 14 of the FTA on Services defined
health care management as a 'commercial service' rather than a 'social'
or 'public' service . . . It opened the door for private foreign firms to
enter into an array of health services, including hospitals, nursing
homes, homes for the disabled, ambulance services, rehabilitation
clinics, home care services, laboratories and blood banks."[13]

Under NAFTA rules, medicare was further threatened. A study
prepared for the Canadian Health Coalition and the Canadian Union
of Public Employees by Manitoba law professor Bryan Schwartz concluded that parts of the agreement that were supposed to protect
medicare were so vague that they were open to all sorts of challenges.

While corporations wanted the area of health care opened up, they
wanted environmental protection closed down. A number of trends
in environmental deregulation have been identified in the aftermath
of FTA/NAFTA. There has been a shift, promoted by TNCs, towards
establishing continental and international regulations, a trend that
makes national initiatives more difficult and restricts citizens' access to
the process. The language of "sustainability" is gradually giving way
to that of "competitiveness," reflecting the fact that policy makers are
adopting the corporate perspective.

Perhaps most alarming is the trend away from regulatory regimes
to ones of "voluntary compliance." A comprehensive 1994 survey by
the forecasting firm KPMG of Canadian corporations and public institutions revealed that whereas 69 percent had an environmental
management plan, only 2.5 percent could claim to have incorporated
all the vital components. Ninety-five percent said compliance with
existing state regulations was their strongest motivation. Determined
lobbying from corporations on both sides of the border convinced
the Chrétien government to introduce the Regulatory Efficiency
Act, which would have allowed corporations to seek waivers from

environmental laws. The federal government is devolving its authority over the environment to the provinces, which are in the process of "harmonizing" their regimes. That means harmonizing them with the province whose level of protection is the lowest and whose enforcement is weakest.

The FTA provisions on energy and natural resources, repeated in NAFTA, make conservation next to impossible. Under the "proportionality clause," Canada is obliged to export the same proportion of energy and other natural resources to American corporations as it does currently, even in times of shortage. This not only undermines conservation goals. In the event of an energy emergency it subordinates the interests of Canada to the abstract principles of economic efficiency and free trade. We could face a situation where we would have to shut down Canadian industries to be able to meet our natural gas commitments to U.S. energy corporations.

It is difficult to find a more compelling example of how the free-trade agreements put commercial contracts between corporations ahead of the interests of a nation and its citizens. Had Canada been militarily conquered, its humiliation might have been understandable. This humiliation, however, was gleefully imposed by the Canadian government at the urging of TNCs and domestic corporations.

Of all the areas of government policy that have been affected by free trade, the protection of Canadian culture has been one to which the federal government has been forced to pay lip service. As we saw, the long-term strategy of the TNCs is built on a foundation of marketing the mass consumer culture to every corner of the planet. As Sony's Akio Morita proclaimed, culture is a trade barrier to building a global mass consumer society. The federal government's schizophrenic record on cultural issues reveals its basic support for the corporate position and its countervailing need to appear protective.

The widespread attacks compelled Mulroney to negotiate a cultural "exemption" in both the FTA and NAFTA. But the exemption included what amounted to a poison pill. It allowed American corporations, through the U.S. government, to punish Canada for taking measures to protect Canadian culture. The U.S. can implement measures of "equivalent commercial effect" against Canada.

The result of the poison pill has been a whole series of decisions by Canada to either back off new support for culture or directly favour U.S. conglomerates. Legislation to restrict foreign takeovers of Canadian publishers was dropped; soon after that the educational publisher Ginn was bought by Paramount. When the CRTC forced the American Country Music Channel off the air in favour of the Canadian New Country Network, the U.S. threatened all sorts of retaliatory action. Part of the resulting compromise was a promise by Canada that it would not "de-list" any other cable service.

In 1997, Canada put a brave defensive face on a World Trade Organization ruling against protecting Canadian magazines — the so-called split-run issue involving *Sports Illustrated* — a decision reflecting the principles behind free trade. But promised legislation to help Canadian books and sound recordings to increase their share of the market has been dropped, and continued huge cuts to the CBC mean that private broadcasters have less competition and a weakened standard of genuinely Canadian programming to live up to. Cuts to the National Film Board and Telefilm Canada, like those to the CBC, were far out of proportion to cuts to other areas and saved relatively small amounts of money, indicating that Ottawa is essentially committed to bringing down the cultural barriers to investment so detested by global corporations.

Perhaps the most important overarching principle enshrined in the FTA and NAFTA is that of national treatment. National treatment means that the rights of citizenship, already accorded to the fictitious corporate person in Canada, are now extended to American and Mexican corporations. What this means is that Canadian governments must treat American and Mexican corporations no differently than they treat Canadian ones.

Clearly these deals represent a serious erosion of democracy and the democratic rights of citizens to determine the future of their country. They so fundamentally shift power in favour of corporations that they are the equivalent to constitutional changes. Here are some other ways these deals undermine democratic governance.

· The dispute settlement mechanism of NAFTA allows corporations to challenge government actions at international arbitration panels. Just the threat of such actions will put a chill on policies that encroach upon corporate interests. A 1997 case was seen as a harbinger of things to come. The American firm Ethyl Corporation demanded $350 million in compensation from Ottawa, claiming that new legislation banning one of its products, the fuel additive MMT, because of its health threat, amounts to "expropriation without compensation."

· Not only do the FTA and NAFTA restrict how crown corporations can be used, they make the establishment of new ones difficult if not impossible. The best example of this was the decision by the Ontario government of Bob Rae to back off its election promise to establish public auto insurance. Rae, to his lasting shame, declined to challenge the FTA by proceeding with such insurance and even declined to make it clear to the public that the FTA was the reason for his decision. Yet the American insurance industry had made it abundantly clear that it was poised to demand billions in compensation if the government made such a move.

· The rationale corporations and the Mulroney government put forward for pursuing free trade was that the agreements would protect Canada from U.S. "trade remedy" laws — in other words, punitive retaliation (countervailing duties and anti-dumping duties). Canada got no such thing, of course, and is just as subject to these laws as it was before the deals. All the dispute settlement mechanism now in place provides is a method of ensuring that U.S. laws are applied fairly.

Many critics saw the trade remedy argument as simply a pretext for the free-trade negotiations from the beginning, as trade experts knew all along that GATT negotiations would have provided Canada with the same trade remedy measures within a few years. Mel Clark, formerly a senior Canadian trade negotiator, did a comprehensive cost-benefit analysis comparing the FTA to GATT in those areas he calculated would "especially impinge on Canada's interest." His conclusion: "The FTA ceded to the U.S. and the private sector the right to shape many of Canada's economic, social, environmental and cultural policies . . . If one assumes the Mulroney government was guided by even a normal regard for the national interest, the FTA defies understanding . . . while vital national powers are protected under GATT, the same cannot be said of the FTA."[14]

Analysis shows that Canada would have been better off with GATT. But even more important is that the free-trade deals were the models for changes to GATT that now threaten to apply to every country in the world the corporate libertarian rules at the core of FTA/NAFTA. This reinforces the claim of many critics that the free-trade deals were intended as stalking horses for global trade and investment regimes, and Canada as a guinea pig in an experiment in corporate rule.

THE WORLD TRADE ORGANIZATION

On January 1, 1995, the multilateral agreement known as GATT became the World Trade Organization, heralding a frightening era of world corporate domination. In the words of the Common Front on the WTO, a Canadian coalition opposed to its initiatives, "The establishment of the WTO represents a watershed in the process of establishing a truly global economic order and it is likely to exert a more profound influence over the course of human affairs than any other institution in history."[15] Yet despite the implications of this development, it received almost no publicity in Canada. It was slipped through Parliament in late 1994 as legislation ratifying the latest GATT agreement, with virtually no public attention let alone any debate. It was scarcely even announced.

While it might be argued that this is true of other multilateral accords, there is something terribly wrong when an agreement with profound implications for national sovereignty is designed in such a way that it can become law with no effort to inform the public, literally unbeknownst to the millions whose lives will be affected. By allowing trade to be defined narrowly as something of interest only to corporations that engage in it, nation-states implicitly surrender their sovereignty as if it were a trifle.

With the advent of the WTO, says David Korten, "a trade body with an independent legal identity and staff similar to that of the World

Bank and the IMF is now in place, with a mandate to press forward and eliminate barriers to the free movement of goods and capital. The needs of the world's largest corporations are now represented by a global body with legislative and judicial powers that is committed to ensuring their right against the intrusions of democratic governments."[16]

For transnational corporations the WTO is the long-awaited third leg in their decades-long campaign for complete liberation from government interference. The IMF and the World Bank successfully established corporate rights throughout the less developed countries of the world. With the WTO it is now the turn of the industrialized countries to turn over their decision-making authority to global corporations.

In transforming itself into the World Trade Organization, the GATT evolved by a huge leap. Its importance, according to the Common Front, is threefold. First is simply the increasingly important role of trade in the world economy: international trade grew by 9.5 percent in 1994 alone. The TNCs control more than a third of the world's productive assets and they organize them — or try to — without reference to national borders. A growing portion of world trade, now at 40 percent, takes place between corporations owned by the same TNC conglomerate.

Second, trade is no longer trade as we used to understand it, that is, the buying and selling of goods across borders. Trade and investment are now indistinguishable and virtually inseparable. With so much trade taking place within corporations, any rule affecting investment — local sourcing, performance requirements, technology transfers — has consequences for "trade" between the companies of the affected TNC.

Perhaps most important, the WTO has extremely powerful enforcement rules that even the largest nations cannot easily ignore. Under GATT strong sanctions existed but were imposed only if there was consensus amongst its 120 members, including the offending country. The rulings of the WTO bureaucracy are now automatically implemented unless a consensus of members (including the member bringing the complaint) votes against the sanction. These are not puny penalties. The first WTO trade complaint was a challenge to the U.S. Clean Air Act. Its regulations were found to be in violation of

WTO rules and the U.S. would have faced a penalty of $150 million each year had it not withdrawn the offending measures.

The World Trade Organization is the institution of choice for transnational corporations quite simply because it works. The ramifications of its decisions far exceed those of the General Assembly of the U.N. and even those of the Security Council. The lives of the vast majority of people in the world are affected by investment decisions, and those are increasingly made by TNCs. The WTO, essentially designed for and dominated by the transnational corporate agenda, is effectively a United Nations for TNCs, providing corporations with the powers of an international state.

Yet, as we will see in the discussion of one WTO initiative, the Multilateral Investment Agreement, there is a crucial difference between the WTO and its two sister organizations, the IMF and World Bank. Decision making in the WTO is based on one country, one vote and not weighted by financial contributions as in the IMF and World Bank. Decisions are made with the unanimous agreement of all member countries. It is a key contradiction, and reflects the world forum in which corporations face down what remains of the sovereignty of nation-states.

As early as 1972, the U.S., on behalf of domestically based TNCs, began shifting its attention away from the United Nations and towards other forums in order to achieve open investment rules. That year the less developed countries, looking for some system to curb the abuses of TNCs, used their voting majority in the General Assembly to set up the Group of Eminent Persons. Its mandate was to examine transnational corporations and their impact on host countries. With the release of their report in 1973 it was clear that U.N. action on a code governing the behaviour of TNCs was near completion.

From that point on it was clear to the U.S. and its corporate clients that a regime to liberate corporate investment from the performance requirements, technology transfers, and controls over foreign exchange established by national governments was not going to be achieved through the U.N. At first that meant pursuing those goals through other means. But in recent years the political leadership of the U.S., media pundits, and corporate spokespeople have conducted an all-out assault on the United Nations.

With their relentless campaign to cast the U.N. as inept, unrepresentative, dominated by an unaccountable, self-serving, and bloated bureaucracy, the political representatives of TNCs have tried to denigrate the world body while creating another one that will speak unflinchingly for their interests. Just as the Free Trade Agreement's promoters tried to put it in place by stealth and negotiated it behind closed doors, TNCs at the international level circumvented the only democratic forum for the world's nations.

One of the enormous advantages of the WTO is that negotiations take place in almost total secrecy, away from the prying eyes of the media and citizens. When a corporation challenges a law under the WTO (or NAFTA), both parties present their arguments to a panel of three trade experts, usually trade lawyers with experience representing corporations. This hearing is held in secret, and the documents presented are secret. Although the ruling itself is made public, the WTO forbids revealing how the panelists voted or what they said.

In short, citizens have absolutely no way of knowing why — or by whom — their democratically determined laws have been declared null and void. As for those defending the said law, they are obliged under WTO rules to prove that the law is not a restriction of trade — that is, countries are guilty until they prove their innocence. Corporations, on whose behalf complaints are made, cannot be charged or found "guilty" of anything or held accountable in any way in any international forum.

It is not just ordinary citizens who are kept in the dark. According to Martin Khor, director of the Malaysia-based Third World Network, the leaders of dozens of the poorest countries are excluded from negotiations and often do not have the sophisticated trade expertise to effectively represent their people when they are presented with agreements signed by the major industrial countries.

The negotiations involve corporations and nation-states to the virtual exclusion of all other interests, reflecting the historical pattern of trade being the sole purview of those doing the trading. Government negotiating teams, particularly the American and Canadian delegations, are heavily dominated by corporate advisory committees and representatives.

One of the most important of these corporate groups was the

Advisory Committees for Trade Policy and Negotiations on GATT in the U.S. Its members, all members of the Business Roundtable (the American equivalent of the Business Council on National Issues), included IBM, AT&T, Bethlehem Steel, Time Warner, 3M, Corning, BankAmerica, American Express, Dow Chemical, Boeing, Eastman Kodak, Mobil, Pfizer, Hewlett Packard, and General Motors. Again, corporations have a legitimate interest in trade issues, but so do ordinary citizens. Workers, environmentalists, the churches, women, consumers, educators, health-care providers, and many more are affected by such agreements. Yet of the 111 members of the three main U.S. advisory committees only two represented unions; the single environmental position was not filled, and there was no consumer representative. All meetings were closed to the public.[17]

In contrast to the U.S. government, which makes public the names of its corporate advisory committees, the Canadian government refuses to do so. Brian MacKay, the deputy director of the Advisory Secretariat for the department of foreign affairs, pointedly refused to reveal the names of any corporations involved in the sixteen sectoral committees advising the government on the MAI. When asked why the names were not public information, MacKay replied, "The corporations asked that their names not be made public." Asked if the corporations individually requested that their names be kept secret, he replied, "Yes." The BCNI in Canada and the European Round Table of Industrialists have been in the forefront of pushing for these deals and the advantages they provide. Japanese corporations have historically worked closely with their governments on all trade and investment policies. It is inconceivable that transnational corporations from these countries would not dominate the process that works out the details of the deals they lobbied for. The whole process is immersed in the corporate culture and reflective of corporate objectives. The bureaucrats who negotiate with each other are trade department officials, many of whom came from the corporate sector and see no difference between the corporate and public interests. While the Canadian government keeps the names of its corporate advisers secret, there is no question that corporations completely dominate the shape of the MAI, here and elsewhere.

Of all the areas on which TNCs have set their libertarian sights, that of investment is by far the most important, both to their interests and to nations and communities. For communities the attraction or loss of capital investment are life and death events, and unregulated investment can be catastrophic. Corporations are pre-occupied with investment because they are driven by an imperative of unrestrained growth. And countries, dozens of them impoverished from years of debt strangulation, are competing desperately for that capital.

THE MULTILATERAL AGREEMENT ON INVESTMENT

The initiative for a global treaty on investment was begun as early as 1986, when the U.S. challenged Canada's Foreign Investment Review Agency (FIRA) under GATT rules. American corporations did not get everything they wanted but they got enough that their foot was in the door. By 1987, GATT articles were being reviewed and dis-cussions were taking place about which government investment measures could be considered trade related.

From the beginning the struggle was between the capital-export-ing industrial countries and the less developed countries, which opposed restrictions on their laws regulating foreign investment. Efforts to get a multilateral investment agreement through GATT continually ran up against resistance from less developed nations, often led by India. TNCs made slow progress under GATT, and in 1992 a number of international business groups approached the OECD through its business advisory committee, pressing it to take the initiative.[18]

The corporate advisory committee to the U.S commerce depart-ment was also pushing for an OECD initiative, and the U.S. made it clear that it wanted "to develop a full treaty it could fast track through Congress and would bind states."[19] There were two advantages to going through the OECD. First, it would prevent backsliding within OECD countries. Second, it would establish a precedent; these stan-dards could then be promoted outside the OECD. The OECD as a consensus-building organization for the dominant market economies thus played the role of missionary for neo-liberal policies.

The U.S. also supported the OECD track because it was confident that it could get a much tougher investment regime negotiated amongst industrialized countries in the absence of non–OECD countries. It was clear from U.S. actions that American-based transnationals believed an OECD treaty would have the advantage of leveraging poorer countries into line with a promise of access to markets in return for increased liberalization. In the end, both sides of the debate amongst developed countries agreed to a two-track approach, pressing for an investment agreement in the World Trade Organization while getting one in place through the OECD, with each initiative reinforcing the other.

In 1995, an OECD report on a multilateral agreement on investment launched negotiations between the twenty-nine developed countries. The target date for a deal was just two years away. The MAI was designed to set a high standard for the treatment of investors and provide transparent rules on liberalization, dispute settlement, and investor protection. More important, the OECD's 1995 *Multilateral Agreement on Investment Report* stated: "The MAI would provide a benchmark against which potential investors would assess the openness and legal security offered by countries as investment locations. This would in turn act as a spur to further liberalization."[20]

A key meeting for the WTO initiative on the multilateral investment agreement was held in Singapore in 1996. By the previous June opposition amongst the less developed countries was growing. In September, India hosted a meeting of fourteen countries and raised the possibility of shifting the discussion to the U.N.'s responsible body, UNCTAD, the U.N. Commission on Trade and Development.

There was no consensus by the time the Singapore meeting was held, and the ministerial declaration outlining the meeting's agenda barely mentioned investment as a major consideration. Opposition from the less developed countries prevented the agreement from getting off the ground, in large part because WTO decisions are all made by consensus. Technically, a single no vote can scuttle any agreement. But the way the industrialized countries attempted to get the agreement through revealed just how the poorest countries are treated by their more powerful neighbours to the north.

The agenda at Singapore was to have focussed on GATT-related problems for the less developed countries. Instead, the developed countries hijacked the conference. The official conference featured ministers from each country giving their speeches in a great hall holding three thousand people. But there was, according to Martin Khor of the Third World Network, no discussion, no debate. According to Khor, "After the first morning no one attended any-more. So, that hall for three thousand people had five people inside. By the second afternoon, the chairman and general secretary of the WTO called an informal meeting of thirty countries which they selected. They did not inform the hall of this meeting; did not tell who the thirty were or how they were selected. They met for five days . . . [and] decided the whole agenda."[21]

The agenda focussed on how the WTO was going to expand its mandate beyond trade in the years to come. That expansion would include not only investment but two other major areas of economic policy, both part of the transnational corporate agenda. The first was competition, by which the agenda setters meant government "monopolies" — state-owned enterprises and state-sanctioned private monopolies granted their status for public policy purposes. The second mandated expansion would be the elimination of "discri-mination" in favour of national and local suppliers in the area of government procurement.

The transparency of the manipulation at the WTO was in large measure responsible for a core of about a dozen developing countries firmly rejecting the investment agreement. Despite this initial victory, Martin Khor is not optimistic. In the high-powered world of WTO politics, the poorest countries are most often ill equipped to see the implications of what they are agreeing to. Says Khor, "The WTO rep visits the country and says you have to change your laws in this way. 'Why?' Because you signed this agreement. 'But the agreement goes against our constitution.' Yes, we know — it goes against it in five ways and we have some constitutional amendments for you to take account of that."[22]

Nonetheless, the WTO is still a democratic organization, and any agreement eventually will have to be voted on. Khor believes that the fight against agreements like the WTO's investment agreement will be determined by how quickly and thoroughly developing countries can learn the rules of the game. "If [developing countries] are saying 'Liberalization has gone too far' but the U.S. wants to push it forward they will, because if [less developed countries] are not prepared they will not even know how to articulate that you want to push it backward."[23]

The failure of the WTO track for a global investment treaty put the ball firmly back in the OECD court, where the U.S. government and American-based TNCs had wanted it all along. Given the secrecy surrounding the affairs of global corporations, few people in any of the OECD countries had ever heard of the agreement. In Canada word didn't get out until a couple of months before the 1997 federal election, just two months before the deal was supposed to have been signed.

CORPORATIONS = NATIONS

The MAI confers on transnational corporations comprehensive political powers that they have not had since the early nineteenth century. This transfer of power is a deliberate act of nation-states; a collaboration between states and TNCs that in effect sees a willing surrender of authority from one institutional structure to another, within a single elite class that increasingly sees itself as international.

As Tony Clarke pointed out in his analysis of the MAI for the Canadian Centre for Policy Alternatives, the MAI throughout its text refers to investors when it means corporations. The agreement confers upon corporations exactly the same political status as nation-states. The precise expression of this status is still being debated, but some of the delegations "go so far as to propose investors (i.e. corporations) and the 'contracting parties' (i.e. governments) be given the same definition in the MAI." Provisions dealing with how corporations entering Canada will be treated serve "to establish corporations as having a superior class of citizenship rights."[24]

Canadian corporations already have extensive citizenship rights in Canada, but under the MAI foreign corporations operating in Canada could be afforded more favourable treatment than even domestic corporations. This is because the agreement provides for treatment of such corporations that is "no less favourable" than that given to Canadian companies. This treatment must also provide foreign corporations "equality of competitive opportunity." This means that governments cannot provide Canadian corporations with any unfair advantages. But in practice Canada may treat foreign corporations *more favourably* than domestic corporations to induce them to invest here.

The final piece to this revolutionary set of rules is that Canada will not be able to impose performance requirements on foreign corporations — things like job content, use of local suppliers, transfer of technology — even if it does so with domestic companies. In other words, if the Canadian government wants to use performance requirements to pursue social, employment, or environmental objectives it will have to discriminate *against* Canadian corporations to do so, holding them to a higher standard of corporate responsibility than it can foreign corporations.

The majority of OECD members, including Japan and the U.S., want the MAI to apply to all levels of government so that provincial and municipal governments would face the same dilemma. This has enormous implications for provincial constitutional powers, which, if there is a conflict between these and the provisions of the MAI, will be superseded by the MAI.

One of the most striking aspects of the MAI is the degree to which it explicitly shifts power away from communities and into the hands of corporations. Historically, one way that governments have attempted to ensure that citizens benefit from the investment of capital is the myriad of regulations that are a prime target of the MAI and of NAFTA before it. But the other, more direct method has been the use of direct capital investment by governments.

Crown corporations in Canada have played a vital role in building communities and defining the nature of the country. Power and natural gas utilities, publicly owned telephone companies, the post office, joint ventures with private corporations, ferry services, airlines, bus companies, the CBC and other cultural agencies — there are hundreds of examples of crown enterprises that provided services that corporations either refused to provide or would have done so at much higher cost.

In Saskatchewan, telephone service, electricity, and natural gas reached the remote areas many years earlier than if a private corporation had been in charge. All of these people's corporations had policies of purchasing and hiring locally where possible. As well, no private bus service would have provided transportation to the hundreds of small towns that were a feature of settlement in the west; the government bus service has provided subsidized service to small communities for decades. When the potash industry brought lengthy court challenges to government increases in taxes and royalties in the 1970s, the Saskatchewan government nationalized the industry and subsequently made hundreds of millions of dollars by developing a resource that belonged to the citizens of the province. (The Tory government of Grant Devine privatized it, selling it for half its assessed value.)

The MAI will make such community investment next to impossible. The WTO has identified crown corporations, pejoratively called state monopolies, as its next target for a multilateral deal, but the MAI begins the process. Severe restraints are placed on what governments can do with their own enterprises and assets. Governments could no longer treat these enterprises any differently than they do foreign corporations. They could not instruct them to buy local goods, nor could they establish noncompetitive prices for their goods or services. They would be required to act "solely in accordance with commercial considerations" and not with a public purpose.[25] Had this rule been in place in Saskatchewan in the 1940s, none of the public service enterprises just described could have been established. In effect, the MAI wipes from the map any competition that nations or communities might present to TNCs.

If a government privatizes a state enterprise, the MAI requires that the "national treatment" principle be applied so that any foreign corporation be allowed to bid on the assets. Some OECD members are pushing for a rule that would also prevent any "special share arrangements" that allocate a certain percentage of shares to the general public or that allows employees or the community to buy the company. At every turn, the MAI demonstrates the ruthless determination of transnational corporations to eliminate any measure that would guarantee either democratic control or a community benefit from an investment decision.

The corporate authors of the MAI have left nothing to chance. Other rules give corporations unprecedented legal protection in terms that would have pleased the merchant colonial states of two centuries ago: no government is permitted to "impair . . . the operation, management, maintenance, use, enjoyment or disposal of investments in its territory of investors of another Contracting Party."[26]

The most powerful aspect of the MAI is its mechanism for enforcing all the corporate rights it establishes. What is called the investor-state dispute mechanism, like NAFTA, provides an almost unlimited scope for corporations to sue a government over any breach of the provisions "which causes (or is likely to cause) loss or damage to the investor or his investment." Even "a lost opportunity to profit from a planned investment" would be just cause for a corporation to bring suit against a government.[27]

A sovereign government would have no choice but to appear before the tribunal set up to hear the corporate complaint, regardless of how frivolous or vexatious that complaint might be. The tribunal judges the case exclusively on the basis of the MAI provisions, with no reference to the laws of the sovereign state. The decisions of the unelected and politically unaccountable panel are binding and are enforced "as if it were a final judgment of [the country's] courts."[28] A footnote to this provision explains that it is intended to ensure that no government declines to accept a judgment on the basis that it would be "contrary to its public policy."

Not satisfied with having countries sign a deal giving up huge chunks of their sovereignty, those drawing up the MAI have built in "political security" provisions, which ensure that even without amendments or additions to the MAI it will continue to liberalize investment beyond the terms already signed by the governments. The MAI contains two provisions, one called rollback and the other a "standstill" provision, that together produce a ratchet effect, clawing away at government regulations and democratic authority long after the ink has dried on the deal.

The rollback provision states that "any regulatory measures of nation-states which do not conform with the principles and conditions of the MAI are to be reduced and eventually eliminated."[29] Even current levels of corporate taxation could be challenged as "creeping expropriation," in other words the illegal seizure of a company's "property" in the form of its rightful return on investment.

The standstill provision commits governments to "agree not to introduce any new non-conforming laws, policies or programs." For example, if a newly elected social democratic government wanted to regain some control over its economy through even a modest amount of public ownership, it could not do so. If it wished to reintroduce environmental regulations to address a growing crisis, any corporation affected by the move could prevent it.

Of all the ground-breaking aspects of the MAI, the most extraordinary is the provision providing for cancellation, or, as the agreement says, "withdrawal." Once the deal is signed, "Contracting Parties" (even the language suggests countries are now just parties to a commercial contract) will have to wait five years before they can withdraw. In addition, all investments made during those five years would are governed by the agreement for a further fifteen years. In short, if this agreement is ratified by the twenty-nine countries of the OECD, the democratic rights of their citizens will be suspended for an entire generation. At least with the FTA and NAFTA, the deals could be cancelled with six months' notice.

What do Canadians get in return for this unprecedented loss of sovereignty? According to its promoters, more of the same benefits we were supposed to achieve through NAFTA — that is, increased foreign investment. But the record of the FTA and NAFTA demonstrates that the promise of these agreements has not been fulfilled. According to Simon Fraser University political economist Marjorie Cohen, the trade deals have led to a huge increase in Canadian investment abroad. The outflow of direct and portfolio (stocks and bonds) Canadian investment was around 5 percent of total business investment in 1993; by 1997 it was 14 percent. There was a net outflow of capital from Canada in 1996 of $3 billion in direct investment and $8 billion in portfolio investment. Says Cohen, "Even when direct investment occurs, it does not necessarily improve the productive capacity or employment levels in Canada . . . Direct foreign investment most often takes the form of acquisition of existing corporations."[30]

THE CORPORATE BLUEPRINT FOR THE MAI

The MAI is so transparently a corporate rights document that it scarcely matters who determined its main features. Yet the key document that determined those features, obtained by the Council of

Canadians in late 1997, revealed just how integrated the developed nations and the TNCs have become. Entitled "Multilateral Rules for Investment," it was produced by the International Chamber of Commerce (ICC).[31]

The document was, in effect, the first draft of the MAI. All of the key aspects of the MAI described above are present in the ICC document. Amongst the critical elements was the description of a global marketplace in which "trade and investment become indistinguishable parts of single strategy except to the extent that national regulation demands distinction."

Under "Requirements for an International Investment Regime," the now famous phrase "high standard" agreement is front and centre. The ICC calls for a "broad definition of investment"; national treatment; an extremely broad definition of what corporations can "repatriate" without interference; and a dispute settlement procedure in which the corporation gets to choose the type of arbitration rules.

As is the case in the MAI text, the ICC insists on very broad definitions of the terms of the agreement, including "investor," "investment," "returns" on investment ("profit, capital gains, interest, dividends, royalties, and fees"), and the term "national," which should include not just persons but any "corporation, trust, partnership, joint venture" of the party in question. The ICC document also calls for the MAI to apply to all subnational levels of government. It provides many of the terms found in the 1997 drafts of the deal — including "standstill" and "rollback" — proposes tax policy as a barrier to investment, and contains the principle that "the MAI should prohibit screening for economic policy purposes."[32]

Corporations have driven the MAI from the beginning but were able to do so only because there is now almost no difference between global corporations and those aspects of state dealing with trade, investment, and foreign affairs. Merging these elements of the state and the business organizations representing TNCs results in an almost seamless institutional regime. The corporatized market state systematically excludes any other elements of civil society and therefore excises any internal dissent or debate. Thus, when business speaks there is no civil-society filter for the message to go through; it is in effect received wisdom. This truncated version of the state, effectively reduced to bureaucrats from finance, trade, and foreign affairs, has the same objectives as the TNCs it deals with.

The MAI is arguably the most important "law" Canada will be faced with in its history. Yet Canadians have had absolutely no say in the negotiation of this treaty. A bureaucrat, Bill Dymond, of the International Trade Branch of the foreign affairs department, speaks for all of us when he sits at the OECD table for Canada. He never consults with ordinary Canadians and speaks only to a very select group of elected officials. He gets his direction mostly from other unelected bureaucrats. To be sure, it is the minister in charge and the cabinet that will officially make any decision. But even here it is trade bureaucrats, committed to liberalization, who advise the ministers in charge. These men and women are politicians who, with little or no knowledge of trade matters, are totally dependent on the expert advice they receive. These advisers are preoccupied with trade and investment issues; ministers and officials of other departments who might be able to warn of the social and environmental consequences of the MAI are not involved. For example, when the Council of Canadians contacted Heritage Minister Sheila Copps's office about the MAI in the spring of 1997, she and her staff had not heard of the agreement.

The perception that the MAI is just another trade deal, of interest only to narrow interests, permeates the department of foreign affairs and international trade. Nicole Bourget, an assistant to then trade minister Art Eggleton, revealed just how disconnected the government is from any notion of accountability. Bourget declared that "there's nothing secret" about the talks, which were in fact going on behind closed doors. Casually confirming exactly what the MAI's critics were saying, Bourget told the *Globe and Mail* that negotiations for other trade deals "proceeded in a similar fashion. Ottawa regularly consults the provinces and has met and sought advice of industry groups, which will also be affected by any agreement."[33]

The apparent innocence of this response is more frightening than one with a public relations gloss. It demonstrates that the lack of awareness regarding who will be "affected" by such deals and the resulting absence of any understanding of public accountability is now firmly entrenched in the public service.

Indeed, while Canadians were kept in the dark about the agreement, the government was busy briefing Canadian business organizations throughout the entire process. One of those organizations was the Canadian Chamber of Commerce. On the occasion of Art Eggleton's appointment as minister for international trade, the chamber's chairman, Gary Campbell, and president, Timothy Reid, wrote to congratulate him. They also took the opportunity to lobby him with the chamber's position paper on the MAI and thanked a trade department official, Phil Somerville, "for the thorough briefing on the MAI that he provided to a select group of our corporate members."[34] Over a year later Eggleton would publicly deny that any such agreement was even being considered. In April 1997, just weeks before the deal was to have been signed, he told *Maclean's* magazine, "It's too early" to debate the agreement.[35]

Eggleton played down Canada's role in the MAI, but his protests were undermined by others closer to the scene. Reinforcing the claim that the politicians are just cheerleaders in the process, Eggleton denied any special role, saying, "As far as I know — I am sure somebody told me this not too long ago — we did not initiate this matter." Not so, according to Alan Rugman, a University of Toronto business professor who prepared the 1995 OECD background study. Rugman claims that Chrétien himself gave the MAI his okay at the G7 meeting in 1995. Donald Johnston, a former Trudeau cabinet minister, now heads the OECD, arguably the most aggressive promoter of trade and investment liberalization of any international agency. Said Rugman, "There are Canadian fingerprints all over the MAI. The untold story is that we're the real heroes getting it going."[36]

ASIA PACIFIC ECONOMIC CO-OPERATION

The multilateral investment initiatives are only the most grandiose schemes being undertaken by transnational corporations. If they cannot push their way through one door they will try another, and another, until their global regime of corporate libertarianism is in place. The most comprehensive efforts outside the formal jurisdiction of either the OECD or WTO is the Asia Pacific Economic Co-operation (APEC) forum, a free-trade initiative encompassing eighteen countries, including Canada and the U.S.

APEC is the free-trade equivalent of a floating crap game: it does not involve binding agreements or enforcement measures and does not have a large bureaucracy like the OECD and WTO. It exists only as an annual series of ministerial meetings prepared by a small secretariat in Singapore. But that is where the dissimilarities end. With its secrecy, its unabashed adherence to the imperatives of corporate rule, the source of its policy advice, and the nature of its ideology, APEC is very much a cousin of the MAI.

❖

APEC is made up of Malaysia, Singapore, Indonesia, Thailand, the Philippines, Brunei, Canada, Australia, New Zealand, Chile, Mexico, China, Taiwan, Hong Kong, Japan, Papua New Guinea, South Korea, and the U.S. According to New Zealand political analyst Jane Kelsey, "APEC has always been market driven and is heavily influenced by big business and the private sector free marketeers. It mainly relies for its research on the tripartite think tank of business representatives, academics and [state] officials . . . known as Pacific Economic Advisory Council."[37]

Its members have committed themselves to trade and investment liberalization. Its agenda includes a long list of "freedoms" for corporations, from deregulation, privatization, market-driven services, minimal controls on resource exploitation, and completely unrestricted foreign investment. Indeed, APEC has added a new twist to the new-right manipulation of language by referring to its members as economies rather than countries, a convenient fiction that allows them to deal with each other as if none of them actually had any responsibility for flesh-and-blood citizens. As TNCs become increasingly like states in their reach and power, and states devolve their role to being corporate facilitators, the distinctions between them begin to blur.

APEC did not start out as a free-trade group. It was formed in the late 1980s as a counterweight to the emerging trade blocs in Europe and North America. It was intended as a regional forum for economic cooperation. The U.S. was not initially invited (neither was Canada) but forced itself in and in 1993 used its influence to see APEC develop its current investment liberalization direction. Canada has been a major booster of this agenda and, with the other English-speaking developed nations, has been pressing for a more legalistic, binding approach. For this reason the leading powers in APEC have insisted that the IMF and World Bank be a part of the deliberations.

Canada's commitment to corporate libertarian principles is contained in a document entitled "Canada's Individual Action Plan," which details Ottawa's efforts at compliance with the goals of APEC.[38] Among the commitments under the heading "Deregulation" is the Regulatory Efficiency Act (REA), which the Chrétien government withdrew in 1996 after considerable public pressure. The REA is designed, says the document, "to encourage sensible regulation conducive to business growth thereby enhancing Canada's global competitiveness."

In its application, the REA allows for the waiving of environmental impact hearings, compliance with existing pollution limits, and other environmental regulations. This same approach, says the "Action Plan," will be applied in other areas. "When regulating, authorities must ensure that government intervention is justified, that Canadians are consulted, that benefits outweigh costs, that adverse economic impacts are minimized."[39] Just which Canadians will be consulted is not made clear, but the trend suggests a narrow definition of those "affected" by trade and investment matters, that is, corporations.

The "Action Plan" reveals a whole variety of changes to the way governments work, changes that Canada is committing itself to in the total absence of any public consultation or even knowledge. For example, it reveals that Canada is working on a series of bilateral deals that will protect the interests of investors, implicitly protecting them against government action. Eighteen of these Foreign Investment Protection Agreements have already been signed and others are being negotiated.

Throughout the "Action Plan" the government makes clear that APEC negotiations and principles are being coordinated with the WTO and OECD initiatives on multilateral investment agreements. These coordinated and reinforcing multilateral deals paint a picture of a government hell bent on surrendering the most important aspects of Canadian sovereignty as fast as it can. Canada now applies the high

NAFTA investment-review thresholds (the level of investment at which review kicks in) to all WTO members. Ottawa is also busy signing deals and making unannounced commitments to liberalize government procurement regulations — in short, reducing government's ability to purchase goods and services from Canadian suppliers. The authority and power of governments to enhance their communities are being rapidly eroded through agreements that are, as far as the public is concerned, clandestine. Only a handful of Canadians, excluding most parliamentarians and premiers, have heard of the Bogor Declaration, the Ministers for Cartagena, or the Osaka Action Agenda.

As with all of these multilateral agreements, the negotiations nominally take place between governments, masking the fact that the exclusive beneficiaries are corporations. Evidence does occasionally emerge, however, of just how crucial these deals are to large corporations. The merging of the market state and corporations was revealed in the days leading up to the APEC summit in Vancouver in 1997. Sixty-seven corporations contributed $9.1 million towards the $57.4-million cost of the summit. Seven corporations contributed half a million each: Canadian Airlines (infamous for squeezing its employees for wage concessions), TD Bank, Federal Express, BC Tel, Nortel, General Motors of Canada, and the Export Development Corporation. Other big contributors included the Royal Bank ($250,000), Panasonic ($250,000), and SunLife ($320,000). These contributions, raised by former TD Bank chair Richard Thompson at Prime Minister Chrétien's request, are a powerful reminder of who APEC is intended to benefit. Equally important, they strengthen the hand of these huge corporations in their efforts to control the outcome of negotiations. Whoever pays the APEC piper calls the APEC tune.[40]

There are other initiatives in corporate libertarianism in various regions around the world. Some are just multilateral agreements like the recent one deregulating telephone services (expected to dramatically increase local-use charges). Others are corporate-state initiatives meant to drive the free-trade initiative faster. This is the case with the Enterprise for the Americas Initiative (EAI), announced by George Bush in 1990 and aimed at creating a hemispheric free-trade zone and liberalized investment and debt restructuring. The U.S has already signed more than thirty framework agreements with Caribbean and Latin American governments. If they wish to get on the NAFTA train, each country must commit to "opening markets in goods and services; removing barriers to investment, and safeguarding intellectual property."[41]

The U.S. is prepared to sign "mini-agreements" on investment and intellectual property rights with Latin American states while it continues its efforts to get a hemispheric free-trade deal. Chile, one of the most aggressively market-oriented countries in the Americas, has already joined a free-trade deal with Canada. These bilateral deals represent the second of a two-track strategy and became more important in late 1997 when President Clinton failed to get approval for so-called fast-track authority for deals like the EAI and MAI.

Common to all of these deals and potential deals is the complete absence of any reference to social, environmental, or labour standards or human rights. In the developed countries, governments have responded to this criticism with what are now commonly referred to as "side deals." These usually concern labour and the environment, the two areas where the protest has been the most effective, and a social charter. So far, under the FTA and NAFTA, the side deals have proven ineffective, though supporters suggest the jury is still out.

There is a fatal flaw in the notion of social charters being attached to liberalizing multinational agreements. Pressing for improved labour, social and environmental standards fundamentally contradicts the whole point of these deals, which is to lower costs and investment barriers to transnational corporations. Free trade and investment demand deregulatory requirements that make social protection ideologically and politically unacceptable. It would be difficult to make them effective precisely because, to the extent that they are effective, they undermine the purpose of the agreement and its corporate libertarian philosophy. You might just as well try to add rabbit-like features to a fox to make it behave more like a rabbit.

The same is true of international environmental protection agreements. Unlike trade and investment regimes, they have no teeth. The Rio Summit of 1992 is a good example. The record of governments "promising" to meet environmental goals established in Rio de Janeiro is appalling because there are no consequences for breaking the promises. And that's how corporations wish to keep it. It is for this reason that they insist on having such issues dealt with, if at all, in side deals rather than integrated into the main agreement.

As for the willingness of corporations to entertain even these toothless "protections," the heavy hitters behind the MAI have drawn a line in the sand. The U.S. Council for International Business, the most powerful lobby speaking for U.S. TNCs, wrote to senior U.S. officials in 1997. "The MAI is an agreement by governments to protect international investors and their investments and to liberalize investment regimes. We will oppose any and all measures to create or even imply binding obligations for governments or business related to environment or labor."[42]

Viable or not, side agreements on labour and the environment have not been pursued by Canadian negotiators in MAI negotiations. In late 1997 it was revealed that Canada was not among those nations speaking up on the issue during the most recent negotiations. Instead, the government accepted weak and nonbinding language in the preamble of the agreement. This is not the only area in which the Canadian government is failing to protect the country's interests. In response to charges that the MAI threatens medicare, education, and social services, the government declared that key areas of the economy and social infrastructure will be listed as Canadian "reservations," allegedly protecting them from the terms of the agreement.

But according to a study by trade lawyer Barry Appleton, commissioned by the Council of Canadians, the way the specific Canadian reservations are worded makes them virtually meaningless. Appleton, who is acting for the Ethyl Corporation against Canada on the MMT case, pointed out that reservations in the context of international treaties are always interpreted restrictively. "Reservations are a form of exception to international treaty commitments and are interpreted narrowly by international courts and tribunals."[43] As well, the definition of "measures" to be reserved in the MAI is itself very narrow compared to the definition in NAFTA, which explicitly lists "laws, regulations, procedures, requirements or practices."[44]

Appleton stated unequivocally that, judged on this basis, Canada's reservations intended to protect social services, health care, and public education are, because they protect only the federal government's programs, "inadequate to permit provincial governments to provide these services without compensating affected foreign investors."[45]

As worded, the reservations would protect only public law enforcement and correctional services.

The environment too is left exposed. According to Appleton, Canada has "chosen to voluntarily bind itself, its provinces and its municipalities to obligations which protect investments over the environment."[46] And culture is left even more vulnerable, since the government made no reservations at all in this area. Appleton's report concluded: "Any policy or program that advantaged Canadian culture or content directly or indirectly, would run afoul of the national treatment or performance requirements obligations."[47] Six areas, including Canadian content in TV, Canadian film distribution policy, and postal subsidies to Canadian publications, require specific reservations; otherwise, they are subject to demands for compensation from foreign corporations.

Reservations to treaties are problematic at the best of times. With the MAI, of course, they also face the rollback clause. In effect, the reservations that are made become a corporate hit-list — conveniently targeted areas of public policy that the government is committed to gradually eliminating.

Transnational corporations, in the process of becoming the most powerful organized force on the planet, have made huge steps towards effectively ruling the world. Corporate influence in public life has always been a reality in capitalist economies, and that influence has always been characterized by a lack of democracy. The last quarter of the twentieth century, however, has witnessed a profound change in the exercise of corporate power and influence.

Going beyond the exercise of influence on individual national politics, corporations are now circumventing the institutions of democracy and creating their own supra-national institutions of domination, institutions that are inaccessible to ordinary citizens, whose laws supersede those passed by democratic legislatures, and whose express purpose is to choke off the ability of communities to control their own destiny. Most alarming of all is the willing collusion of our democratically elected governments in this global counter-revolution.

The Multilateral Agreement on Investment and APEC, like the FTA and NAFTA before them, will make enemies of citizens and their government. By aligning themselves so exclusively with transnational corporations, governments virtually by definition declare a kind of social war on their own citizens, a declaration of acceptance of permanent class divisions as a feature of modern society. Most of what government does, for ordinary citizens, involves moderating the unequal effects of the marketplace. If we see democracy as principally a process of and for equality, then the fruits of democracy can be achieved only by exercising significant control over the market economy.

Transnational corporations have transcended the national governments that gave them identity and corporate status, but only with the aid of those governments. If nations can sign multilateral agreements ceding their individual sovereignty to the so-called larger purpose of international trade, they could create international agencies of democratic governance. Yet no major nation-state has proposed an international tax scheme, an enforceable labour code, an enforceable environmental code, or international standards for health and education assured by international financing. What explains the fact that nation-states are willing to surrender sovereignty to transnational corporations but not to a world government? Only that the economic and political elites that currently rule the developed nations are complicit in the development of corporate rule over their own citizens.

The speed with which global corporate rule is being implemented is breathtaking; the eagerness of democratically elected governments to dismantle what they have constructed over three generations is just as stunning. The headlong rush into a totally deregulated world is a kind of social madness or, as John McMurtry says in his book *The Global Market as an Ethical System*, a cancer, eating away at a body politic whose immune system no longer recognizes the mortal danger. We are creating ever greater poverty at home and in less developed countries, contrasted by ever greater obscene wealth concentrated in fewer and fewer hands. The rulers and the ruled have not been divided by such an economic, social, and moral gulf since the Great Depression.

6

Rulers and Ruled in the New World Order

The total cost of the 700 social events laid on for delegates during the single week was estimated at $10 million . . . A single formal dinner catered by Ridgewells cost $200 per person. Guests began with crab cakes, caviar and crème fraiche, smoked salmon and beef Wellington. The fish course was lobster . . . the entrée was duck with lime sauce, served with artichoke bottoms filled with baby carrots. Dessert was a German chocolate turnip sauced with raspberry coulis, ice cream bonbons and flaming coffee royale.
— Journalist Graham Hancock, describing a joint IMF–World Bank meeting in Washington, in *Lords of Poverty*

Potential troublemakers were threatened with arrest and violence. The Philippine government put out a blacklist of undesirable anti-APEC visitors, and turned away, among others, the east Timorese activist and Nobel Peace Prize winner Jose Ramos Horta, for fear of upsetting Indonesian President Suharto. The shanties of over 400,000 families were demolished in an attempt to create an "eyesore free zone" for visiting dignitaries . . .
Their land, which has been confiscated . . . is slated for the largest super-mall in the world, which will house the first Disneyworld of the region.
— Maude Barlow, Council of Canadians delegate to People's Summit on APEC, 1996

Ruling elites and demonstrations of their power are as old as human organization itself, and in modern times those elites have been easily identified, whether in communist, capitalist, democratic, or authoritarian regimes. Yet the elites in the age of transnational corporations are playing a particular role. Increasingly we are witnessing an international ruling elite developing apace with international capital and the institutions of global governance such as the WTO, the OECD, and the multilateral deals they design and implement.

As we will see in the next chapter, underlying this global ruling elite is an unprecedented political and ideological consensus. The speed with which the new order is being put in place owes a great deal to this consensus. But for the flesh-and-blood individuals who constitute that elite it also has to do with how they make their money, the things they buy, and who they identify with and have contact with. Their wealth depends on giant corporations and currency speculation, their work has been internationalized, and they take comfort in the decline of civil society by agreeing, with a hint of regret, that the great social experiment in egalitarianism simply didn't work.

The rich are different from us. Of course, they have always had more money and have always gained it at the expense of the huge majority who don't have as much, or any. But today they are even more different from us. The rulers of the world are not only are getting obscenely rich. They are getting rich through increasingly unchallenged corporate rule and through the exponential growth of the power of transnational corporations, both financial and political.

There are now so many billionaires in the world that *Fortune* magazine's list no longer names them all. So many are added each year that only the "Top" 200 are now rich enough to warrant being listed. The 1997 list nearly surpassed 500; in 1996 it was 447. In 1995 there were "only" 357 billionaires. Their net worth was $760 billion, more wealth than the bottom 45 percent of humanity. That is, 357 people in the world owned more combined wealth than 2.7 billion other people. And this, we are told, is the result of the "market," the invisible hand by which each individual's pursuit of wealth is alleged to benefit the whole of humanity.[1]

And the billionaires are just at the very top of the human pyramid. Below them are tens of thousands of multimillionaires and millions who have assets of more than a million dollars. The inequality is staggering. It is, nonetheless, portrayed in the popular culture as natural.

The egalitarian state, on the other hand, has always been denounced by free marketeers as social engineering.

Yet what the world has experienced over the past twenty years is a massive and accelerating transfer of wealth from the poor to the rich, a social engineering project matched only during colonial times. When wealth is created it is divided between those who labour and those who invest; between owners and workers. And everywhere that division is becoming more unequal.

This is just as true with nations as it is with individuals, with the less developed world every year pouring billions of dollars into the pockets of the elites in the developed world. It is also true within developed countries. A 1993 U.N. Human Development Report revealed that in 1960 the richest fifth of the world's population was thirty times better off than the poorest fifth. The latest estimate is that they are now 150 times better off.[2]

In Canada the situation parallels the international scene. *Financial Post* magazine reports that the wealthiest fifty Canadians now have assets of $39 billion, equivalent to two and a half times the total income of more than five million Canadians who earn less than $10,000 a year.[3] In 1993 alone, according to Statistics Canada, the top 30 percent of Canadian families "took an extra $14.3 billion over and above the amount they would have received had their share of the income pie not increased since 1973. And virtually all of their income was siphoned off the bottom 50 percent."[4]

The wealth transfer has been accelerating, with the share going to the wealthy growing two to three times faster from 1987 to 1993 than from 1973 to 1987. A November 1997 Ernst and Young survey revealed that Canada was home to 220,000 millionaires, an incredible threefold increase since 1989. The number is expected to triple again by 2005. (The millionaire status was determined by liquid assets and did not include home equity or pension plans.)[5]

The transfer of wealth has a variety of sources. Much of it, according to Ernst and Young, comes from inheritances, which in Canada are not taxed. (Canada is the only OECD country, other than Australia, without such a tax.) In addition, the speculation-driven stock market has made millionaires out of many who used to consider themselves middle class. Ironically, a large part of the new wealth comes from interest on government debt, paid by average taxpayers to the wealthy who hold government debt. The incomes of managers and professionals have gone up much faster than average earnings. The wealthy have also benefited from the years of high interest rates on their assets. Tax breaks and lower marginal tax rates have helped, too. After two decades of tax reform Canada has a virtually flat tax system, where everyone pays the same rate. A Carleton University study revealed that, taking all taxes into account — income, sales, payroll, property, and others — those earning between $100,000 and $150,000 pay 32.6 percent of their total in taxes; those earning between $40,000 and $50,000 pay 34.1 percent, and those earning less than $10,000 pay 30.1 percent.[6]

The ruling elite consists of those who make the most important decisions that affect our daily lives. What aspects of life do we normally consider the most important? At the top of the list for most people is the ability to make a decent living. Living in a community and neighbourhood in which you feel not only safe but a part of that community is a key aspect of daily life. So too is access to safe food, clean air, drinkable water, and an environment that is generally free of threats of any kind. Housing, transportation, and access to services such as medicare and education are also high on the list.

When we talk about who "rules," we necessarily contrast how many of these aspects of daily life are determined by government, over which ordinary people have some nominal influence, and how many are determined by corporations and, more specifically, those who run them. Even a cursory examination of what government does reveals its efforts to moderate the "normal" behaviour of corporations in the economy either by regulating them or by providing public services that corporations won't provide equitably.

For most people the ability to make a living depends on whether private capital invests in some activity. Yet how capital behaves in providing that living is not entirely in its hands. Labour laws have something to say about child labour, working hours, minimum wages, employer deductions for pensions and EI, protection of employees' health and safety, and last but not least their right to form a union to speak for themselves collectively. A similar list could be drawn up for other areas of daily life.

But when government withdraws from these areas, or cuts back its involvement, it does not mean that no one is left governing. When government abandons its responsibility to create jobs or loosens regulations about working conditions or passes "regulatory efficiency" laws that bypass environmental protection, then the economic elites simply increase the social territory over which they rule.

Countries maintain the trappings of democratic, popular governance while CEOs of large corporations, hidden from public view, seize more and more of the ground of governance and make more and more of the decisions that affect our daily lives. This shift from democratic governance to corporate rule takes place incrementally, each step carefully rationalized by the purveyors of market ideology. The state still governs, but corporations rule.

It is not just the decisions these individuals make in their capacity as corporate executives that constitute corporate rule; neither is it just those at the pinnacle of the corporate order who are part of the ruling elite. This corporate upper echelon has always made decisions that affect the lives of millions of people. Corporate rule's "governing" elite involves two other dimensions. First, the role that the truly powerful play goes beyond the decisions they make for their corporations. Their role in lobbying government and political parties, their support for and involvement in think-tanks, their networking with other elite members through company directorships, their personal alliances with national and international corporate leaders, their private and occasional public intervention on policy issues, all of these activities extend their ruling capacity beyond the confines of the corporate suite.

The second dimension of the ruling corporate elite is its wider base, today including those who share the power, influence, and financial benefits with the top 1 percent of the truly powerful. The large numbers who populate the managerial class of corporations and the law firms, accounting firms, brokerages, and financial houses that make up the modern corporate world are all part of that elite, sharing in the privileges and adopting the perspectives and depending on the dominance of those at the top. Add to that the political class of senior university administrators and academics, newspaper publishers and other guardians of information, senior bureaucrats and senior cabinet ministers and you have a conglomeration of people who constitute the ruling elite.

This class has always been integral to the functioning of a liberal democratic society. But two things have changed in the past twenty years. First, there is stronger consensus about the direction of the state than there has been for decades, and it is radically different from the one that arose in the post-war period. That consensus amounts to a virtual counter-revolution against the egalitarian state, a determination to turn back the clock on social programs, regulatory regimes, development aid, human rights, and the commitment to social equality that has been the definition, or at least the operating myth, of the Canadian nation-state for almost three generations.

The second change, and indeed part of what drives the radical new consensus, is the international perspective of this reconstituted ruling elite. The attachment to market ideology is at least in part a rationalization for the source of the new elite's vast new economic wealth and its future well-being. With the advent of free-trade deals, the power of transnational corporations to manipulate the world economy, and the wealth to be made in stock and speculative markets, the rulers have lost interest in their local domain. Their dominion, like the mercantile class of the eighteenth century, is now the world.

THE SECESSION OF THE SUCCESSFUL

One of the keys to the development of this neo-mercantilist elite is how they make their money. Those who work directly in the highest ranks of the private sector not only engineer profits for their companies through the international markets in goods, services, and currencies. They are in many ways more linked to that international world than they are to their own communities or country. Robert Reich, a Harvard economist who became Bill Clinton's labour secretary, describes the new elite this way: "The highest earners now occupy a different economy from other Americans. The new elite is connected by jet, fax, modem, satellite and fiber-optic to the great commercial and recreational centers of the world but not particularly to the rest of the nation."[7]

Not all countries have devolved their civil societies to the extent that the U.S. has, but it is instructive to examine the American experience as a window on the future everywhere if current trends continue. In a piece for the *New York Times Magazine* called "Secession of the Successful," Reich describes the work of the American equivalent of this elite as symbolic analyzers. "Most of their work consists of analyzing and manipulating symbols — words, numbers or visual images. Among the most prominent of these 'symbolic analyzers' are management consultants, lawyers, software and design engineers, research scientists, corporate executives, financial advisers, strategic planners, advertising executives, television and movie producers, and other workers whose job titles include terms like 'strategy,' 'planning,' 'consultant,' 'policy,' 'resources,' or 'engineer.'"[8]

It is a long time since Henry Ford realized that his new mass production methods were so efficient that he was making more cars than there were Americans who could afford to buy them. His solution, to double the wages of his workers so they *could* afford the sticker price, was dubbed Fordism. Reich's anecdotal version is the rich industrialist on the hill who worries about his workers down below — because they produce his wealth through their work. No work, no wealth. That scenario is pretty much history. In the post-Fordist world, the ruler on top of the hill doesn't care if the ruled at the bottom works; he doesn't ever see him. His wealth, in any case, is more likely produced by the labour of a Mexican or Filipino or Thai worker whom he doesn't see either. He doesn't even care if that worker buys his product so long as some middle-class consumer somewhere buys it.

Reich argues in his article and in his book *The Work of Nations* that the "fortunate fifth," the wealthiest 20 percent of Americans, were "quietly seceding from the rest of the nation." That trend is now highly advanced in the U.S. Reich cites many examples, beginning with the fact that the wealthy now pay only a fraction of the taxes they used to pay, decimating public finances and services. They can thus justify shelling out even greater amounts of money for private services provided in what have become known as gated cities. Everything from libraries, street repair, fire service, and police are now privately funded. Much of America is becoming characterized by a kind of social apartheid. The elite "feel increasingly justified in paying only what is necessary to insure that everyone in their community is sufficiently well educated and has access to the public

services they need to succeed."⁹ The social solidarity that characterized the recent past is being replaced by class solidarity at the top.

Large U.S. urban centres are being "splintered into two separate
cities. One is composed of those whose symbolic and analytic services
are linked to the world economy" while the other is the whole
panoply of service workers who depend on the "other" city for their
employment. Most blue-collar jobs have disappeared from big cities.
Between 1953 and 1984, New York lost 600,000 manufacturing
jobs while gaining 700,000 "symbolic analyst" and service jobs.
Wealth-creating jobs, which used to link the social classes, have
gone elsewhere.

The symbolic analysts no longer even live in the cores of the big
cities. Many, connected from home to the centre of trade and finance
around the world, live in pastoral settings far from the eroding cities
and the lives of their marginalized fellow citizens. Those still living in
the urban centres create their own cities within cities. "One such
New York district, between 38th and 48th streets and Second and
Fifth Avenues," writes Reich, "raised $4.7 million from its residents
in 1989, of which $1 million underwrote a private force of uniformed
guards and plainclothes investigators."¹⁰

The trend to private security is now so advanced that there are
three times as many private cops as there are public police. And rather
than deal with the poverty of the "other cities" the U.S. is putting
people in jail at a record-setting pace. It now jails 2 percent of
its working-age population, at a rate of 529 inmates for every 100,000
population.¹¹ This is nothing more than warehousing of the unemployed, as the record shows that being tougher on crime in this
manner has no effect on crime rates.

The use of private cops suggests more than just a "secession" of the
elite. It also suggests that they believe they can protect themselves
from threats from the underclass they are helping create. Though the
private police do not yet have the same powers of coercion as their
public counterparts, the lines between them are blurring. The wealthy
are gradually seizing the "right" to use violence now exclusively in
the hands of the democratic state.

THE ELITE SECESSION IN CANADA

The international orientation of the ruling elite is a generally accurate description of Canada's economy, too; however, because so many TNCs are centred in the U.S., the role of symbolic analyzers is necessarily larger in that country. But what Canada lacks in that global field it makes up for in the export economy. Since the first free-trade deal was passed, the government and the business elite, as represented by the Business Council on National Issues, have focussed almost exclusively on policies promoting international trade, to the detriment of the domestic economy.

The great puzzle of the "jobless recovery" is no puzzle at all when one examines the extent to which the domestic economy has been savaged by government spending cuts, the erosion of income redistribution, the flattening of the tax system, and the loss of more than 200,000 industrial jobs. These are all deliberate government policies, not some globally dictated inevitability. It is not just that the domestic economy is being neglected. It is, as we will see later in this chapter, being subjected to a "controlled economic stagnation" whose purpose is to discipline labour and check inflation to ensure the international competitiveness of the corporations oriented to international trade.

The trade economy, while constantly touted in government and business propaganda as key to Canada's future, is dominated by large corporations, which are the big job destroyers. Despite our loss of jobs, there has been an enormous increase in overall trade: 33.2 percent of GDP went to exports in 1994, compared with 26.3 percent in 1988, while imports increased from 25.8 percent of GDP to 32.5 percent. The majority of that increase has been with the U.S. as the result of free trade. And 90 percent of the trade with the U.S. is accounted for by the two hundred largest exporters.[12]

Robert Reich's description of the secession of the successful does not fit what's happening in Canada, at least not yet. But like so many trends connected to economic development, especially given the pressures for "harmonization" from the FTA and NAFTA, there are clear signs that Canada is headed in the same direction. We can simply look at the U.S. to see where we will be ten or fifteen years from now.

As Canadian budgets for social programs and infrastructure steadily erode it is hard to imagine Canada not following the same path as the

U.S. One of the key developments leading to the "two separate cities" phenomenon in the U.S. is diminishing federal funding to the cities, from 25 percent of their budgets in the 1970s to 17 percent in the mid-1990s. The same trend is developing here as provincial governments, facing cuts in federal transfers, download costs to municipalities. Canada is also following the U.S. trend of putting more of the poor and marginalized in jail.

The evidence that the Canadian ruling elite is seceding is mounting. The anecdotal evidence is everywhere, of course; editorials and columnists in almost every newspaper in the country rail against "big government," and the vast majority of academics on radio and TV panels express the same consensus. Polls show that the elite in this country are gradually withdrawing their commitment to social equality. The social contract "signed" by their predecessors is being unilaterally broken.

A 1994 project launched by the Ekos research and polling group, called "Rethinking Government," interviewed 1,000 of the key decision makers in the country — top civil servants, elected officials, and corporate executives — and 2,500 members of the general public. The results were dramatic. "The comparison between the elites and the general public suggests that . . . a profound gap exists between the public and decision-makers in the area of preferred government values."[13] Given twenty-two value choices for government action, the two groups' attitudes are almost totally reversed. "Competitiveness" and "minimal government" ranked first and third for the elite but at the bottom of the list, numbers 20 and 22, for the general public. Virtually all of the policy values related to equality, social justice, collective rights, full employment and regulation of business, and even personal privacy were low on the elite's list of priorities and high on the general public's.

The overall conclusion of this study was that the elites look at government through the other end of the public's telescope. Everything is attenuated. Not only is everything related to government reduced, it is also purged of its moral content. One finding of the study was the degree to which the elite was "homogeneous in their values and attitudes . . . due to both their shared social class and internal cohesion . . . A chasm exists between those charged with governing and those being governed."[14]

THE MYTH OF THE GOOD CORPORATE CITIZEN

The Ekos poll is far from the only sign of the elite's abandonment of nation building and social justice. One of the results of the elite's resentment of enforced social solidarity is an unprecedented increase in tax evasion. *Taipan*, one of many "insider" financial newsletters, shamelessly promoted illegal tax evasion: "You'll be able to conduct your financial life in absolute privacy and security . . . The government won't know whom you're sending money to or getting money from. The whole transaction will disappear from the face of the earth . . . Those who amass wealth and profits will be able to keep it. The tax burden will shift towards those who make money in the traditional way."[15] A book of advice on tax avoidance, *Take Your Money and Run*, sold eighty thousand copies in Canada.

As of 1995, Canadian wealth sitting in off-shore tax havens already amounted to tens of billions of dollars. By diverting their wealth off-shore, the elites don't have to bother demanding lower tax rates, already slashed during the 1980s; they just don't pay taxes, period.

Secession is well under way. The *Financial Post*, in an article entitled "A System for the Rich," described how millionaires bypass the public medicare system to get the very best treatment immediately from specialist clinics in the U.S.[16] As the elite avail themselves of private services they increasingly resent paying taxes for public services they no longer use. And as public services decline in the face of lost revenue, the wealthy abandon them even more, widening the gap between public and private, rich and poor. And with the principle of universality now breached with respect to pensions, the wealthy feel even more that they pay for programs that they won't benefit from.

The restructured ruling elite has managed to create a broad social base for its continuing counter-revolution. As we will see later in this chapter, the traditional middle class in Canada and elsewhere is fracturing. Once the very expression of social solidarity, it is now a class with no clear social role. Those who have managed to attach themselves to the new economy now identify with the elite and have done extremely well. The result is a portion of society — the most politically literate and class conscious — that now accounts for nearly 40 percent of the population.

The willingness of the elite, and by default their followers, to abandon the historic compromise is rationalized, according to the Ekos study, by a stated belief that the whole post-war project failed to deliver the goods. But the ease with which many in this upper social class savage their fellow human beings goes well beyond any such practical conviction. The ruthlessness of the corporate world and the esteem with which downsizing CEOs are held in that class cannot help but infect the elite as a whole. The moral detachment of money traders and speculators adds to that sense of separateness and secession.

One of these traders, Dennis Levine, eventually imprisoned for insider trading, described how the whole Wall Street culture was like a big game. "When a company was identified as an acquisition target, we declared that it was 'in play.' We designated the playing pieces and strategies in whimsical terms: white knight, target, shark repellent, the Pac-Man defense, poison pill . . . Keeping a scorecard was easy — the winner was the one who finalized the most deals and took home the most money . . . It was easy to forget the . . . material impact upon the jobs, and thus the lives, of millions of Americans."[17]

In the U.S., the twenty-year exodus from the cities, now accelerated by changes in communications, is creating two class solitudes, which increasingly never see or experience each other. It isn't just the elite that gets isolated. The poor do as well, as the high-poverty ghettoes grow at an alarming rate, from four million ten years ago to eight million today. There have always been geographic class divisions, yet the current trend to both extreme poverty and extreme wealth is changing the character of U.S. cities. American sociologist William Wilson, author of *When Work Disappears*, argues that the poor are becoming so hostile that widespread social unrest is increasingly likely within the next ten years.

Yet the elites seem complacent about the possibility of such unrest, confident that increased private security will be enough. A combination of blaming the poor, which prevents a moral response, and a blind confidence in their continued success absolves them from taking any action to address the issues. And why would we expect anything else? The downsizing champions carry on with impunity. They trash the lives of thousands of their employees and the other shoe never drops. With the exception of a mere handful of dissenting voices, mostly private sector, this sociopathic behaviour is endorsed by default.

Canada has not yet created the terrible divisions we see south of the border. But all the ingredients for that class division and potential class violence are now in place in Canada. There is nothing to suggest that the new global-oriented elite here is any more conscious of its history, more aware of its amorality, or any less arrogant in its triumphalism than its American counterpart. Giddy with its success, content to blame the poor and count on the police, the rulers in Canada have left themselves no way out.

THE RULED

The historic efforts at democratic self-determination of anti-colonial governments, socialist Third World states, and the unique one-party democracies of Africa have long since disappeared. Subjected to the geopolitics of the cold war and the pro-corporate machinations of the IMF and the World Bank, dozens of less developed countries were never given the chance to develop civil societies. And now that communism is dead the U.S. has lost interest in democracy and human rights, one of its tools in its cold war battle with the Soviet Union. Many of these nations are, as a result, now governed by the opportunists and thugs recruited by the U.S. to fight communism.

Or they now have peace with no justice, as in the states of Central America where the same economic elites and the same political gangs who spoke for them in the past still run their countries. The poverty, unemployment, and exploitation are exactly the same, and the leaders of the developed world expect the exploited to be thankful that they are not being dragged from their beds in the middle of the night and murdered.

The best the ruled can hope for is that the transnational corporations' expectation that countries play by accepted rules, will mean no surprises. That is the substance of the democracy being promoted by TNCs and their state allies. Perhaps the only benefit of NAFTA for the people of Mexico is that pressure from the U.S. and the TNCs to end rampant corruption and political dictatorship has helped bring a greater semblance of parliamentary democracy to that country. Jack Warnock, author of *The Other Mexico*, says, "The free trade move undermined the old way of doing business in Mexico. TNCs want transparency in dealing with government. They want . . . assurances that contracts will be honoured." Also, Mexico has become a more open society. "The foreign press, business interests, and some governments have felt free to criticize the Mexican government for its corruption, ties with the drug industry, and human rights abuses."[18]

Transparency involves rules, not the conditions under which wealth is created and labour exploited. And that is the irony in this moderate democratic opening. For while it arrives in part because of NAFTA, the very fact of NAFTA and economic liberalization renders the democratic state virtually powerless to improve the lives of its citizens. The corporate and political power brokers of the world are delivering on a decades-old promise of institutional democracy only when it is bereft of any meaning, stripped of its egalitarian essence, and reduced to little more than a service to transnational corporations. Indeed, judging just by economic and social conditions, most Mexicans were far better off before the democratic opening.

Before the signing of NAFTA, Mexico went through a radical restructuring based on the same neo-liberal principles underlying free trade. That restructuring, which followed Mexico's debt repayment crisis in 1982, involved replacing its longstanding import-substitution strategy with an export-driven strategy. In effect, NAFTA was just another step along the road to the neo-liberal game plan. The results for ordinary Mexicans have been devastating.

Despite its much-touted low-wage advantage, Mexico has experienced the same de-industrialization that Canada and the U.S. have experienced since the early 1980s. In 1994, about 60 percent of the membership of the chambers of commerce in Mexico reported that they were in "dire need of assistance." The competition with the U.S. (indirectly, competition with extremely low-wage-based imports from Asia) saw the number of sporting goods manufacturers drop from 150 to 38; 114 drug companies were reduced to 40. In 1993–94, fully 40 percent of Mexican clothing manufacturers went bankrupt. The shift to exports was supposed to help Mexico's debt situation, but in 1992 the country had a balance-of-payments deficit of $18.8 billion. In 1994, the first year of NAFTA, that deficit rose to $28 billion.[19]

The fall-out for the average Mexican worker has been a cruel ratcheting down of living standards. The share of GDP going to wages dropped from 37 percent in 1980 to 24 percent in 1991, and real wages (money wages corrected for inflation) of Mexican workers dropped by 40 percent. A major factor in this catastrophic drop was the decline in real minimum wage from $7.49 a day in 1981 to $2.65 in 1994.[20] The jobs created by NAFTA have actually tended to bring down the average. The overall average industrial wage was $2.61 an hour in 1994, while in the *maquiladoras* (where the number of plants has increased by six hundred since NAFTA was signed in 1993) the average is $1.75 an hour.[21]

The enormous disparities in wealth in Mexico, historically very high, have become even worse with NAFTA and neo-liberal policies. The selling of billions of dollars in state assets has created over two dozen new billionaires; 54 percent of the country's total wealth is now held by its richest thirty-six families. Far from helping to bring Mexico into the "first world" as promised, NAFTA and corporate libertarianism have driven Mexico closer to the bottom of the Latin American ladder.

The race to the bottom that has been unleashed on the peoples of the world has profound consequences for hundreds of millions of workers and their families. The drive to externalize the costs of production is most ruthless in the very countries that are supposed to benefit from off-shore production and investment. The competition for the lowest wages, taxes, and environmental and human rights standards produces predictable results.

According to the International Labour Organization, the most reliable figure on the level of child labour for 1997 was 250 million. This is not just children working for their families' businesses or assisting at home. This is also factory labour, much of it extremely hazardous. It is indentured labour, in which the children's pay is never enough to pay back the employer's "costs" of keeping them alive; it is children making the things Canadians purchase from transnational corporations like Disney, Nike, and dozens of other corporations who contract out their production to the contractor with the lowest bid.

The race to the bottom involves everyone, everywhere. If democratic reforms and workers' fights for better wages improve conditions in one developing country, corporations move to one where labour is cheaper. An exposé of conditions in Thailand followed a fire at a toy factory in which 188 workers, mostly thirteen-year-old girls, lost their lives because the owner violated safety laws. As a result of improved law enforcement, companies moved toy production from Thailand, Indonesia, and the Philippines to plants in free-trade zones in southern China. There the daily wages averaged 80 cents compared with $5.52 in Thailand.[22]

South Korea, emerging from decades of military dictatorship, implemented democratic reforms that resulted in unions gaining a tripling in wages for Nike shoemakers and workers in general. Nike led the way in reacting to these changes. The company contracted factories in China, Indonesia, and Vietnam, where hourly wages are as low as seventeen cents an hour.

Nike, the target of citizen campaigns around the world, is a quintessential TNC. Its products are "global," providing middle-class kids everywhere with the kind of product identification that is the envy of other corporations. It does not have factories of its own but hires thousands of subcontractors who employ half a million workers. For these employees, who labour sixty to seventy-five hours a week, corporate rule directly determines working conditions, which for many are appalling.

A 1997 report by Hong Kong human rights groups revealed conditions at a Wellco subcontractor in Dongguan, China, employing children as young as thirteen "that have resulted in workers losing fingers and hands; beatings by security guards; . . . fines levied for workers who talk to each other on the job; 72 hour work weeks; and pay less than the . . . minimum wage of US$.24 an hour." In Vietnam workers for another Nike subcontractor had their mouths taped shut for talking on the job.[23] Meanwhile, Nike pays its star advertiser, Michael Jordan, $20 million a year, just about the same as it pays in one year to its twelve thousand Indonesian workers, most of whom are young girls who work fifteen hours a day.[24]

In country after country competing for TNC investment, unions are smashed, their organizers beaten or killed, and human rights violated. In 1996 workers and others in El Salvador signed a letter asking the GAP clothing company to allow independent investigation of conditions in its Mandarin International plant. In response, the Salvadorean minister of the interior threatened the death penalty for the signers and deportation for foreigners.

The family of Ken Saro-Wiwa has filed suit in the New York District Court against Royal/Dutch Shell for its collusion with the Nigerian military dictatorship in the detention, trial, and subsequent judicial murder of the poet-activist and eight colleagues. The suit will include evidence that Shell called in the military to suppress demonstrations, bribed witnesses at the trial, and had direct involvement in human rights violations against the Ogoni people.

THE RACE TO THE BOTTOM

The impact of transnational corporate power on social life and democracy is not limited to developing countries or military dictatorships. As dropping real wages combine with the steady shredding of the safety net, more and more working people in Canada and other developed countries fall into a social class characterized by almost constant insecurity. The benefits to corporations driving this agenda are both economic and political.

The economic benefits are obvious. The political benefits are more subtle. But the decline in democratic participation by working people is every bit as important to corporations as the decline in wages and social programs. The historic battle for who gets the biggest share of new wealth produced by corporations — employees or shareholders — turned in favour of workers in the 1960s and early 1970s. Full employment gave working people the upper hand in a sellers' labour market.

And workers achieved success not only at the bargaining table. They achieved equally important gains at the polling booth. A revitalized and militant labour movement combined with dynamic and forceful social movements of women, youth, aboriginal people, and the poor wrenched away some of the formally exclusive influence of corporations on government. It was this brief flowering of democratic participation that drove the social policy agenda in that period.

The changes affecting the security of working people and their communities are easy to identify. Restructuring the world economy and the TNCs that dominate it has created dual economies in two quite different ways. Within TNCs, according to David Korten, the corporation's internal operations are reduced to its core competencies, "generally the finance, marketing, and proprietary technology functions that represent the firm's primary source of economic power." These core functions are centralized at company headquarters and the employees performing these functions "are well compensated, with full benefits and attractive working conditions."

The second tier of employees are in what is now called peripheral functions, which, ironically for firms known for their products, includes manufacturing jobs. These are the functions that are most often farmed out to independent contractors or foreign-based units of the company. The pattern here is extremely low paid work, often by part-time employees who have few if any benefits.[25]

Not only are these functions of the TNC seen as peripheral and therefore given no commitment but they are also the areas in which competition is the most fierce. These production units, even the ones remaining in the firm, function as independent small contractors forced to compete with each other for the firm's business.

With the de-industrialization of North America, and the major investments in labour-displacing technologies, the job market in Canada and the U.S. is characterized by a good job/bad job phenomenon. The good jobs are just like the good jobs of old: well paid, generous benefits, a promise of career advancement, and a measure of security. The bad jobs — and these are the ones the economy is mostly creating — offer almost no hope of advancement. These jobs are designed to be dead-end, for the just-in-time contingent workers who must be on call twenty-four hours a day if they want work. These workers are effectively competing with those in the developing countries.

The trend to part-time work is developing with astonishing speed and throughout the whole economy. A 1996 study done for the *Globe and Mail Report on Business* revealed that "part-timers now make up 29 percent of the average firm's total workforce, more than triple the 1989 level." More than half of Canadian companies now employ part-timers, compared with a little over a third in 1989. In construction the increase between 1989 and 1996 was from 8.7 percent to 34.7 percent; in finance, from 2.4 percent to 16.3 percent. The trend is most dramatic amongst the largest firms, with 69 percent employing over 250 employees using part-timers.[26]

The combination of technological change, downsizing, two-tier wage agreements, and the proliferation of part-time jobs has resulted in a dramatic worsening of the income levels for the bottom rung of wage earners. A study by McMaster University economists Peter Kuhn and Leslie Robb revealed that the poorest 10 percent of men saw their income drop by a full 28 percent between 1977 and 1991. The trend to contracting out, a major issue in the 1996 confrontation between the Canadian Auto Workers union and General Motors, is slowly eroding high-wage jobs, too.

A 1996 Statistics Canada report shows another result of the increase in the number of contingent, part-time workers. In 1995 just over half of Canadian workers worked a traditional thirty-five-hour week, down from 67 percent in the mid-1970s. This change was triggered by the recession of the early 1980s but, said the report, "seems to have entrenched itself as a permanent feature in the Canadian labour market framework." While unskilled workers find themselves in the part-time job ghetto, there is a growing use of overtime with skilled workers and university graduates. Corporations can treat unskilled workers who require little training "as roughly interchange-able." This, said the report, gives employers "flexibility and saves money on fringe benefits."[27]

Unskilled workers in Canada are rapidly becoming a permanent underclass. As of October 1997, only 43.5 percent of Canadians with only some high school education were employed. Between October 1996 and October 1997, fully 319,000 new jobs were added to the economy. But Canadians with only some high school education lost 67,000 jobs. Canada now has the second highest percentage of low-paid jobs of any industrial country, with 25 percent of full-time jobs falling into this category. It helps produce the fifth-highest poverty rate in the OECD.[28]

Overlaid on all of these disparate trends is the increasing insecurity of all but the highest-paid workers. Few now express a desire for a shorter work week, fearing that they may not have a work week at all in the near future. Statistics Canada reported in 1997 that only 6 percent of paid workers preferred a shorter work week even if it meant less pay. When the Conference Board asked the same question in 1987, fully 17 percent gave that answer. Now almost a third of workers want more hours.

The work world thus reflects another duality, the overworked and the underemployed. This pattern has become a key feature of the race to the bottom. Says labour market analyst Armine Yalnizyan: "The approach taken must reinforce one's primary link to the world through providing one's labour services. This is to be achieved by handcuffing people ever more tightly to the labour market, which increasingly demands a twenty-four-hour-a-day, seven-days-a-week, on-call-as-needed commitment. The propelling force behind getting people to accept this model is a pervasive sense of insecurity and rapid change."[29]

WOMEN AND YOUTH: NOWHERE TO GO BUT DOWN

The new forces at work have hit women by far the hardest of any group. According to researcher Jane Jenson, throughout developed countries, "while women are not confined to this non-standard labor force they are disproportionately located in it rather than in the core sectors."[30] Part-time work remains "a female ghetto." The loss of thousands of full-time private-sector jobs in the clerical, banking, and receptionist fields, traditional employers of women, accounts for much of this shift. A 1996 International Labour Organization report confirmed this view: "While more and more women are working, the vast majority of them are simply swelling the ranks of the working poor."[31] This is not just a truth in the industrialized nations. In the developing countries, women provide 80 percent of the cheap labour for export industries.

Huge cuts to social programs, medicare, and education in Canada and elsewhere have a double impact on women. Two-thirds of union jobs in the public sector, such as health, education, social services, and the postal service, historically have been held by women, and cuts there hurt them the most. When they lose those jobs because of cutbacks, they also suffer because of the loss of the services. As well, women involuntarily take up the slack of the eroded social services. An enormous part of the newly "externalized" costs of production, once covered by state programs, is now increasingly provided as unpaid work by women. Thousands of young women who had been living independently, once able to rely on UI or social assistance when unemployed, now end up back at home. The cutbacks in health care have meant that elder care falls increasingly on families; that is, on women.

The other group that has suffered disproportionately under restructuring is young people. Canadians are aware of the high rates of joblessness of young people but few realize that jobs for young people are declining. Since the recession of 1992, the situation has been getting worse. Between January 1996 and July 1997, there were 330,000 jobs created for adults, while jobs for young people fell by 74,000.[32]

The high rate of youth joblessness has remained extremely high (at 16 percent almost double the average) even though the number of young people actively in the workforce has dropped dramatically. In 1989, 71 percent of people between the ages of fifteen and twenty-four were working or looking for work. That figure hit 61 percent in December 1996.[33] There are many unskilled workers in this age group, yet there are many others who are overeducated and to get an entry-level job have to "dummy down" their résumés, putting in question the current elite infatuation with training as a solution to unemployment.

The overall pattern of low-paying part-time jobs is worsened by the steady twenty-year erosion of the minimum wage. In 1976 the minimum wage in all provinces except Ontario provided an income above the poverty line, and the federal government provided an income equivalent to 106 percent of the poverty line. By 1994 the federal minimum was at 53 percent of the poverty line, and in the provinces it ranged from 67 percent to 89 percent.[34]

Driving this pattern of low-wage and part-time jobs is the persistently high level of unemployment. If those who have stopped job hunting are included, the rate exceeds 14 percent, and if those who want full-time work are added it shoots up to at least 17 percent. These figures would be alarming enough if the social programs of the early 1980s were still in place. But in every case the safety net has been shredded. Welfare rates have been slashed so severely that many provinces now have rates lower than most U.S. states. Out of sixty-two jurisdictions, B.C. placed highest in Canada but just sixteenth best in North America; Nova Scotia was thirtieth, Saskatchewan fifty-third.[35] Only 46 percent of the unemployed now qualify for the EI they paid into. Several provincial governments are introducing workfare schemes, making welfare recipients work or enroll in training as a condition to receiving benefits.

THE PERMANENT RECESSION

Of all the government strategies to reverse the political and economic gains of labour, the use of monetary and fiscal policy has been the most powerful and effective. Jim Stanford, of the Canadian Centre for Policy Alternatives, argues that since 1981 Canada's monetarist, anti-inflationary strategy has kept the country in a state of permanent recession. Even periods of "recovery," such as that experienced in 1997, hardly seem worthy of the term.

The reason, according to Stanford, is that "elected and unelected economic institutions have since [1981] embarked on a policy that deliberately fostered a state of controlled economic stagnation. Permanent unemployment was reestablished in order to repair the 'damage' done to the profit system by 30 years of full employment, rising wages, growing unions and an increasingly interventionist public sector."[36]

It may be hard to credit that democratically elected governments would deliberately create permanent high levels of joblessness. But in following this path the Canadian government and the Bank of Canada were simply falling in line with the IMF, the OECD, and other agencies devising ways out of the capitalist crisis of falling profits and increasing inflation.

The IMF criticized countries for their policies aimed at "the achievement and maintenance of unduly low unemployment rates." The IMF went on to recommend wage limits and tight monetary policies to "crush" inflation. The Bank for International Settlements, the central bankers' central bank, concluded with satisfaction in 1981: "Many if not most governments now appear to believe that restrictive demand management offers the main — and perhaps only — hope of a gradual return to more satisfactory levels of unemployment."[37]

The permanent recession is referred to in the language of the downsized state as the non-accelerating inflationary rate of unemployment, the so-called NAIRU rate. It is that rate that must be maintained to keep inflation, the scourge of the bondholders, in check. Governments used to set the maximum socially acceptable level of unemployment based on workers' interests; it now sets a minimum level based on the interests of corporate investors.

While unions in Canada have maintained an almost 35-percent level of unionization, their ability to defend their members' interests is being steadily eroded. In nonunion workplaces the situation is so desperate that Statscan reported that almost 20 percent of Canadians worked overtime in the first quarter of 1997 and 60 percent of them earned no extra pay. In addition, thousands of employees put up with blatant violations of the labour codes, from sexual harassment to unsafe working conditions to unannounced cuts in pay, because they are desperate to keep their jobs.

The poverty rate in Canada has been increasing since the early 1980s and has accelerated to 18 percent in 1996. A European study comparing the ratio of the highest and lowest income earners of seventeen developed nations showed that Canada was fourth-worst in terms of income inequality, behind only the U.S., Ireland, and Italy.[38] The 1994 World Competitiveness report compared thirty countries, developed and less developed, examining the amount of household income going to the lowest quintile. This study revealed that Canada, with just 5.7 percent of income going to the bottom 20 percent of the population, placed twenty-second, behind Indonesia, the Philippines, Thailand, and South Korea.[39] This study was done in 1994, before the huge cuts to social transfers and the devastating loss of full-time jobs. A Statscan study of the wage gap, comparing 1990 with 1996, revealed that 5.4 million Canadians reported income of less than $10,000 a year; over 300,000 reported income of more than $100,000.[40]

The attack on the living standards of millions of Canadian workers has two distinct but closely connected objectives. One is to simply reduce the costs of production through lower wages and greater flexibility in the use of labour. But equally important is the effect of this chronic insecurity on the functioning of democracy. During the period of rising expectations in the 1960s and early 1970s, democratic participation in Canada reached a height not achieved since the years immediately before and after the Second World War. The economy was at near full employment and the expression of dissent both in the workplace, regarding working conditions, and outside it, regarding the role of government, was driven by a sense of security and a vision of a more equal society.

Ten years of high unemployment, the loss of hundreds of thousands of high-paying jobs, the advent of part-time and temporary job ghettoes, and the discovery that education is no longer a ticket to economic security have had the effect of shutting down democratic participation for hundreds of thousands of Canadians. Two and half million workers are now either unemployed or face the very real possibility of becoming unemployed.

Poverty, near poverty, and the economic insecurity generated by cutbacks and corporate downsizing increase social isolation and exclusion. The poor are disenfranchised because to take part in any meaningful way in the political life of the community you need, at a minimum, to be free of fear of where your or your child's next meal is coming from. This insecurity can cripple an individual's ability and motivation to engage with the community, to take part in the political process.

Overrepresented in low-waged work and in the ranks of the un- and underemployed, women and youth, two of the groups most active in the sixties movements for social justice and equality, are now the ones most likely to be effectively disenfranchised by their economic situation. Many women, who are consistently to the left of men when it comes to social policy and the role of government, are being slowly silenced by poverty; nearly half of young people, with arguably the greatest interest in maintaining government as a force for equality, are socially and culturally isolated and excluded from the political life of the country.

For working people the only effective political voice most ever have is through their unions. Trade and investment agreements, however, are undermining this collective voice. The trend in the U.S. is alarming. An analysis of the NAFTA Labor Commission's study "Final Report: The Effects of Plant Closing or Threat of Plant Closing on the Right of Workers to Organize" showed that "plant-closing threats and actual plant closings are extremely pervasive and effective components of U.S. employer anti-union strategies. From 1993 to 1995, employers threatened to close the plant in 50 percent of all union certification elections and in 52 percent of all instances where the union withdrew from its organizing drive." After a certification victory, 15 percent of employers followed through on threats made during the organizing campaign, triple the rate before NAFTA went into effect.[41]

The use of threats to close plants is symbolic of what is happening to democracy in the new global economic order. The fundamental right of workers — the right of association — which is protected in human rights covenants around the world, is gradually being eroded or made irrelevant by the increasing "rights" of so-called corporate citizens. This is not only a direct assault on a fundamental human right, it is also an attack on democracy in that it prevents workers from speaking with a collective voice.

Another corporate tactic to undermine the unions' collective voice turned up in the aftermath of an extremely bitter two-year strike at the Irving oil refinery in St. John's. Returning strikers were obliged to go through what union leaders called a "brainwashing" and political cleansing program. "Former strikers must socialize with replacement workers who crossed the picket line . . .; they must be co-operative; they must be appreciative of work and they must accept that the union was wrong." The shop-floor "test" lasted four weeks and workers were assessed every day. They had to pass the test before they received full pay.[42]

Nearly every aspect of these developments is either designed by government policies or it is allowed to flourish because governments refuse to act to change it. It is governments that have refused to maintain the minimum wage above the poverty level; it is govern- ments that have savaged the unemployment insurance system; it is governments that have cut back on enforcing labour standards and workplace health and safety, and it is governments that have established draconian and punitive welfare policies.

THE MIDDLE CLASS: CAUGHT IN THE MIDDLE

When it comes to nation building it has historically been the middle class that has provided much of the commitment, the imagination, and the defining characteristics of the national project. No nation can be built without the cooperation of the ruling economic elite, but it was the broad middle class, whose numbers were large enough and whose political motivation was strong enough to command the attention of the elites, who were critical to the process.

Within the middle class were writers, academics, journalists, broadcasters, those occupying all the areas of the arts and culture and also those who chose to put their time and money into supporting the arts and cultural activities. They had the background, the resources, the education, the motivation, and the self-confidence to take on the task of shaping their communities and, as a result, the nation. In Canada this group included the thousands of cultural workers and planners in the dozens of publicly funded institutions such as the CBC, the National Film Board, the Canada Council, and the National Arts Board. Included in this class as well were the key public policy thinkers at all levels of government, from those imagining a national health-care system to those designing provincial public parks or municipal recreation programs.

This is not to say that other social classes had nothing to do with nation building. The historic compromise of the post-war period obliged the Canadian elite to support state policies that were nation building in their consequences if not their design. Indeed, Canadians today identify the broad range of social programs and the social equality they bring as the defining characteristic of their country. It was the working class's struggles for social justice in the 1930s that created the conditions for that compromise and for the subsequent egalitarian state. But once the compromise was reached it was the broad middle class that worked out the details and coloured the national landscape.

Today the middle class might well be called the muddle class. No longer imbued with a clear view of what the nation means, they have lost that cultural and ideological homogeneity that was key to their success and their influence. The unity that characterized the middle class now belongs to the ruling elite. The political power of the middle class is waning because it is divided between old notions of social solidarity and acceptance of the new global view promoted by the elites. No longer a single coherent force in society, the middle class has lost its mediating role.

A large portion of the middle class has seen its dream of steadily increasing living standards dashed with a brutal finality and breathtaking speed. The victims are left in stunned disbelief as they go through the doors of the welfare office for the first time. Another portion has hit the global gravy train. They are among the "symbolic analyzers" that Reich talks about.

For them the adaptation is not to a shocking new insecurity and even poverty but to membership in a new elite, one that requires a major ideological shift, from a conviction that government can be a force for good to a belief in the essential virtue of the market. With the spectre of their middle-class friends living steps away from poverty, they don't want to look back and they don't dare do anything that might send them there, too.

A study by Clarence Lochhead and Vivian Shalla revealed this split reality of the Canadian middle class. To make comparisons, researchers in income distribution typically divide the population into five quintiles, or fifths of the population. Between 1984 and 1993, the top 20 percent saw their income increase 5 percent (to $102,792). The next quintile, that segment of the middle class benefiting from the new corporate order, saw their incomes rise by 3.6 percent (to $61,333). But the next two quintiles, the middle- and lower-middle-income groups, both saw declines, of 2.68 percent (to $43,103) and 10.2 percent (to $26,291) respectively. The lowest 20 percent of the population was by far the hardest hit, with a 31.9 percent drop (to $5,325).

The decline of market income of the three bottom groups was not insignificant. Had they maintained their 1984 levels they would have had another $5.2 billion a year to spend. The overall average income for a family with children was at a virtual standstill between 1984 and 1993, rising from $47,663 to $47,777.[43] The beleaguered middle class is getting poorer, paying more taxes, and getting fewer services. That is a recipe for a decline in the support of government, except that the insecure middle class still relies heavily on transfers and other programs for their standard of living.

There are other pressures, too. Many of those who have lost full-time jobs are now "self-employed." Too often that is a euphemism for having to administer your own downward spiral in living standards. The self-employed fall disproportionately into two large categories, those earning $100,000 or more and those earning $20,000 or less.

The trend to self-employment has been portrayed as a return to the free-market era of small independent producers. In fact, this self-employment, in the trucking industry, for example, reflects the efforts of large corporations to externalize their costs and the associated risks. The self-employed, whether truck drivers or those in the consulting business, are now just as dependent on large corporations — and often the same corporation — as when they received a salary.

Much of the middle class are maintaining their status by going ever deeper into debt, using credit as a private-sector safety net. In the twelve months ending March 1997, consumer spending increased by 5.1 percent. The only problem was that this amount was seven times greater than the increase in income. Personal debt as of mid-1997 outpaced Ottawa's debt by $75 billion, a level very close to 100 percent of personal disposable income, the highest level in Canada's history. The personal savings rate is plummeting as personal debt rises. According to Statscan, the savings rate was 17.8 percent in 1982. It dropped to 10 percent by 1993 and to 5.4 percent by June of 1996.[44] In the first three months of 1997 it sank almost out of sight, to 1.7 percent.[45]

The fracturing of the middle class into "self-employment" means that tens of thousands of Canadians have now entered a much more individualistic economic and social subculture. Instead of relying on stable employment, it is now every man and woman for themselves. Many of the self-employed left voluntarily to escape the pressures of the downsized workplace, where layoffs have meant a sometimes doubled workload for those remaining. Whatever their reasons, the exodus of the middle class from the traditional work world disengages them from the workplace community and leaves them more isolated. It has also meant a greater reliance on investment income for those who have any money to invest.

There is, of course, an enormous irony in those affected by the downsizing mania turning to investments to survive or prosper. The billions of dollars pouring into mutual funds and employee pension funds are being used to finance the very corporations that are doing the downsizing. Indeed, the reason that a mutual fund buys a stock is quite likely to involve the company's dedication to cutting costs. The laid-off employee of Bell Canada who puts part of her severance money into a mutual fund reinforces Bell's antisocial behaviour. Hundreds of thousands of Canadians are unwitting accomplices in their own declining economic security at the same time that they reinforce the logic of the market and corporate domination.

Yet as Canadian attitudes become increasingly characterized by possessive individualism there is little practical choice for many. Whatever a person's values may be, however much one would like the world to be different, the world people face when they get up in the morning is no less real because they had no say in making it. A large portion of the middle class who were the foundation of the communitarian character of Canada for two generations now find themselves thrown into the dog-eat-dog marketplace. They don't have the option of refusing to go along.

Not only does this force them to adopt market values that aren't theirs, or at least behaviour that reflects those values, but it leaves many unable to find work that reflects their old values. The hundreds of thousands of civil servants, CBC broadcasters, artists, writers, librarians, people in the publishing business, in public recreation and theatre, and in public education have been thrust not just out of jobs but out of the work that is the basis for a communitarian culture. The work available in the private sector is simply not the same.

The change is in both the content of the work and the attitude required in a high-pressure private sector focussed on profits and obsessed with efficiency. Former journalists working for public relations firms, ex-public policy analysts working for corporations, former public teachers working in private schools, independent university researchers going begging for corporate research money, former tax auditors working for corporate tax law firms — all of these changes augur profound long-term consequences for the political culture of the country.

The decline of much of the middle class has an immediate effect on government legitimacy. The propaganda about the inefficient public sector, failed social programs, bloated bureaucracies, and wasted taxpayer money is far more effective if the middle class has lost faith in government. As we will see in the next chapter, this loss of legitimacy in the eyes of citizens, instead of creating a crisis for the state, has so far allowed it to dramatically reduce Canadians' expectations of what government can or will do.

The apparent ease with which the radical restructuring of democracy has proceeded is explained not in the change in Canadians' values but in the simple fact that the majority of Canadians now have to cope with a situation for which the politics of the country has never prepared them. So long as the shifts in policy implemented by the governing elite took place within certain parameters, proscribed by the forty-year-old historic compromise, we could cope. These were, after all, incremental changes, and the consensus, though often challenged and always vulnerable, had never been rejected outright. Until now. What Canada is experiencing is nothing short of a counter-revolution in the role of government, imposed from the top, designed by and carried out openly in the interests of transnational corporations.

The corporate domination of the world was no more an accident of history than was the struggle of ordinary people for progressive government. Corporations have waged a twenty-year campaign to regain the power they lost in the post-war period. They have carried out a deliberate propaganda campaign, built around the deficit and debt and aimed at lowering people's expectations of government. It has been carried out with the ruthless determination of rich and powerful people protecting their hold on that wealth and power. And the state, "our" government, has been enlisted to serve the corporate agenda despite the opposition to it by the vast majority of citizens.

But guiding this broad campaign to change the political culture of Canada and the developed world in general was a process of building a consensus amongst the world's elites and within the elites of the most important developed countries. The world's most powerful corporate executives, its most influential political leaders, together with supportive opinion makers, senior government officials, and academics meet regularly in a number of high-profile but largely secret forums. They plan the future of the world, and their power and influence are such that their conclusions are directly reflected in the decisions our governments make. That most citizens have no idea of this powerful influence on their democratic governments is no accident.

7

CREATING THE ELITE CONSENSUS

Some of the problems of governance in the United States today stem from an excess of democracy.
— *THE CRISIS OF DEMOCRACY*, TRILATERAL COMMISSION, 1975

Revolution is never brought about by mass armies. Every revolution whether you look at Lenin's or Castro's or any other . . . [is] led by a small group of people with powerful ideas.
— TOM D'AQUINO, PRESIDENT AND CEO OF THE BUSINESS COUNCIL ON NATIONAL ISSUES

If we were to create an image of the advent of global corporate rule we would first have to picture dozens of democratic institutions, parliaments, legislatures, congresses, supreme courts, the offices of senior government planners and bureaucrats, the United Nations, all as facades, with familiar and reassuring fronts, like the main street set in a western movie. Empty vessels, these physical trappings of what used to be governing bodies and agencies maintain the fiction that societies and communities are engaged in making choices about what kind of society they will have, about the prospects for their children.

It is here, according to the old script, that elected representatives, duly chosen by the people, debate and decide these questions. And of course the representatives are still there and elections do still happen.

Important laws are passed and repealed. The democratic authority to make decisions still resides in these institutions. But in reality the script has changed. The pomp and ceremony of Parliament's opening, the acrimonious debates, and the occasional scandals are becoming little more than ritual. There is a new script, one that ordinary citizens don't even get to see.

For almost twenty years the most important policy directions taken by Western governments have been discussed, refined, and agreed upon not in the established democratic forums but in closed, exclusive clubs established for this purpose. Such consensus-building organizations and forums as the Trilateral Commission, the World Economic Forum, and the Bilderberg forum have not been established by or even acknowledged by governments. Yet they, and their nationally based counterparts like the Business Council on National Issues, are among the most important policy forums in the world. Officially recognized or not, they have an enormous influence on the lives of ordinary citizens in every country, in every village, in the world.

Elite consensus, then, is no longer determined in democratic forums where, ostensibly at least, people of all classes, and parties of various world-views, contribute to some semblance of pluralist compromise. Abandoning the social contract in the mid-1970s entailed abandoning the democratic traditions that both created the historic compromise and became part of it. Just as there is no longer an elite commitment to the welfare state, there is no longer a commitment to democracy.

The proper place for developing a consensus on corporate libertarianism is away from the compromising "art" of politics, from the prying eyes of citizens and the media. Indeed, corporate libertarianism is by its very nature totalitarian, and it follows that its planning would be carried out in private, where the interests of others need not be taken into account.

The organizations that have fostered the development of an elite consensus operate at both the national and international levels. At the international level some have been operating for almost as long as the United Nations, which was supposed to be the international forum for consensus building. Today, virtually none of the important decisions affecting the world's nations are taken there. Drained of its prestige, moral authority, and power, it is of all the democratic institutions in the world the most thoroughly reduced to ritualistic pretence.

There are numerous international forums in which political leaders and corporate executives get to mingle informally, but two go back several decades and have proven to be extremely influential in directing the world's economic order. One of these is so informal that it has no name other than that of the hotel where its first meeting was held in Oosterbreek, the Netherlands. Prince Bernhard of the Netherlands founded the Bilderberg forum in 1954 to address the broad issue of managing world capitalism. The U.S. was concerned about the Soviet threat but even more about a repeat of the national rivalries within Europe that led to the Second World War. In the 1920s, it had pushed for a "United States of Europe" that would have provided a stable European entity to participate in managing the world economy. Bilderberg was, in part, a response to the failure of these pre-war efforts. It was a forum for informal deliberations by the most important political and corporate players in the European movement for unification.

Joseph Retinger, a key figure in the Polish government in exile during the war, headed the organization and saw it as a way of addressing the historic weakness of Europe. The solution was to move towards a federation of European countries in which states would "relinquish part of their sovereignty."[1] The Bilderberg meetings are credited more than any other forum with building the foundation for European unity and the European Union itself.

The Bilderberg has no permanent membership. It includes some of the most influential people on the planet — heads of state, other leading political figures, key industrialists and financiers. It also includes academics, diplomats, sympathetic media figures, and a smattering of trade unionists to round out the broader definition of the ruling elite. Prince Bernhard (who resigned in 1976 after being implicated in the Lockheed bribery scandal), at the head of a core of fewer than half a dozen officials, appointed all members of the steering committee and decided who would be invited. No invitations were ever sent out to representatives of developing countries.

Bilderberg is exceptionally secretive; the confidential report drafted after each meeting contains no names, just the speaker's nationality.

The Bilderberg has no institutional powers but, according to researcher Peter Thompson, "Bilderbergers are in positions of such considerable executive power that if a consensus is reached and acted upon, the advanced capitalist West is likely to act more or less as a unit."[2] A German participant claimed that through the Bilderberg elite network a dozen people got the world's monetary system working again after the OPEC crisis.

As early as 1968 Bilderberg was to have taken up the issue of the internationalization of the economy but was prevented by the Vietnam War and student revolts in France. Nonetheless, the issue of managing global capitalism was the forum's constant preoccupation. It played a key role in creating out of the OECD a club of rich nations and global corporations. Its members were also instrumental in the establishment of the Trilateral Commission, the pre-eminent establishment consensus body.

The Bilderberg was not a decision-making body. The consensus it develops is much more general and gradual. In the words of Joseph Retinger:

> Even if a participant is a member of a government, a leader of a political party, an official of an international organization or of a commercial concern, he does not commit his government, his party or his organization by anything he may say . . . Bilderberg does not make policy. Its aim is to reduce differences of opinion and resolve conflicting trends and to further understanding, if not agreement, by hearing and considering various points of view and trying to find a common approach to major problems. [3]

As an informal forum for developing and refining an international elite consensus, the Bilderberg is challenged only by the World Economic Forum (WEF). The forum was established in 1970 by its president, Professor Klaus Schwab. Its Web page openly describes its role: "The Annual Meeting in Davos, Switzerland, sets the world agenda for the year to come. Members of the foundation, represented at the CEO level, converge on the Swiss ski resort of Davos at the end of January for six days of intensive discussion on those issues of greatest relevance to the future of world business."[4] In 1997, fully 1,000

CEOs of the world's largest corporations, 200 senior government officials, 40 heads of state, and 300 "experts" gathered to take in 236 seminars, plenaries, social events, and so-called brainstorming sessions.

The WEF, like Bilderberg, provides the perfect format for corporate governance. It is not an organization, has no administrative staff, and is very protective of its exclusivity. In his gushing praise of the forum, *Globe and Mail* publisher William Thorsell described it as "a set of circumstances rather than a place, a network rather than an organization. It integrates the most powerful, wealthiest and most capable sector of global society — corporations — with the most important governments . . . It lowers the stakes for the main political players precisely because it involves so many others with significant power."[5]

Apparently sanguine about the world being run by a secret club of fifteen hundred men, Thorsell declares, "The World Economic Forum is very much a precursor to 21st century institutions . . . [It is] one of the informal, unofficial . . . agents of communication and decision-making now emerging as the operative instruments in human affairs."[6]

Some of the corporate delegates at the 1997 meeting were Matthew Barrett, Bank of Montreal CEO; Thomas Bata, the right-wing chairman of Bata Shoes; Jacques Bougie, CEO of Alcan; Jacques Lamarre, president of SNC-Lavalin; and Charles Sirois, chairman of Teleglobe. All were there hoping to be wooed by government ministers from the hot economies of Asia, all offering up their workers, their environment, and their police protection in return for investment dollars.[7]

A recent initiative of the WEF is its computer-networking service, intended to keep the world's elite in constant touch with each other, sharing ideas and helping each other deal with "crises." The forum's Web page service, called WELCOM, promises "crisis-management support and direct access to experts and media leaders. Direct face-to-face counselling with experts at leading business and knowledge centres around the globe, such as the John F. Kennedy School of Government, Harvard University, the Brookings Institution, the MIT Laboratory for Computer Science and the Hong Kong University of Science and Technology."

THE OECD

The Organization for Economic Co-operation and Development is not usually seen as a consensus builder, and in most public references to the organization it is portrayed as little more than a research institute for the developed Western countries. But the OECD goes far beyond being a source of the statistics we see in newspapers. Its key role in pushing the MAI has in effect revealed the true power and influence of this elite-nation organization.

The OECD in the 1970s comprised almost exclusively advanced, industrial nations (it now includes Mexico, Poland, the Czech Republic, Hungary, and Korea). Among its key founding goals were "efforts to reduce and abolish obstacles to the exchange of goods and services and current payments and maintain and extend the liberalization of capital movements."[8]

During the 1970s efforts to establish favourable rights for transnational corporations occurred within the OECD, for obvious reasons. This was an organization whose membership was restricted to those nations that were the home base for all the world's transnationals and provided a forum for developing global policy; unlike the U.N., then, it excluded developing countries. The organization has been used extensively by developed countries to prepare consensus positions that were then taken to broader and more democratic forums, such as the U.N. or GATT. This was particularly true when developing countries began to challenge the role of multinational and transnational corporations.

THE TRILATERAL COMMISSION

Of all the consensus-building forums of the world's economic and political elites, the Trilateral Commission stands out as the most important and the best known. Less secretive than either Bilderberg or the World Economic Forum, the Trilateral Commission has permanent offices in the three regions it was established to represent: Japan, North America, and Europe. It commissions and publishes studies that, along with the names of its members, are available to the public. It meets yearly and produces a report on its proceedings.

The Trilateral Commission was formed in 1973 in response to a series of crises and worsening chronic problems facing the world capitalist system. First, the consensus so carefully built up over the previous twenty-five years was suddenly violated by President Richard Nixon, head of the very country that had worked so hard to establish it. Second, the oil-producing countries of the Middle East created a crisis for the world economy by dramatically increasing the price of oil — a move that would result in the transfer of huge numbers of American dollars to countries that previously had Third World status. And within the rest of the Third World, many countries were vigorously pursuing a policy of anti-colonialism through self-sufficiency, which, if successful, could shut the door on foreign investment or place restrictions on how it operated.

Perhaps more important, because it affected the way the developed countries could deal with these problems, there was a surge of participatory democratic activity throughout the developed world, particularly at its imperial centre, the United States. This increased involvement in democratic politics was threatening the elite governance that had prevailed to the end of the 1950s. And it was threatening at the very time that concerted elite action was crucial for the stability and even the survival of the world economic system.

But the immediate incentive for the commission was the crisis precipitated by Nixon, who was determined to reverse the gradual decline of the U.S. as an economic superpower. As part of his New Economic Policy, Nixon unilaterally delinked the U.S. dollar from the gold standard, violating an IMF agreement to which the U.S. was a signatory. He also violated the General Agreement on Tariffs and Trade by slapping a 10 percent tariff on most goods entering the U.S. With these two moves Nixon declared the U.S. intention to reassert its economic dominance over Japan and Europe. But he also effectively declared war on the most powerful corporate groups in the world: the increasingly dominant transnational corporations and international financiers whose interests lay in even freer trade, free investment, and a completely interdependent capitalist economy.

The result of the "Nixon shocks" in the transnational camp was almost immediate. Several key administration officials resigned and went to work for groups promoting the interests of finance capital, groups like the Brookings Institution and the Council on Foreign

Relations. Some of the biggest names in finance capital, including David Rockefeller, as well as Zbigniew Brzezinski, George Ball, and Cyrus Vance, and European and Japanese representatives began to blitz the Nixon administration through a series of high-profile articles, conferences, and exchanges of opinion.[9]

These actions led in early 1973 to the formation of the Trilateral Commission, an organization that has been described by author Holly Sklar as "the executive advisory committee to transnational finance capital."[10] According to Richard Falk, writing in the *Yale Law Review*, "The vistas of the Trilateral Commission can be understood as the ideological perspective representing the transnational outlook of the multinational corporation [which] seeks to subordinate territorial politics to non-territorial economic goals."[11]

The Trilateral Commission was also going to be assigned another difficult and growing problem. Brzezinski (who would become Jimmy Carter's secretary of state), credited along with Rockefeller with founding the commission, described the problem of the developing world as follows: "Today we find the international scene dominated . . . by conflict between the advanced world and the developing world than by conflict between trilateral democracies . . . The new aspirations of the Third and Fourth worlds united together seems to me to pose a very major threat to the nature of the international system and ultimately to our own societies."[12]

For the trilateralists, whose deliberations and global prescriptions came to be known as the Washington consensus, the weapon of choice, argues Sklar, would be debt dependency, a neo-colonial "leash around a Third World country's neck. The leash is let out to allow Western-directed development projects to gallop ahead . . . Or the debt leash can be pulled in tight — as part of an economic and political destabilization campaign — to strangle a rebellious nation into submission."[13]

The Trilateral Commission was initially designed to operate for just three years, enough time, it was thought, to create a foreign and domestic policy framework for the trilateral areas. But it kept renewing its three-year mandates and has become the permanent forum for global trade and investment policy making. Its initial funding came from some of the elite from the American corporate world — General

Motors, Sears Roebuck, Caterpillar Tractor, Exxon, Texas Instruments, Coke, Time, CBS, Wells Fargo Bank — as well as numerous foundations, with the Ford Foundation putting up $500,000 and the Rockefellers' Fund $150,000.

The commission is more than just a consensus-building organization amongst policy intellectuals. It is explicitly an action-oriented body that develops consensus through studies and consultation and then makes concerted efforts to implement that consensus. The whole membership of the Trilateral Commission (it started with 180 and is now about 300) meets once a year in one of the three regions. Keynote speakers address key issues of the day and task forces present reports. These plenary meetings, as well as executive meetings, are highlighted by meetings with heads of state and high government officials.

The commission's task forces are its key policy development tool. Each task force is coordinated by three "rapporteurs," one each from the three regions. But it is the direct lobbying of decision makers that gives the task force reports (and their subsequent refinement) their clout. The commission holds "impact meetings" in order to "sharpen the impact of its work among decision-makers." The meetings, often facilitated by former political leaders in its membership, take place with the media, legislators, "executive and congressional staffers; embassy officials, leaders of international organizations and political bodies and top government officials . . . In this fashion the circle of 'influential persons' directly in contact with the Commission is widened considerably."[14]

The original Canadian membership was dominated by Liberal politicians, government officials, and academics. The current Canadian membership is equally high profile but completely dominated by business. Since 1991 it has been chaired by Allan Gotlieb, former ambassador to the U.S., a key promoter of free trade and NAFTA, and an influential member of the Canadian establishment. Gotlieb joined the commission in 1989 just as the Free Trade Agreement came into force. At the same time, he was appointed senior trade adviser to Burson-Marsteller, the world's largest public relations and lobbying firm, which that same year bought a 49-percent interest in Executive Consultants, one of the oldest government relations firms in Ottawa.

Burson-Marsteller was eager to have more lobbying clout with the Canadian government. Its list of clients includes many of the trilaterally represented corporations: AT&T, DuPont, GE, Shell, Westinghouse, Coca-Cola, and Bank of America. It is not surprising, then, that Burson-Marsteller and Gotlieb were among the most aggressive promoters of NAFTA. Reinforcing the original goal of the Trilateral Commission, Gotlieb told a meeting of the Americas Society in 1991 that NAFTA was critical to the completion of "the new world order [in which] the withering of the nation-state . . . is the dominant feature."[15]

Among the thirteen Canadian commissioners are Hollinger's Conrad Black; Jacques Bougie, CEO of Alcan; Mickey Cohen, CEO of Molson's and former finance department architect of many of Ottawa's corporate tax breaks; Yves Fortier, former ambassador, and Paul Desmarais, head of Power Corporation, a man who has helped finance the careers of three prime ministers.

The membership is rounded out by three powerful western millionaires: Jimmy Pattison, of Vancouver car dealership fame; Ron Southern, of Calgary-based ATCO, and Michael Phelps, CEO of Westcoast Energy. Of the thirteen Canadian members in 1996, eight were CEOs; one was a current MP; three were in the diplomatic or civil service corps, and one was an academic, Marie-Josée Drouin, a member of the powerful Washington-based Council on Foreign Relations and former executive director of the conservative Hudson Institute. All the companies represented are also on the Business Council on National Issues, except for Black's Hollinger (privately owned companies are not invited into the BCNI).[16]

For the first three years the commission was run by Brzezinski, reflecting the fact that American finance capital took the initiative in redirecting international policy. And although it was the Nixon shocks that ignited this effort, the commission's founders were also concerned with chronic political problems with American democracy.

The issue was quickly addressed in one of the Trilateral Commission's first commissioned studies, entitled "The Governability of Democracies." Eventually published as *The Crisis of Democracy*, the study detailed what the most vigorous proponents of the global economy and transnational corporations believed was the gravest threat to the future of capitalism: the growing demands of citizens on Western democratic governments. The major conclusion of the study was summed up in the section on the U.S. authored by Samuel P. Huntington. "Al Smith once remarked that 'the only cure for the ills of democracy is more democracy.' Our analysis suggests . . . [that] instead, some of the problems of governance in the United States today stem from an excess of democracy . . . Needed, instead, is a greater degree of moderation in democracy."[17]

The study looked fondly back at the days when American democracy was run quietly by an elite of political figures, industrialists, academics, and media owners. "Truman had been able to govern the country with the co-operation of a relatively small number of Wall Street lawyers and bankers," states Huntington.[18] By the early 1970s that era was long past and government authority weakened. The public now questioned "the legitimacy of hierarchy, coercion, discipline, secrecy, and deception — all of which are in some measure inescapable attributes of the process of government"[19] and "no longer felt the same compulsion to obey those whom they had previously considered superior to themselves in age, rank, status, expertise, characters or talents."[20]

Stating that a "governable" democracy requires "apathy and non-involvement" on the part of marginalized groups, Huntington describes the current crisis as it developed in the sixties and seventies: "Previously passive and unorganized groups in the population, blacks, Indians, Chicanos, white ethnic groups, students, and women now embarked on concerted efforts to establish their claims to opportunities, positions, rewards and privileges, which they had not considered themselves entitled to before."[21]

The principle of democracy was infecting all sorts of American (and other Western nations') institutions, which were better run as autocracies loyal to the capitalistic ethic. The study identified universities and the media as needing major reform, for their role in turning the American public against the war in Vietnam was particularly galling to trilateralists. The study called for action to restore a balance between government and the media through more rigorous self-censorship.

The anti-war upheaval on U.S. campuses was seen as a deadly threat to the functioning of American democracy. "This development constitutes a challenge to democratic government which is potentially at least as serious as those posed in the past by the aristocratic cliques, fascist movements and communist parties."[22]

The trilateralists' solution was that rather than have "value oriented intellectuals," there was a need for "technocratic policy-oriented intellectuals." As for students, the study suggested that more teenagers from the previously marginalized groups should be steered towards vocational training. In addition, "an attempt should be made to lower the expectations of 'surplus' people with college degrees."

The trilateralists' fears of the threat of democracy extended well beyond its effects at home. Indeed, it was on foreign policy and the freedom of transnational corporations that much of the discussion focussed. In Huntington's words: "If American citizens challenge the authority of American government, why shouldn't unfriendly governments? . . . A decline in the governability of democracy at home means a decline in the influence of democracy abroad."[23]

The kind of democracy the trilateralists wanted reflected the future strategy of TNCs, discussed in chapter 3. It was the democracy of consumption. The success of American democracy had been, according to Huntington, the adoption by millions of Americans of middle-class values and "consumption patterns." An article by Daniel Boorstin in *Fortune* described that democracy as the "Consumption Community." "Consumption Community is democratic. This is the great American democracy of cash which has so exasperated the aristocrats of all older worlds. Consumption Communities generally welcome peoples of all races, ancestry, occupations and income levels, provided they have the price of admission."[24]

Applying this principle of consumption democracy to all those, worldwide, with the price of admission is now the global strategy of the TNCs. This not just an economic strategy. One of the most advantageous aspects of the consumption community is social control, for this community is by its nature politically apathetic.

At the time that *The Crisis of Democracy* was published the elite consensus in Canada was not in sync with that of the Americans. The reaction of Canadian commission members and others invited to a Montreal forum to discuss the study was disagreement verging on alarm. The political elite, at least, was going in the opposite direction — supporting Pierre Trudeau's participatory democracy initiatives, which actually nurtured the kind of interest in politics that Huntington equated with the threat of fascism.[25]

Canadian business, however, like its counterpart in the U.S., was alarmed at political developments. It is interesting to note that of all the participants in that forum on the governability of Canadian democracy there was only one business representative. That man was Simon Reisman, who would twenty-two years later negotiate the Canada-U.S. Free Trade Agreement, which did more to make Canadian democracy "governable" than any other single government initiative. That business was not invited to the forum was in marked contrast to how the Trilateral Commission functioned in the U.S. and it may have reflected the fact that in Canada the political elite and the business elite were more separate than at any time in the country's post-war history.

The Canadian business elite was acutely aware of something the Trudeau government, from the business perspective, seemed oblivious to. The so-called golden era of capitalism was over. Though Canada did have a modest public sector, mostly in utilities, for three decades the private sector had taken care of job creation and investment more or less by itself. An almost unprecedented profit boom, reinforced by the multiplier effect of higher wages and mass consumerism, had given the federal government the resources to expand social programs, increase the public sector, and introduce measures to reduce poverty.

But the end of that economic expansion suddenly left the corporate world with major problems. As economist Jim Stanford notes, "The bottom-line consequence for employers . . . was a long historic rise in the wage share of output, mirrored by a decline in the profit share . . . Full employment and expanded unionization enhanced labour's bargaining power over both wages and work practices, and expanded social programs provided workers with a degree of social and economic security," and thus independence from employer power.[26]

International competition and new tax measures, combined with low productivity, pressured CEOs and boards of directors to find solutions. In a few short years, from 1974 to 1976, powerful business figures would take major initiatives to reverse the trend of participatory democracy, labour power, and a social safety net that tipped the balance of power towards workers.

THE BUSINESS COUNCIL ON NATIONAL ISSUES

Few people took much notice when three groups formed to pursue this objective in their own ways. The Business Council on National Issues (BCNI), the Fraser Institute, and the National Citizens' Coalition would each play a key role in fashioning a new elite consensus and changing the political culture to make it amenable to that consensus. The Fraser Institute and the National Citizens' Coalition focussed their attention on public opinion and will be examined in the next chapter. The BCNI was the Canadian branch of trilateral elite consensus.

One of the reasons that the business elite in Canada was seemingly absent from policy making had to do with the nature of the Trudeau government and the makeup of Parliament itself. Trudeau did not come out of the business community and was not easily accessible to it; in fact he publicly criticized the role of corporations. The leader of the Conservative Party, Robert Stanfield, was a Red Tory and generally supportive of a policy of state intervention. And David Lewis of the NDP gained the balance of power in the House of Commons on the strength of a campaign that branded big business as "corporate welfare bums" because of the tax breaks and subsidies they received. Not only was the business elite disconnected from its political counterpart but corporations had hit a new low in public opinion. It, more than government, was blamed for the economic ills of the country.

But more important, the political voice of business had become weak. The imposition of wage and price controls in 1975 politicized the economic sphere, and the Trudeau government was eager to consult more closely with business. The trouble was, there was no one to effectively consult. Michael Pitfield, the powerful secretary to the cabinet, claimed that "the existing business organizations had atrophied so badly they had become part of the problem."[27] No organization addressed the issues and implications of an increasingly internationalist capitalist economy.

That changed in 1976 when two powerful corporate executives created that voice in the form of the Business Council on National

Issues. W. O. Twaits, retiring chairman of Imperial Oil, and Alfred Powis, president of Noranda, were the first co-chairs of the new organization. This would be an organization that would go beyond the "carping and special pleading" with which business groups had become identified in the public mind. It would, in Twaits's words, "strengthen the voice of business on issues of national importance and put forward constructive courses of action for the country."[28]

The BCNI modelled itself after the Business Roundtable in the U.S., an organization whose members were the CEOs of the 192 largest corporations in the country. Only active CEOs could be BCNI members, a strategy aimed at solving one of the problems of the traditional business lobby groups, whose spokespeople and staff could not make decisions quickly; because they did not speak for their corporations it was impossible to develop a consensus. The BCNI began as an organization of the CEOs of the 150 largest corporations in the country. Careful not to offend existing business groups, the council included senior officers of the Canadian Chamber of Commerce, the Canadian Manufacturers' Association, and the Conseil du Patronat du Québec as associate members and ex-officio members of the Policy Committee.

The BCNI also copied the structure and general approach of its American counterpart. It was the perfect national complement to the Trilateral Commission in the sense that it tried to speak for the system as a whole. Just as the Trilateral Commission was a conglomerate of all sectors and interests addressing issues of global capital, the BCNI addressed those same issues in the Canadian context.

It was clear from the beginning that the council would be fundamentally different from any other business organization in Canadian history. According to York University political scientist David Langille, it would explicitly reflect the interests of multinational and transnational corporations under the leadership of finance capital, led by the chartered banks. Long before the term *global economy* had become a common phrase, the BCNI was organized to reinvent the Canadian state in order to facilitate globalization.

The coalition of sectors in the council was consistent with Canadian capitalist history. The alliance between finance capital and companies involved in resource extraction and primary manufacturing dominated the council and its thirty-member Policy Committee just as they did the economy as a whole. Nearly a third of the BCNI members are foreign-owned corporations.

The most important purpose for which the BCNI was established was to transform public policy. Here, too, its approach was critically different from the crude lobbying of the past. The BCNI's efforts were cast in the mould of a newly enlightened business class. Its public relations spin claimed that "members were sought for their public spiritedness and commitment to the betterment of public policies, for their leadership abilities." The council's approach was to address carefully chosen and broad areas of public policy on which to influence the government. According to former council president William Archibald, the council aimed at taking a pre-emptive approach "at emerging public policy areas" and would "develop approaches and solutions . . . that they can put forward early in the process so that they have a chance of being considered."[29]

The council thus presented to senior civil servants and cabinet ministers business-oriented policies that also addressed the potential political problems of those policies. In effect, with its high quality of research the BCNI would become virtually a parallel government, combining the skills of the senior policy analyst with the sensitivity of a politician. In many instances, BCNI policy papers proposed the wording of legislation that would reflect their recommendations.

Indeed, the BCNI's structure of task forces made it a virtual shadow cabinet. The task forces were established and dissolved according to the political priorities of the day. Among the task forces were those addressing national finance (that is, taxation), international economy and trade, social policy and regional development, labour relations and manpower, government organization and regulation, foreign policy and defence, competition policy, education, and corporate governance. The BCNI has a small staff compared to other business organizations but its task forces draw on the staff of its member organizations and the resources of the C. D. Howe Institute, another consensus-building agency funded by many of the same corporations.

Until the early 1980s the BCNI had such a low profile that few Canadians ever heard of it. But that changed when Tom d'Aquino was chosen president and CEO of the council. A former Trudeau trade adviser, d'Aquino would give the council a greater public profile and influence just at a time when the Trudeau government, in trouble with its traditional business supporters over its National Energy Program, felt obliged to make overtures to corporate Canada. It was also at a time when key corporate leaders and d'Aquino had decided to push within the corporate elite for a consensus on a free-trade agreement with the U.S.

With d'Aquino at its helm, the BCNI effectively seized control of national policy making. It began with the Trudeau Liberals as they faced the new reality of a hostile and aggressive corporate class, moved effortlessly into the regime of the Mulroney Tories, who despite a landslide victory in 1984 had no clear agenda for the country, and picked up again with the Paul Martin and Jean Chrétien Liberals after 1993. Governments and prime ministers come and go, but the BCNI, the voice and organizational embodiment of corporate rule, is a permanent presence.

The rejection of the historic compromise by business cannot be traced neatly to any single expression or event. But perhaps the clearest and most brutal chapter in the Liberals' awakening to the new corporate agenda was the response of the corporate elite, all BCNI charter members, to the government's efforts at tax reform in 1981.

When Allan MacEachen was appointed finance minister in 1980 big business requested that government examine the tax system with a view to making changes. But MacEachen's senior advisers soon focussed his attention on how billions of dollars were being lost yearly to scores of dubious corporate tax breaks. Finance officials put together a tax reform package designed, among other things, to eliminate 165 of the most costly and counter-productive tax expenditure measures and in the process increase revenue by close to $3 billion. When he introduced the legislation it caused a firestorm of protest from the corporate elite.

Neil Brooks, now professor of tax law at Osgoode Hall Law School, was working for the finance department on the tax reform package and has recalled the tactics of the large corporations. "It's almost a classic example of what's called a capital strike. I mean, business simply said to the government that if you go ahead with these measures we will stop investing in Canada." The development industry reacted instantly. "Literally the next day they were closing jobs down and . . . pulling cranes off construction jobs." Measures designed to prevent developers from deducting up to 30 percent of the cost of construction as an immediate expense were "reversed on very quickly, within a week and a half."[30]

Life insurance companies had their own strategy. The industry, which for years had paid income tax rates of close to zero, wrote to every one of its policyholders, telling them the new measures to tax investment revenue would greatly increase their premiums. "The government," says Brooks, "at one point was receiving thousands of letters a day from people across the country."

The ferocious assault by the corporate and wealthy elite proved to be the wakeup call that moved the Liberals off their social agenda and back to business. The government's signal that it was serious about an improved relationship with business was Trudeau's dumping of MacEachen as finance minister. His replacement was Montreal lawyer Marc Lalonde. Formerly in the social liberal camp, Lalonde changed colours quickly, meeting with and smoothing the feathers of a stream of representatives from various sectors in the economy. But, in a move pregnant with the symbolism of BCNI power, Lalonde went to the home of Tom d'Aquino in the tony Rockcliffe area of Ottawa to meet with council leaders. There, according to David Langille, "he is alleged to have signed a peace pact with the business leaders and to have promised them the government's support."[31]

That support wasn't long in coming and it set a precedent for how corporate-government public policy making would take place in the new era. The BCNI's role in remaking Canadian energy policy illustrates its role in elite consensus building, a process that included reconnecting the previously divided political and business elites. The council arranged a series of secret meetings involving oil executives, the government of Alberta, industrial representatives, and the Ontario and federal governments, and managed to create a temporary peace.

But the BCNI was always anticipating problems. Its Task Force on Energy Policy, headed by the CEO of Imperial Oil, sent d'Aquino and Union Gas president Darcy McKeough on a mission to Alberta premier Peter Lougheed, Ontario premier Bill Davis, and energy minister Jean Chrétien. Out of that junket came a two-day high-level secret meeting held at the Niagara Institute. Eight months later, in June 1984, a deal was hammered out at another high-level meeting. The new legislation was a virtual carbon copy of most of the BCNI's key proposals, including deregulating Canadian oil and gas prices, lowering federal taxes and provincial royalties (thus contributing to the federal debt), and shifting government incentive grants to the tax expenditure system, where they would be less visible.

A good example of the BCNI's approach to rewriting government policy involved its intervention on anti-combines legislation. A year before the Trudeau government introduced its own discussion paper, the BCNI put twenty-five corporate legal counsels to work and literally wrote a new act. The 236-page report, released in 1981, was comprehensive, with precise recommendations and detailed statutory amendments that it stated were intended to "ensure that the public interest in having Canadian business compete vigorously in domestic and international markets can be served." Included in the amendments were several that addressed interests "outside the business community" so as to "reach a 'reasonable consensus' that would be 'practically workable.'"[32] The new Competition Act was virtually the same as the BCNI's recommended package of changes. It generated almost no comment let alone opposition, and business got just what it wanted, legislation that did almost nothing to promote competition.

By far the most important initiative taken by the BCNI was its early decision to pursue a free-trade deal with the U.S. More than any other policy area, the council's position on trade represented the interests of transnational corporations in Canada. And more than any other political victory, its initiative and lobbying on free trade fundamentally altered Canadian democracy and public policy.

Until the early 1980s the capitalist class in Canada was divided over freer trade versus protectionism. But that changed by 1983, according to David Langille. "As oil prices dropped and the National Energy Program came apart, so did any hopes of repatriating the Canadian economy. For their efforts, Canadian government and business leaders were so severely chastised by the Reagan administration that they [were] unwilling to attempt further experiments in economic nationalism which might jeopardize their 'special relationship' with the Americans."[33]

The push for free trade was in the interests of the U.S. simply by virtue of its status as the home base for so many of the world's transnational corporations. But by the mid-eighties Canadian capital was onside, with the manufacturing sector ready to join the finance and resource sectors in a continentalist strategy vis-à-vis the U.S. Growing international competition and the trend towards ever larger corporations were forcing a consensus amongst Canadian business. The BCNI was able to bring all sectors of capital together to support a comprehensive deal with the U.S.

It was left to d'Aquino to state the broad objectives of a free-trade deal and other policy initiatives of big business. He gave a speech to Toronto's Empire Club, responding to a highly publicized statement by Canadian bishops calling for less corporate greed. D'Aquino said that he and the BCNI were working on a plan to "reconstruct" Canada. "And by reconstruction we mean fundamental change in some of the attitudes, some of the structures and some of the laws that shape our lives."[34]

Having achieved consensus amongst the business and corporate elite in Canada, the BCNI turned to the other players who needed to be onside: the government of Brian Mulroney (who had opposed free trade during the 1984 election) and the top echelons of U.S. corporate and political leadership. To help accomplish the first task, the BCNI initiated a forty-five-member task force to present a united front to the government.

The BCNI's initiative on free trade was taking place at the same time that the Royal Commission on the Economic Union and Development Prospects for Canada, the Macdonald Commission, was deliberating. Rather than mount a frontal assault on the government itself, d'Aquino launched a coordinated corporate campaign to determine the outcome of the commission. The council orchestrated a host of presentations to the commission by some of its key member companies, all calling for free trade. Combined with a strategically timed media blitz, the council virtually determined the commission's report. The commission, in an unprecedented move, came out in favour of free trade, calling for a "leap of faith" before its own researchers had even completed their work.

The spring of 1985 saw the council and its allies promoting a trade deal on both sides of the border. In March the council dispatched seventeen representatives on a three-day blitz of Washington, meeting with key corporate leaders and some of the top representatives of the Republican political elite: Secretary of State George Shultz, Defense Secretary Caspar Weinberger, Senate Majority Leader Robert Dole, and the chair of the Senate's International Trade Subcommittee, John Danforth.

By April, after the "successful" Shamrock Summit between Mulroney and Ronald Reagan, d'Aquino felt the time was right to ask the Conservative prime minister to seek early discussions with the U.S. about a comprehensive deal on trade liberalization. That task turned out to be little more than a formality. So complete was the business consensus that the story is told of d'Aquino convincing Mulroney of free trade in a fifteen-minute conversation on an Ottawa street. More than any other victory, the BCNI's consensus building on free trade would turn out to be the key to achieving d'Aquino's goal of "reconstructing" Canada.

But it by no means stopped there. Having set the framework by persuading the Tories to move on free trade, the council continued to add other elements to its corporate libertarian agenda. Perhaps the most important of these was its relentless campaign to set an inflation target of 2 percent or lower. As we will see in chapter 9, the war on inflation accomplished several corporate objectives: it protected corporate assets (the alleged motivation for low inflation) and at the same time accomplished the crucial political objective of lowering expectations among working and middle-class Canadians.

One of the other BCNI initiatives worthy of mention was its determined support for the goods and services tax. So powerful was the corporate consensus on this issue that the Conservative government of Brian Mulroney virtually committed political suicide to get it through. Dedicating themselves to a corporate initiative (the GST transferred $18 billion in taxes from corporations to individuals), the Tories showed just how much the political elite and its agenda are now virtually indistinguishable from the wishes of corporate Canada.

❖

The BCNI's success in writing public policy during the Mulroney years is breathtaking. The council's defence paper, for example, was so closely mimicked by the government's own White Paper that the magnanimous d'Aquino agreed to delay its release for several months so as not to embarrass the government.

In 1981, the BCNI had established a task force on foreign policy and defence, and "discovered, in painful detail, how manifestly incapable this country is of defending itself from external aggression and effectively protecting and asserting Canadian sovereignty." D'Aquino declared it was "scandalous" that Canada did not have modern submarines.[35]

In 1984, the BCNI was saying universality in social programs should be abandoned and was recommending that $5 billion be cut from federal spending. Yet it said military spending should be increased by 6 percent after inflation each year for ten years. Fortunately, this is one instance where the council did not prevail. Had it done so, national defence spending in 1995 would have been $25 billion rather than the $11 billion budgeted. Yet the BCNI campaign for a military buildup did not exactly fall on deaf ears. The federal government increased military spending by 40 percent after inflation through the 1980s and the military's budget has never returned to where it was before the buildup rationalized by the cold war.

The BCNI is responsible for two long-lasting changes to the very nature of how the federal government works. First, in its pro-business victories with free trade, taxation, competition policy, and regional development (the latter killed any sort of industrial policy at the national level, the only place it counts), the BCNI put into place a policy environment that is a permanent feature of federal governments, regardless who is in power.

Second, and related to that policy environment, the BCNI's approach to corporate intervention has permanently changed the way that public policy is made in Canada. It's almost as if the traditional forums for debating and determining a public consensus are now little more than bread and circuses, rituals tossed out to the public as a sop to democratic legitimacy.

The BCNI's control of both the policy process and the federal agenda is so effective that prime ministers are reduced almost to the status of figureheads. Within months of taking power the Chrétien government, elected on a promised return to social liberalism, was receiving its marching orders from the BCNI. Jean Chrétien was, in any case, long accustomed to listening to Tom d'Aquino. During a brief stint as finance minister in the early 1980s he had declared that he never prepared a budget without seeking the opinion of the BCNI. In fact, long before the 1993 election, d'Aquino had begun getting close to the Liberal Party, partly through the vehicle of corporate funding. According to Duncan Cameron of the Canadian Centre for Policy Alternatives, "While other people were debating with the Tories about free trade and other issues, d'Aquino was quietly briefing the Liberals in opposition on the deficit issue and on how to deal with the NAFTA issue. He was back-rooming it with the Liberals because he knew the Tories were going to lose. By the time of the election the transition was almost seamless."[36]

Most of the policies of the Mulroney government dealing with the economy had been written by the BCNI and delivered to Brian Mulroney for the formality of implementation. The first term of the Chrétien government delivered on most of the BCNI's social policy agenda. And in 1994, the BCNI in effect delivered to the Liberal government instructions for the next phase of corporate governance. Its plan, "A Ten-Point Growth and Employment Strategy," covered almost every area of government policy.[37]

In social policy the Liberals were urged to make the huge cuts that the Tories had failed to make, to end universality, and to revamp programs like UI to remove alleged disincentives to work. The 150 member CEOs insisted that, though the battle with inflation had been largely won, the government must continue with a policy of "non-inflationary growth." The ten-point plan recommended that the government eliminate the deficit entirely by 1998–99.

And on trade it pushed for more of the same along the lines of NAFTA, calling for the elimination of provincial trade barriers and telling the government to continue, at the international level, to pursue aggressive international trade development and diversification. Finally, signalling that it really would like to see the federal government decamp from national governance altogether, the strategy document called for a more decentralized federation.

The BCNI's plan is well on its way to completion as the Liberals enter their second term. The Red Book of Liberal promises is now little more than a historical curiosity, a testament to political duplicity and government subservience. Yet in a sense the BCNI had just provided its particular preferences for the further liberalization of the economy. One wing of the Liberal Party had been onside all along. While the social liberals provided the deception needed for an election victory, Chrétien and Paul Martin and the party's business Liberals had been primed to implement the BCNI's wish list.

At the most important policy conference the party had held in years, the Liberals gathered at Aylmer, Quebec, in the fall of 1991 to hammer out their direction for the new millennium. Here, consolidation of the elite consensus took a huge step, with the Liberal Party decisively shifting in favour of its business faction. According to Maude Barlow and Bruce Campbell, "Chrétien declared that the old left-right split in the party was obsolete; from now on there was only the inevitability of the global economy, and Canada would have to adapt. 'Globalization is not right wing or left wing. It is simply a fact of life.'"[38]

At the Aylmer gathering, the presentation that heralded the transformation of the Liberal Party was given by Peter Nicholson, a Nova Scotia Liberal and free marketeer. In his speech "Nowhere to Hide" he endorsed the economic rationalism that now guided nearly all of the English-speaking developed world. "What seems beyond question is that the world has entered an era where the objectives of economic efficiency . . . will hold sway virtually everywhere. Societies which fail to respond effectively to the market test can, at best, look forward to a life of genteel decline, and at worst a descent into social chaos."[39]

The most dramatic demonstration that business was back and firmly in control, and that the elite consensus was solidified, was the cabinet choices Chrétien made upon achieving power. Chrétien himself had impeccable corporate credentials and his previous cabinet posts — finance; national revenue; industry, trade, and commerce; energy and mines; and Treasury Board — had brought him into contact with the most powerful business sectors in the country. After his defeat in 1988 he worked for corporate lawyers Lang Michener and sat on the boards of Toronto Dominion Bank, Stone Consolidated, and Viceroy Resources.

He was also close to Quebec power broker Paul Desmarais, who agreed to be his chief fundraiser in his bid for the Liberal leadership.

Chrétien's cabinet choices reinforced business Liberals' control over the cabinet and the national agenda. Finance Minister Paul Martin owns Canada Steamship Lines, one of the most notorious tax-dodging companies in the country. The other economic ministries went to people like businessman John Manley at industry, the hard-right Doug Young at transport, former Toronto mayor Art Eggleton at the Treasury Board, and the right-wing friend of the oil industry, Alberta's Anne McLellan, in natural resources. Marcel Massé, head of the Privy Council, was former Canadian director of the IMF and once president of CIDA, and is a hard liner on structural adjustment who had already helped apply the program in the Third World. "It isn't just the Third World that needs structural adjustment," Massé once opined. "We all do, in one form or another. We should avoid the temptation to let our desires for justice in the world obscure the view of reality."[40]

Perhaps most important, next to Martin himself, was Chrétien's choice for minister of international trade. Roy MacLaren had been the point man in setting up formal contacts between the Trudeau cabinet and the BCNI. MacLaren, as Chrétien's trade critic in opposition, worked closely with Tom d'Aquino in developing a position on NAFTA intended to appease the social liberals while it assured the corporate elite that its agenda was still in place.

Interviewed for *Canadian Forum* magazine in 1992, Tom d'Aquino scoffed at the idea that he was the de facto prime minister. It was false modesty. Yet it is important to note that d'Aquino, able as he is, speaks on behalf of his corporate cabinet. Its members, who make up the all-important Policy Committee of the council, are the cream of the corporate CEO crop.

Amongst the thirty members of this group, which effectively determines social and economic policy for the country, are the CEOs of three of the big banks, including the Bank of Montreal's Matthew Barrett and A. L. Flood, CEO of CIBC and chair of the BCNI; Brian Levitt of Imasco; David Kerr of Noranda; David O'Brien of Canadian Pacific; Paul Tellier of CN; Guy St. Pierre of SNC-Lavalin; Alfred Powis, the retired founding chairman; John Mayberry of Dofasco;

Loram Corporation's Ronald Mannix, and Jean Monty of Northern Telecom (now at its parent company, BCE).[41] The members reflect the dominant sectors of the Canadian economy, heavily weighted in favour of financial institutions and the resource industry. There is also strong representation from American transnationals (which make up one-third of the council's membership), including Imperial Oil, Cargill, GM, DuPont, and Hewlett-Packard.

In the summer of 1997 the Policy Committee, having gained almost everything it could think of in the way of social, fiscal, and economic policy from three successive governments going back sixteen years, took a political initiative intended to reduce the federal government's role to an absolute minimum. A memo sent to the prime minister reinforced the BCNI's position that the federal government should give up its leadership role to the provinces. With an arrogance befitting a de facto prime minister, d'Aquino states, "Prime Minister, we acknowledge that you too feel passionately about the future of the country." He then goes on to urge Chrétien to surrender leadership on the Quebec issue and support "any worthwhile initiative" that might come from the provinces.[42]

After sending this memo the BCNI conveniently provided the provinces with just such a "worthwhile initiative." In one of its rare high-profile public interventions, it issued a position paper on national unity and ostentatiously gave it to Alberta premier Ralph Klein.[43] Klein, a favourite son of the Western resource companies, was to be the BCNI's errand boy in delivering the national unity word to the annual premiers' conference.

Choosing Klein was no coincidence, as he is onside with the BCNI's call for radically decentralized constitutional powers. While the BCNI and its members are concerned about Quebec separation, the use of the unity issue as a vehicle for the further devolution of the federal government is a theme common to Klein, Ontario's Premier Mike Harris, and the federal Reform Party. And gutting the federal government's authority is consistent with other BCNI initiatives.

Ostensibly about Quebec, the memo to the premiers focusses almost exclusively on shifting powers from Ottawa to the provinces. It states that "all provinces have their right to equal treatment as partners in the Canadian federation."[44] It then lists seven principles that should guide the "evolution" of the federation, almost all of which imply the gutting of the federal government, including the Reform Party's favourite propaganda line that services should "be provided by the level of government that can do so most effectively and efficiently within the framework of the constitution."[45]

The Business Council on National Issues is the quintessential agency of corporate rule, perhaps unique in the developed world. There are more powerful organizations, such as the Business Round-table in the U.S., but none have likely dominated political life to the degree that the BCNI has. It has forged an elite consensus so powerful that, as Duncan Cameron put it, some corporations whose interests have been harmed by free trade, for example, "have fallen on their swords" as a sacrifice to the general good of corporate rule. And the council has conducted its affairs with a strategic intelligence that has, with few exceptions, allowed the state to implement a compre-hensive corporate agenda while appearing to act in the public interest. In classic role-of-the-state terms it has facilitated an enormous increase in the government's "accumulation" role for capital while maintain-ing its legitimacy.

OTHER PLAYERS, DEEPENING CONSENSUS

The BCNI is so dominant in its role of creating elite consensus that its supporting organizations are often overlooked. But it does have help from many other players, and the consensus is as powerful as it is because it has now permeated many other institutions and agencies that once produced broad policy alternatives. Among its most pow-erful allies (and ex-officio members) is the Alliance of Manufacturers and Exporters (formerly the Canadian Manufacturers' Association). In addition, the council and some of its key members have brought onside organizations whose membership is not at all united on the issues at hand.

Two such organizations are the Canadian Chamber of Commerce and the Canadian Federation of Independent Business (CFIB). Both consist for the most part of small and medium-size businesses whose interests depend not on the so-called global economy or even on trade but on the health of the domestic economy. The tens of thousands of bankruptcies over the past ten years have been almost exclusively among smaller firms, and many of those failures can be traced to the permanent recession created at the behest of the country's largest corporations. While only one-third of CFIB members said they would benefit from free trade, its chief at the time, John Bullock, claimed otherwise, and supported it from the start.

There are fundamental conflicts of interest between small and medium businesses and large corporations in Canada, which normally would be reflected in conflicts in public policy needs. Yet the organizations that supposedly speak for small and medium companies are almost always onside with the BCNI. Here, too, the dominant BCNI members have paid attention to strategy and work hard to ensure that there are no cracks in the business consensus. Duncan Cameron gained some insight into how they "manage" their lesser cousins:

> I was invited to speak at the Canadian Chamber of Commerce on a panel to discuss the budget. I arrived there and the banks had funded all the events. The lunch was provided by Scotiabank, the dinner was the Royal Bank and so on down the line. The banks were all over it. They were on the program and on the program committee. I think the chamber is a legitimate representative of small businesses which join at the local level but once it gets to the senior level it's a different story. Which members can afford to fly to an annual meeting and who pays for the tickets? Who's actually running the Chamber of Commerce? When Jean Chrétien says he checks with the Chamber who is he actually checking with? He might as well just check directly with the banks.[46]

The BCNI also has a strong ally in the C. D. Howe Institute, the principal corporate think-tank in the country. The C. D. Howe plays a dual role of helping to create the elite consensus and also helping to change the political culture to reflect it. It has played a major role in bringing key elements of the elite onside, including senior public policy makers at all levels.

As with all such think-tanks, the C. D. Howe provides an air of neutrality and intellectual legitimacy to an ideology that does little more than serve the interests of its large corporate members. The institute's history reflects precisely the shifting consensus in the corporate and political elite. Until the late 1970s it promoted policies of full employment, tax reform, and social program enhancement. By the 1980s it was pressing Ottawa to pursue free trade with the U.S. and urging all governments to attack deficits through massive cuts to social spending. One of its most prominent policy papers, *Social Policy in the 1990s*, by Tom Courchene, provided the ideological foundation for the Liberals' gutting of the UI program, one of the most important elements in the corporate agenda.

Its membership is dominated by the same Canadian corporate heavyweights that dominate the BCNI. There are 280 members and sponsors, including Alcan, Canadian Pacific, GM, MacMillan Bloedel, all the big five banks and the bankers' association, Quebec's Power Corporation, and Great-West Lifeco, as well as such key individuals as Thomas d'Aquino and Peter Bronfman. Its board of directors, like the corporate sector it promotes, is dominated by the financial sector.[47]

Once the ideas of the right were reflected in public policy — ideas of "smaller" government, market solutions to public problems, the debt as the principal issue of society — they began to permeate every public institution that dealt in ideas. Just as Keynesian economic policy had enjoyed this status as "common sense" until the mid-1970s, new-right neo-liberal prescriptions achieved that status within government by the late 1980s. And the aggressive corporate promotion of these ideas, whose claim was to have simple answers for everything, inevitably infected institutions that were once forums for genuine debate. Business and its ideology are now everywhere. According to Duncan Cameron:

> Any successful operation eventually needs more money. Once you let the business groups use their network to invite people to the Canadian Club, for example, pretty soon they're going to be invited to be on the executive, and the next thing you know they're going to be inviting businesspeople to come and talk.
>
> For example, once the Canadian Institute of International Affairs got a journal going it was sort of natural to reach beyond its immediate membership. And the corporations, once they

became international, got interested in international affairs, so they got involved and started providing funding. The department of external affairs got interested and soon the institute is dominated by a certain way of thinking.[48]

Universities, too, are rapidly changing, partly because of the dominant ideology but more because of huge funding cuts. The battle between public space and private space is determined by the withdrawal of public monies. Says Cameron: "The entire university community in Canada has become hostage to the new type of university president, who is in large part a fundraiser. The university president is no longer someone who takes a leadership role and speaks out on matters concerning society. They lunch, they raise money, and the terms of the relationship are quite clear. Money for services rendered."[49]

Notwithstanding the economic power of corporations and the political power of the state, decision making must still appear to be democratic. And indeed it is still politicians who vote in Parliament. The crude application of elite rule, especially when contrasted with a recent history of more open democracy, would have been unacceptable. Government must still balance its two key roles in a liberal democratic capitalist society: accumulation and legitimation. Without coercion the first cannot succeed in the long term without the second.

We grudgingly accept the new world order being created by transnational corporations only because of an unprecedented ideological assault on Canada's communitarian political culture by corporate-funded think-tanks, lobby groups, right-wing populist organizations, Preston Manning's Reformers, conservative foundations, and the corporate media. This relentless attack on social programs, public services, the idea of government, and the ideas of the Left and small-l liberals has smoothed the way for the corporate domination of the country. In an effort to foment a counter-revolution of falling expectations, the free-market propaganda machinery has tried to bully Canadians out of their expectations of government and their own vision of the country. It is machinery largely designed and paid for by the corporations that stand to gain from the changes.

8

CHANGING THE IDEOLOGICAL FABRIC OF CANADA

If you really want to change the world you have to change the ideological fabric of the world.

— MICHAEL WALKER OF THE FRASER INSTITUTE

I understand: the Fraser Institute is the wholesaler and the NCC is the retailer!

— MILTON FRIEDMAN

Alfred Powis was a busy man in 1975. Chairman of the powerful Noranda Corporation, he was also a founder and the first chair of the Business Council on National Issues, a lobby group that would redefine the political role of corporations in Canada. He was motivated by the waning influence of corporations and believed fervently in the role they should play. It angered him that corporations had hit rock-bottom in the polls. He complained in an address to the Canadian Club that "the private sector is increasingly subject to uninformed, but strident and highly publicized attacks which seem to have a pervasive impact on government policies."[1]

Even in times of relative public disfavour, CEOs can depend on two key factors to tilt the political scales towards corporations. The media's newsrooms are, in theory, independent of their advertising departments, but in practice their dependence on corporate advertising exerts a powerful pull towards corporate views. Corporate funds also play a significant role in the finances of most Canadian political parties, making it unlikely that politicians will bite the hand that feeds them.

In the mid-1970s, though, Powis and other key executives of transnational corporations felt that these pro-business filters were letting too many critical voices through. While corporations needed a powerful voice through an organization like the BCNI, they needed something else, too. They needed an organization that could counter the ideas of the Left.

This was clear to others in the corporate world, especially in B.C., where the NDP government of Dave Barrett was not just expressing ideas of social justice, human rights, and public ownership. It was implementing them, and by doing so was giving broad public legitimacy to ideas that until then were more or less confined to marginal groups with no claims on power. What was needed was a think-tank that would re-establish the dominance of free-enterprise ideas, the value of the market, and property rights. To fill this need, Alfred Powis joined other corporate heavyweights and created the Fraser Institute, the now famous right-wing think-tank headed by the ubiquitous Michael Walker.

At about the same time, another businessman, not nearly so well connected but certainly well heeled, was getting just as angry at what he viewed as the dominance of unions, a growing and alarming presence of the government in the economy, a plethora of universal social programs like medicare, and a general loss of economic freedom. For Colin M. Brown Sr., "big government" was a threat to everything he held dear. He had been acting on his beliefs for several years but in 1975, on the advice of his friend retired Alberta premier Ernest Manning, he formally established the National Citizens' Coalition. It would become the pit-bull terrier in the corporate assault on government and communitarian values.

Of all the institutes and organizations working to promote minimalist government and market solutions, the NCC and the Fraser Institute are among the most important. This chapter deals with them more extensively than other agents of right-wing change because they were established to undermine public support for public programs. Their strategy and tactics, their reliance on corporate funding, and their questionable claims to legitimacy all need to be exposed. We need to understand how corporations, by changing the political culture of Canada, have made the country more amenable to corporate rule.

The Fraser Institute has worked systematically to change the country's "ideological fabric," focussing on media coverage, and on grooming a right-wing intellectual elite. The NCC, as its long-time president (until 1998) David Somerville says, is "very directly engaged with the political process" and has more leeway than the Fraser Institute because it is set up as a nonprofit organization rather than as a charitable organization. Through its political activism, the NCC has provided a model for a variety of pro-business groups such as the Canadian Taxpayers' Federation and the Canadian Progressive Group for Independent Business. The NCC's successful court challenges to limitations on third-party spending in elections have opened the door for money to play an even greater role in Canadian politics.

The role these organizations play can scarcely be exaggerated. They and other agencies such as the media, public relations firms, and the Reform Party, also examined in this chapter, have been key players in the corporate domination of Canada. The development and growth of corporate rule in Canada and elsewhere could not have taken place without an ideological assault on the values and expectations of ordinary citizens. Ideology has been called meaning in the service of power, that is, the creation of rationalizing myths, ideas, and, in today's lexicon, "common sense," that pave the way for people to accept conditions they would otherwise protest against. Had Canadian values and expectations remained untouched from the mid-1970s, the assault on medicare and public education, the casual savaging of people in poverty, and the criminally high levels of unemployment would never have been tolerated. Certainly governments espousing these policies would not have been elected.

It is the job of ideological agencies to scorch the cultural earth to prepare it for the assault on government services, employees, and the environment. The terminology used to describe this ideology is often confusing, as the terms *neo-liberal*, *neo-conservative*, and *new right* often seem to be used interchangeably. Desmond King has described the relationship between neo-liberalism and neo-conservatism this way: "Liberalism is the source of New Right economic and political beliefs and policy objectives; conservatism provides a set of residual claims to cover the consequences of pursuing liberal policies."[2] He gives the example of neo-liberal-inspired cutbacks that force women to take on the burden of social problems. This consequence for women is justified by neo-conservative appeals to "traditional family values" and the traditional role of women. The NCC and the Fraser Institute have been disseminators of both neo-liberal and neo-conservative ideology.

The Fraser Institute's policy prescriptions are the answer to a CEO's prayers. Its likely candidates for membership are, says its literature, "owners of property or those who seek to own property." You can see why by reading any of its annual reports. Seeking legislation that will let your company hop jurisdictions and invest anywhere you get the most favourable terms? The institute campaigns for free trade, removal of interprovincial trade restrictions, and the decentralization of government programs. For people interested in cannibalizing public services for private profit, the Fraser Institute's papers proclaim the failures of the public health and education systems and assure the reader that privatization will offer more "choice." For executives enraged with organized labour, the institute organizes right-to-work conferences promoting legislation that makes it harder for workers to unionize. Are you challenged by women to improve fairness in hiring and promotion? The Fraser Institute's senior analysts deny there is any significant inequality in the workforce or that what does exist is just a result of women's lifestyle choice to bear children. Are you embarrassed by skyrocketing profits as poverty worsens? An institute analysis claims that poverty statistics are overstated. And if you are worried about being sued for faulty products or polluting, the institute undertakes a Law and Markets Project advocating limits on citizens' ability to take you to court.

But the Fraser Institute's work goes beyond the strategic publishing of papers and studies. It is a centre of extreme neo-liberal ideology, an ideology it resolutely promotes. And by implication this ideology is supported by all the executives and senior officials of the corporations that fund the institute.

Does the Bank of Nova Scotia's senior vice-president, Warren Jestin, think employers should be allowed to ask women if they plan to have children and discriminate against them if they do? Does Brian Levitt, president of Imasco, want Canada to model itself on Singapore, where prisoners are beaten so severely they are permanently scarred, citizens can be arrested without warrant, and opposition politicians have been locked up? Does Richard Currie, who received $2.4 million in 1996 as president of Loblaws and George Weston Companies, agree with Michael Walker that "poverty is simply a reflection of the fact that the sufferers were dealt an unlucky intellectual or physical allocation from the roulette wheel of genetic inheritance"?[3]

All of these positions have emerged from the Fraser Institute, self-described as Canada's "largest, privately-funded, public policy research organization."[4] This organization backed by Canada's blue-chip corporations has prospered and become increasingly influential in stamping a right-wing agenda on Canadian public life. More than half of the top one hundred most profitable corporations in Canada have contributed to the Fraser Institute. That is according to a list of corporate donors compiled by the institute in 1989, a practice it has not repeated.[5]

The institute declares it is "an independent Canadian economic and social research and education organization." Its "diversity of revenue" is supposed to guarantee its independence. However, while corporations contribute 31 percent and individual members 11 percent, fully 57 percent of its money comes from business-oriented charitable foundations, such as the John Dobson Foundation, whose declared purpose is to "educate the public with respect to the free enterprise system," or the fabulously wealthy right-wing Donner Foundation, whose stated purpose is to promote market solutions to public policy issues. (The Donner Foundation gave it $450,000 in 1994 to make government debt a dominant public concern.) Foreign foundation donations appear to be increasing rapidly, from $223,000 in 1994 to $342,000 in 1995, so that 17 percent of the institute's funding is now from foreign sources. The Fraser Institute has a small membership of two thousand and is able to raise $2.7 million from a very small pool of donors.[6] The Royal Bank handed over $20,100 to the institute, according to the bank's charitable contributions report for 1996.

Because it can count on such significant donations, the Fraser Institute's fundraising costs are minimal and more than 90 percent of its budget is spent on pursuing its anti-government goals. In 1996, the institute produced eight books, six studies, a monthly issue of *Fraser Forum* magazine, its youth newsletter, *Canadian Student Review*, sixty-five op-ed articles, forty-nine speeches, and four parliamentary submissions, hosted twenty-five luncheons and conferences, and funded six student seminars.

The institute says it takes no government funding. That should be qualified: it takes no direct government funding, but governments in Canada and the U.S. give up tax revenue worth an estimated $1 million to institute donors by allowing them to deduct charitable contributions to the Fraser Institute or its supporting foundations.

The claim is also made in its annual reports that it does not "undertake lobbying activities." However, it does claim credit for "changing the conventional wisdom about many areas of public policy." According to the institute's own documents, the organization offers free dinners to members of Parliament who attend its presentations, packages its products specifically for politicians, holds policy conferences in provinces where it thinks those governments are likely to adopt its ideas, and targets those it approaches for funding on the basis of specific kinds of projects.

Yet, to retain its status as a charity, the institute theoretically is not supposed to be "political." Ron Davis, director of Revenue Canada's charities division, has said that his department defines an organization as political "if its purpose is to affect government directly or indirectly, or to sway public opinion." It is hard to think of a single aspect of the institute, either its self-proclaimed goals or the activities it reports, that would not qualify as political under this definition.[7]

The Fraser Institute is best known for its prescriptions that put the highest value on "freeing" society so that people can pursue wealth. Democratically determined government policies are presented as gross impositions on freedom, as is conveyed in such institute titles as "Breaking the Shackles: Deregulating Canadian Industry."

Executive director Michael Walker is forthright in explaining what he and the institute are up to. In the 1990 annual report, Walker states: "The Institute is in the ideas business. In a way which is not possible for those in business who are perceived as having a vested interest, the Institute forcefully argues the case for the competitive enterprise system at every opportunity and in every forum."

The advantage of concealing vested interests becomes clear in the context of specific institute "products." Executives at major food companies must have been delighted when the institute produced reports slamming marketing boards. Likewise, Bramalea, Equitable Real Estate Investment, the Vancouver Board of Trade, and Vanac Development must have been very pleased with the institute's series of studies attacking rent control and public restrictions on land development in British Columbia.

Although the institute is usually circumspect about its service to the country's largest corporations, someone at head office leaked its five-year plan to the *Edmonton Journal* in 1996. According to the plan, the Fraser will "enlist the help of no less than 25 multinational companies in supporting the development of the [Economic Freedom] index." A person will be hired exclusively "to work with multinational firms and foundations for the purpose of getting more resources to support the Economic Freedom Project."

THE IDEOLOGICAL ENTERPRISE

In the fall of 1973, Michael Walker was working for the federal finance department when he got a call from an old college friend, Csaba Hajdu. Hajdu's boss, MacMillan Bloedel's T. Patrick Boyle, and other business executives in B.C. were greatly agitated by the NDP government of Dave Barrett and wanted advice on how to bring about its demise. In the spring, Walker met with Boyle, who twenty-three years later is still a Fraser Institute trustee. While a think-tank was not an ideal way to deal with the immediate problem of getting rid of the NDP government, Boyle and his mining-executive friends were apparently willing to take the long view. Walker's pitch was good enough to persuade fifteen of them to hand over a total of $200,000 to get the project started.[8] It was the seed money for the Fraser Institute.

Institute publications now brag that the organization's success is reflected in the shift in policies of all federal and provincial governments, regardless of who is in power. The Fraser Institute, in fact, was virtually a Chicago School Trojan horse sent into Canadian political life. Not only was Michael Walker a Milton Friedman follower but over the years they became close friends and racket-ball partners. Friedman does not seek elimination of the state; he wants the state dedicated to the interests of corporations and to social control. This relationship between state and business underlines the international aspect of monetarist, free-market ideology. In some ways, it is a movement, though one with a small and select membership. Throughout Europe, North America, New Zealand, and Australia, Friedmanite "franchises" play a similar role to that of the Fraser Institute.

Inevitably, the Fraser Institute's free-market advocacy conflicts with notions of democratic majority rule. In 1984 that conflict was made explicit with the launching of the Economic Freedom of the World project.

This project is essentially a political effort by the Fraser Institute, and other right-wing institutes collaborating with it, to redefine freedom in the public debate about the direction of governments. The project originated in a 1984 paper Michael Walker presented to the international club of free marketeers who belong to the Mont Pelerin Society. Rather than majority votes, opposition parties, freedom of association and press, or other such criteria commonly used to define the degree of freedom in a country, the freedom for individuals to do whatever they wanted with their wealth was to be the new standard. By this standard, Singapore, a virtual one-party state that administers public beatings to its prisoners, locks up citizens for their religious beliefs, and drives opposition figures into exile, is rated as far more free than Sweden.

Fraser Institute chair R. J. Addington explained the ideological goal underlying the Economic Freedom Index project: "The Institute's ambition in producing the Economic Freedom Index is nothing short of changing the nature of public discourse about the role of government in society. It is our ambition, by creating an international measurement movement, to ensure that adequate attention is paid to the implications of government actions for the level of economic freedom."[9] Under the Fraser Institute's Freedom Index, countries that focus on ensuring the basic needs of all citizens by promoting social equality are given demerits because such policies infringe on the free-dom of investors. The Fraser Institute publication "Economic Freedom: Toward a Theory of Measurement" argues against "value-laden rating systems which indicate that democracy is the best way to advance economic freedom."

The Fraser Institute is forcefully promoting its ideological attack on democracy. In 1996, it hosted a conference in San Francisco that pro-vided ideological training in the use of the index for participants from thirty-seven countries. The American foundation Liberty Fund, with its annual budget of $115 million, is paying for the institute's work on the index.

PURSUING ANTI-DEMOCRATIC ENDS

At a Fraser Institute symposium, "Freedom, Democracy, and Economic Welfare," held in 1986, Milton Friedman went after a speaker who dared to say "democracy is an ultimate value, given protection of minority rights and basic fundamental rights." Friedman said flatly, "You can't say that majority voting is a basic right . . . That's a proposition I object to very strenuously."[10] He argued that the ability to freely pursue the acqui-sition of wealth should be considered the ultimate social value, whereas the pursuit of social justice would "ruin the world." In *Fraser Forum*, Friedman has said: "One of the things that troubles me very much is that I believe a relatively free economy is a necessary condition for a democratic society. But I also believe there is evidence that a democra-tic society, once established, destroys a free economy."[11]

How far would the Fraser Institute roll back democracy? Here are the views of Walter Block, who co-authored the report "Economic Freedom of the World — 1975–1995," worked as the Fraser Institute's senior economist from 1979 to 1991, and whose opinion pieces are still published in *Fraser Forum*. At the 1986 Fraser Institute symposium on democracy, Block said: "Why does it follow that we should have an equal right to vote in the political process? Voting in a political process is not a negative freedom, it is a positive freedom, and it is an aspect of wealth. We don't say that everyone has an equal right to vote in IBM . . . It depends upon how many IBM shares they bought. If we look upon the polity as a voluntary organization, we must recognize the legitimacy for unequal votes."[12]

Block disputes the idea that freedom of assembly and freedom to form unions should be considered positive. He has called unions "bands of criminals," and says, "Unions are just institutions that engage in prohibition of entry into labour markets. They are anti-free labour markets, and I'll be damned if I can see why they get a plus. And the same goes for political demonstrations, which are often organized violations of private property rights."[13] Block also makes comments reminiscent of Nazi philosophers about how human rights are a sign of the decline of the strength of a people: "The first settlers in the land meet harsh conditions and this resolve and strong character carries over until the third or the fourth generation. But eventually later generations get weaker. They become involved in pornography and rights for homosexuals and things like that."[14]

Women's rights are also expendable in Block's world-view, sacrificed on the altar of private property rights: "Consider the sexual harassment which continually occurs between a secretary and a boss . . . While objectionable to many women [it] is not a coercive action. It is rather part of a package deal in which the secretary agrees to all aspects of the job when she agrees to accept the job, and especially when she agrees to keep the job. The office is, after all, private property."[15]

Michael Walker summarized the conference on democracy as finding that "majority rule of itself has no particular virtues."[16] In 1991, when he appeared before the Standing Committee on Finance to lobby for legislated limits on government spending, he argued against the "tyranny of the majority" and said an amendment to the Constitution was needed to place "a limitation on the ability of Parliament to legislate with regard to the extraction of a person's income . . . The Fraser Institute, through its National Tax Limitation Committee, has been investigating ways in which the self-destructive economic forces unleashed by democratic political choice might be restrained."[17]

He made similar arguments in 1993 to Finance Minister Paul Martin, who had invited the institute to an all-day meeting shortly after the Liberals won the 1993 federal election. Walker insisted in a paper entitled "The Political Problem" that just as employers did not downsize on the basis of the votes of their employees, nor should the government base its budgetary decisions on majority opinion.[18]

CHANGING CANADA'S IDEOLOGICAL FABRIC

In the booklet for the Fraser Institute Endowment Fund, Walker promises potential funders that "the organized involvement of informed and concerned individuals can greatly affect Canadians in their choice between two ways of life." Given its ideological project, it is easy to predict how the Fraser Institute would operate. Throughout its twenty-three-year history, it has targeted all the major institutions in the country that influence how Canadians think: the media, churches, political parties, nongovernmental organizations, and universities.

According to the institute's leaked five-year plan, "a central focus of our program . . . during the next five years will be the expansion of our penetration of the national media." The Fraser Institute has so penetrated the Canadian media that it is hard to imagine where it could possibly expand. Its 1996 annual report claims 3,108 references to the institute in the media that year, 51 percent more than the previous year. The institute holds news conferences and issues news releases, and makes sure it always has staff available to be interviewed. Its fax news-broadcasting operation sends a two-page news sheet to 450 radio stations every week. It provides packaged editorials for newspapers and radio designed "to explain the merits of the free-market system, issue by issue." As well, its seminars are extensively covered by cable stations, which gave it 105 hours of coverage in 1996.

The receptivity of the media is not surprising. Over the years, key media institutions have funded the Fraser Institute, including Sterling Newspapers, Southam, Thomson Newspapers, and Standard Broadcasting. David Radler, president of Hollinger, is an institute trustee, and Barbara Amiel Black, another Hollinger executive as well as a columnist for Southam papers, was a trustee until 1996.

Media-friendly gimmicks help the mass media get Fraser Institute views across. The institute's "Tax Freedom Day" — the day in the year when the average family has earned enough to pay its total tax bill to all levels of government — receives wide coverage. Fraser Institute report cards predictably flunk governments that, in the view of institute staffers, have not slashed or privatized enough.

The institute also claims to provide an objective evaluation of media bias through its National Media Archive. The authors of this department's publication, *On Balance*, review major news programs on

CBC and CTV for bias and claim their analyses are "completely objective." However, *On Balance* often demonstrates that these analysts are viewing programs through the coloured glasses of the institute's motto, "Public Problems . . . Private Solutions." For example, they criticized the CBC for emphasizing negative economic news such as youth unemployment rather than broadcasting good-news stories about increases in corporate and bank profits. CBC and CTV were applauded for substituting the term *scabs* with the management-friendly term *replacement workers*.

An independent group, NewsWatch Canada, evaluated seventeen issues of *On Balance* published in 1995 and 1996. It found generally that "while purporting to promote 'objectivity' and expose a lack of balance in journalism, the National Media Archive itself manifests a consistent pattern of innuendo, decontextualized results, and selective interpretation."[19] Yet despite these failings, Fraser Institute staff are sought for comment as experts on the media.

Young people are a particular target of Fraser Institute efforts. According to its 1996 annual report: "Over the years, particular attention has been paid to the development of the student program as the Institute and its supporters recognize the importance of bringing free-market economic ideas to university, college, and high school students in their prime learning years." Through sympathetic professors and students on campuses, the institute distributes twenty thousand free copies annually of its newsletter, *Canadian Student Review*. The institute encourages like-minded professors to place its publications on course lists and to assign its essay contests as part of class work. Typical of the themes for these contests is "Free Market Solutions to Environmental Problems."

Paul Havemann, writing about how right-wing ideas have been marketed in Canada, has described the Fraser Institute as "a finishing school for the salesmen of the new Establishment Ideology."[20] Each year, the institute runs six student seminars in cities across Canada attended by 1,000 students at a cost of $200 per student, and plans to increase the number of seminars to fourteen. Every year, it spends $1,250 per student on an in-depth leadership training colloquium for twenty participants; by 2001, three more will be added. Fourteen graduates from the student seminars have been deemed worthy enough to receive a week's worth of intensive training in right-wing ideology at the Institute for Humane Studies in Fairfax, Virginia. With funds from the Donner Foundation and the Hunter Family Foundation, the Fraser Institute hires seven students as interns.

"We have already had the satisfaction of seeing some of the earlier participants in our programs rise to positions of influence within political parties, or within the policy-making apparatus of government."[21] Ezra Levant, a former columnist for the *Edmonton Sun* and the *Calgary Sun*, and now legislative assistant to Reform Party leader Preston Manning, is perhaps the best-known institute acolyte. Levant worked for the institute in 1995 as an intern. Recently, the institute has published *Youthquake*, his polemic against government social spending. In this book Levant pits young people against baby boomers, accusing the latter of living high off the government hog and leaving the next generation to pick up the tab.

The Fraser Institute brags that "the current public policy agenda reads like an index of past Institute publications." Five programs specifically target politicians and government officials: seminars for MPs; a "hot line" that MPs can phone to get "direct personal assistance"; free copies of all institute publications, including the *Fraser Forum*; a new series of publications, *Public Policy Sources*, which supply short position papers on topical issues, and the National Media Archive, which provides transcripts of all CTV and CBC news programming.

During the 1993–97 Parliament, it often sounded as if the Fraser Institute was the research wing of the Reform Party. Twenty-two of the fifty-one Reform MPs drew on institute materials for their speeches. The party helps promote Fraser Institute gimmicks like Tax Freedom Day, and in return gets advance copies of institute studies; Michael Walker's study on cutting social programs was first presented to a Reform Party policy session. Reform MPs Rob Anders and Jason Kenney are also Fraser Institute members. Support for the institute is not confined to Reform, however. Finance Minister Paul Martin signalled his own comfort in being associated with the institute by presenting the Fraser Institute's $20,000 Prize for Economy in Government in 1994.

The institute is invited to make submissions to parliamentary standing committees and is consulted by civil servants. Some who have made the pilgrimage to the institute include the federal finance department's assistant deputy minister Don Drummond, members of the B.C. premier's round table on social program renewal, and foreign affairs staff accompanied by foreign guests.

INSTITUTE CLAIMS OF LEGITIMACY

Fraser Institute studies are replete with charts, graphs, and numbers that appear to demonstrate the seriousness of a problem, often in terms of what the cost of a program is to the average family. It makes the self-serving claim that it has a "well-deserved reputation for the quality of its work, which earns its recommendations the attention of policy makers around the globe."[22] But the methods used in these studies often would not pass muster in an undergraduate social sciences class.

A much-quoted hospital waiting list released in 1997 provides a glaring example: the survey consists entirely of the "impressions" of medical specialists about how long patients have had to wait for an operation; no random sample is used, and the results compiled are only from those motivated enough to send in their "data" to the institute. It has no more credibility than a TV phone-in survey asking a deliberately provocative question. Steven Lewis, who was head of the National Forum on Health's committee on private versus public medicine, described the survey as "methodological garbage."[23] Obviously, specialists have a vested interest; promoting the notion that there are lengthy waits allows specialists to argue for increased spending on their services.

As if the biases in that survey were not enough, the institute plans to carry out another one on patient satisfaction in conjunction with a vociferous U.S. opponent of public-sector health care, the National Center for Policy Analysis. The survey will double as a media campaign since "patients will be asked to indicate their willingness to give interviews to the press about their experience so that the results of the survey can be translated into terms that are more directly understandable by the general public."[24]

Michael Walker and Walter Block in their 1985 study denouncing employment equity programs reported in a footnote that they were engaged in "an informal competition" with a researcher at the American

Enterprise Institute on who could come up with the better numbers indicating women were faring better in the workforce than men.[25] They also used Helen Gurley Brown's 1964 pop-psychology book, *Sex and the Single Girl*, as reference for their claim that "other things equal, they [women] will accept lower pay for a job which puts them in contact with large numbers of eligible bachelors."[26]

Another example of the quality of the institute's work was reported in the *Vancouver Sun*. The story, headlined "Beloved Regulations Squeeze Us Badly," featured an institute study attacking government regulations.[27] Researcher Fazil Mihlar had used U.S. data compiled by an adviser to President Reagan to claim that government regulation is harmful to the public. His solution: hand regulation over to corporations. Journalists reporting on the proposal seemed blithely unconcerned about its implications for Canadian democracy. Nor did they comment on the fact that not a shred of Canadian data was used.

With the sheer volume of Fraser Institute activity (eleven conferences in 1996 alone), it would take a separate institute to evaluate how well its research stands up to academic standards. However, an international team of economists and labour lawyers did evaluate the presentations made at one of the institute's 1996 conferences. In a report entitled "Bad Work: A Review of Papers from a Fraser Institute Conference on 'Right-to-Work' Laws," they documented a multitude of errors that could only be seen as the result of an anti-union political agenda.[28]

One speaker gave a talk entitled "Closed Shop Provisions Violate Canadian and Provincial Charters of Rights and Freedoms." But he somehow neglected to mention a key Supreme Court ruling that closed-shop provisions do not violate the Charter. Another speaker argued for reform of a B.C. law that he said gave too much power to unions. But the law had been repealed a decade earlier.

The Institute repeatedly demonstrates a willingness to make claims that are unsubtantiated or even contradicted by available data. That the media do not reject them may reflect a bias in favour of the same ideas or may simply be because reporters, stretched to the limit by downsizing, lack the ability or resources to critique the institute's work.

With medicare on the ropes, governments dealing with debt by cutting spending, the CBC in peril, NAFTA in place, and the MAI looming, the Fraser Institute might be expected to be pacified. Not so. Its five-year plan calls for doubling its budget, to $5 million, and aggressively pursuing its radical vision of corporate libertarianism. Public schools, universities, hospitals, and public land all will be on the auction block if the details of this plan are carried out. Unions and environmental organizations could be crippled if government spending is lowered to a minimalist 30 percent of GDP from its current 33 percent. Fazil Mihlar has said that governments should reduce their legislation until all that remains are "framework laws," the ones that protect property and ensure contracts.[29]

THE NATIONAL CITIZENS' COALITION

An insight into the division of labour between the Fraser Institute and the National Citizens' Coalition was provided by NCC president David Somerville at a 1996 gathering of right-wing libertarians. Asked about the merits of joining organizations like the NCC, Somerville replied: "If you want red meat for breakfast then you want to get involved in something like the National Citizens' Coalition. We are very directly engaged with the political process. I just want to offer one caution and that is to do the kind of job that I'm doing you not only have to be strongly intellectually engaged but strongly emotionally engaged."[30]

The NCC's "red meat for breakfast" style of operating was established by its founder, millionaire businessman Colin M. Brown. In 1967 this London Life insurance agent set the pattern for NCC campaigns by placing a full-page ad in the *Globe and Mail* attacking medicare and asking for donations to spread the word. According to an NCC description of Brown's legacy, he waged a "ceaseless battle against big government and big unions."[31] Brown himself described the NCC as "a hobby that went berserk."[32]

The NCC has tried to make secrecy a democratic virtue. The organization has repeatedly refused to reveal who backs it, and does not even provide a breakdown of corporate versus individual supporters. A May 15, 1992, NCC news release criticized a proposal for electoral reform because those who contributed more than $250 to a third-party group would have to reveal their names. Somerville said, "This is an affront to freedom of speech. No Canadian should be forced to divulge his political beliefs," and he compared funding disclosure to the right to a secret ballot.

The NCC campaigns to allow the wealthy to exert a disproportionate influence on Canadian political life. Secret ballots enable all citizens to exercise a right, regardless of wealth. In contrast, keeping secret the names of corporations and individuals who have bankrolled particular campaigns conceals key information about these campaigns. For example, farmers might want to know if Cargill Grain is covering the costs of the NCC's current support for challenges to the Canadian Wheat Board.

In 1985, Canadian Labour Congress president Dennis McDermott accused the National Citizens' Coalition of being "nothing more than a front for some of the wealthiest and most powerful individuals and corporations in the country." Somerville responded, "There's nothing wrong with private associations . . . They're throughout society."[33]

One source of information that lists individuals and corporations willing to be associated with the NCC is the program given out at the NCC's annual Colin M. Brown Freedom Medal awards dinner. At the 1996 dinner for Ontario premier Mike Harris, some of those paying for advertising in the program or named in it as an NCC "Patron of Freedom" include John D. Leitch, Edward Bronfman, Jack Pirie, and Thomas Bata; Upper Lakes Shipping, Magna International, and Rogers Cable; and the John Deere Foundation. The money raised from this dinner-program advertising alone was at least $15,000.[34]

A list of the members of the NCC's advisory council and board of directors is another source of information about its backers. Very powerful members of Canada's corporate establishment have lent the NCC credibility and assisted its fundraising.

John Leitch acted as chair in 1987 and has been a member of the advisory council for more than two decades.[35] Leitch is past-president of Upper Lakes Shipping International and has been a director of ten major corporations, including the Bank of Commerce, Massey-Ferguson, Canada Life, Dofasco, and American Airlines. One-time advisory council member John Clyne was the chair of MacMillan Bloedel for sixteen years. Like Leitch, Clyne was a director of the Bank of Commerce and he has held directorships in five major

corporations. Ernest Manning, yet another Bank of Commerce director, was involved with the NCC. After being the Social Credit premier
of Alberta from 1943 to 1968, Manning went on to sit as a director of
eleven major corporations. Gerald Hobbs brought his connections as
director of the Bank of Nova Scotia to the NCC advisory council.
Hobbs was head of Cominco, and was also a director of B.C. Tel,
North America Life Assurance, MacMillan Bloedel, and Pacific Press.[36]

Nick Fillmore's analysis of key NCC advisory board members in
1986 revealed ties to thirty-nine major Canadian corporations, including, in addition to the above, Canadian Pacific, Brascan, Bank of
Montreal, Royal Trust, Power Corporation, and Bell Canada. There
were also links to "eight major insurance companies, seven advertising
agencies and more than fifty lesser corporations."[37]

Reinforcing its connections with the country's business elite at the
national level, the NCC got Keith Rapsey, the former president of
the Canadian Manufacturers' Association, to serve on its advisory
council during the 1980s. As well as these nationally well-connected
businessmen, the NCC has drawn on the prestige of members of
regional business elites in appointments to its advisory council,
including Harold P. Connor, the former head of National Sea
Products, and Jack Pirie, president of Pirie Resource Management.

In a response to an article critical of the NCC, communications
director Gerry Nicholls claimed: "We do not receive a single cent in
government handouts, and contributions to the NCC are not tax-
deductible."[38] The NCC is registered as a nonprofit society, rather
than a charity, so it cannot issue charitable receipts. However,
Revenue Canada allows businesses to deduct contributions to such
organizations. Businesses can pay to become NCC members and get
its newsletters, then write off this support as business expenses. As
well, businesses that advertise in the programs distributed at NCC
events qualify for tax deductions.

Noted Canadian tax lawyer Arthur Drache, writing in the *Financial
Post*, has said that the deductibility of contributions is how business
lobby groups like the NCC "are able to operate on handsome budgets."
Drache argues that "the end result is that . . . businesses are much
more able to make their views heard with deductible tax dollars than
are individuals."[39]

Every year, the NCC publishes "Tales from the Tax Trough," which ridicules government spending. Grants to organizations like the National Action Committee on the Status of Women come in for particular attack; feminists are portrayed as fat pigs with hairs sprouting from their chins. But government grants to organizations are at least subject to review by democratically elected politicians, whereas the public has no say at all over how the NCC's budget, $2.6 million in 1996, is spent. Yet if businesses are allowed tax deductions for their donations to the NCC, all Canadian taxpayers are forced to support the organization through the revenue the government gives up. This support includes helping to disseminate arguments about why it is not in the nature of the French to be democratic;[40] why Vietnamese refugees should not have been allowed into Canada (because they would bring in thousands of their relatives and would not "fit in" as well as Europeans with the same "blood lines" as Canadians),[41] or how there is almost no real poverty in the U.S.[42]

THE NCC'S GOALS

Colin Brown campaigned against medicare in the 1960s and 1970s and battled in the early 1980s against the Canada Health Act, claiming in an NCC fundraising appeal that people "*would die*" if the act was passed. He asked prospective donors to contemplate "how you would like your open-heart surgery done by a civil servant?"

Brown summarized his anti-government philosophy by claiming, "The less a government does, the more the man-on-the-street has to do. And he enjoys doing it."[43] Articles in NCC publications decry the public school system as a failure, advocate privatization of crown corporations including the post office and the CBC, ridicule government grants for research and the arts, and praise the private health-care system in the U.S. as superior to Canadian medicare. The NCC has organized Canadian speaking tours of British consultant Madsen Pirie, who advocates "the privatization of everything." The NCC sent copies of Pirie's guides on how to privatize to 1,465 federal, provincial, and municipal politicians, as well as to senior civil servants. Alberta premier Ralph Klein made it required reading for every member of his caucus.[44]

Consistent with the views of Milton Friedman, the NCC calls for the elimination of government, except in a policing and military role. Although the NCC's motto is "More Freedom Through Less Government," the organization stands for "a strong defence." Brown and Somerville made a special trip to Washington in 1985 to oppose what they called the "strident anti-Americanism of Canada's peace movement."[45] NCC ads placed in American newspapers said it was time Canadians acknowledged our "debt" to the U.S. While they were in Washington, Brown and Somerville met with Republican senators and members of Congress who opposed arms control; the Canadians promised to maintain contact with them.

The kind of political advocacy the NCC engages in is expensive. One NCC project alone, Ontarians for Responsible Government (O.R.G.), budgeted $560,000 in 1995 to wage what it termed an "all out electoral war" against the provincial NDP.[46] O.R.G. was created in 1991 "to bring down the government of Bob Rae."[47] Billboards with anti-government messages appeared first in downtown Toronto and then right across the province, with pictures of Rae and slogans like "How Do You Like Socialism So Far?" The Ontario news media gave extensive coverage to this campaign.

As community and labour organizations mounted opposition to the cuts introduced after the Conservatives defeated the NDP government, O.R.G. began a counter-campaign, using its substantial media-buying budget to support Premier Mike Harris. O.R.G. spent $20,000 in the week preceding the 1995 general strike in London, Ontario, calling for a "fight back" against the unions. It ran a similar campaign to combat the protest in Hamilton in 1996.

NCC radio and TV commercials in the 1996 B.C. election could hardly have been more direct: "Don't vote for Glen Clark's NDP." Because B.C. law prohibits third parties from buying ads that tell people how to vote, the NCC spent $44,000 to have its message broadcast on American television and radio border stations. Somerville issued a news release saying the law limiting third-party spending should be opposed because it was "dangerous and oppressive" and "citizens who value freedom must resist tyranny."[48] When the NDP had won, Somerville announced the NCC would be funding Kelowna businessman David Stockell's attempt to overturn the election results.

How did the NCC get to play such a major role in Canadian politics? According to writer Nick Fillmore, until 1984 "the coalition was very much an unimportant right-wing fringe group, paid little attention by most politicians, the media and even shunned by other right-wing lobby groups . . . The first breakthrough came in July, 1984, when the NCC successfully used the Alberta Supreme Court to overturn the federal government's bill C-169, a . . . law aimed at preventing third parties . . . from advertising a political position during an election campaign."[49]

Bill C-169, a bill with all-party support, was designed to block spending in elections unless it was approved and accounted for by the party that stood to gain from the spending. Judge Donald Medhurst in striking down the law said there had to be proof that such spending undermined democracy before any government could impose limits on the freedom of expression guarantee in the Charter of Rights and Freedoms.

The NCC's court victory opened the door to virtually unlimited corporate spending in the 1988 federal election, arguably the most important election in Canada in decades. Advocates of free trade were able to far outspend opponents; the Canadian Alliance for Trade and Job Opportunities spent $1.5 million on one booklet alone, double the total amount spent by the Pro-Canada Network to fight the deal.[50]

In 1993 Justice D. I. MacLeod of the Alberta Court of Queen's Bench declared that the renewed federal efforts to prevent third-party spending through Bill C-114 were also unconstitutional. Bill C-114 was partly the result of the Royal Commission on Electoral Reform and Party Financing, which described the 1988 free-trade election as "the most striking intrusion of third-party advertising in a national campaign in over 40 years."[51] The federal government appealed MacLeod's decision, but in 1996 the Alberta Court of Appeal ruled against the government and blocked electoral reform once again.

Along with its campaigns to eliminate funding for social advocacy groups, the NCC has established its reputation in attacking the ability of unions to support social causes. Perhaps inspired by similar and successful action by corporate interests in the U.S., in the 1980s the NCC funded community college teacher Merv Lavigne's court case, which challenged the social-action objectives of Canadian unions.

The argument Lavigne's NCC-paid lawyers made was that his right to freedom of expression as defined in Canada's Charter of Rights was infringed upon by having to pay dues to his union that were used for purposes he personally did not support.

Had the case succeeded, it would have meant that unions would have had to go back to each individual member every time they were deciding whether to spend even a couple of pennies. The Canadian Labour Congress and other unions pointed out that Lavigne had every right to engage in the democratic process within his union to determine what political causes were funded.

The NCC won the case at the Ontario Supreme Court, but the Ontario Court of Appeal overturned the decision in 1989, saying in part that "it is not the courts' job to decide what is collective bargaining and what is not." Lavigne, again financed by the NCC, took the case to the Supreme Court of Canada, where in 1991 the court ruled again in favour of the unions.

In her judgment, Chief Justice Bertha Wilson observed how limits to union social-action spending had worked in the U.S.: "When [American] unions speak out on political matters, for example, they must (upon request) refund to dissenting members the prorated cost of such activity. Corporations do not have this problem; corporations may speak out on political subjects in spite of shareholder dissent. Corporations also speak with a far louder voice, heavily outspending labour on dissemination of their views."

The Lavigne case cost the NCC close to a million dollars, demonstrating just how much its backers were willing to spend to cripple unions. Having lost at the Supreme Court, the NCC kept up its anti-union efforts. In 1995 it launched a project called "Canadians Against Forced Unionism" that was dedicated to the introduction of right-to-work legislation. The project's spokesperson, Robert Anders (now a Reform MP), declared, "The time has come to free Alberta's workers." Ralph Klein's Conservative government decided against right-to-work legislation, partly on the basis that, with the existing laws, the rate of unionization was already decreasing in the province.

NCC LEGITIMACY AND LOBBYING

In the early 1970s many of the social movements the NCC criticized seemed to be reaping the benefits of years of activism: social programs appeared secure, and labour, human rights, and women's groups were having a significant influence on public policy. An NCC newsletter recounts how at one point in this period Ernest Manning "urged our founder to transform his one-man crusade into a citizens' action group. Shortly thereafter, Colin [Brown] incorporated the National Citizens' Coalition." Brown got $100,000 in seed money to do this from wealthy Canadians.[52]

The National Citizens' Coalition may have taken on a grassroots name for Brown's crusade, but it took on nothing of the character of a membership-controlled organization when it was incorporated in 1975. It is not national, its citizen members can't vote, and it is not a coalition. In its bylaws the NCC distinguishes between two categories of membership — public and voting. According to Bylaw 27: "Public members shall not be entitled to receive notice of or to attend any meeting of the members of the Corporation and shall not be entitled to vote at any such meeting."

Voting members, on the other hand, are entitled to receive notification of NCC meetings, attend them, and vote. Voting members choose the board of directors, the president, and the vice-president. The NCC does not reveal who its voting members are (this is a highly select group) and, according to Bylaw 28, *only two* voting members are required to make up a quorum at meetings.

A voting member also qualifies to become one of four NCC directors, and only three of these have to be present at any meeting to conduct NCC business. These three or four people decide who is allowed to become an NCC member, both voting and public, and the fees. Directors can also force members to resign. This structure makes the NCC seem more like a private lobbying firm than a non-profit citizens' organization.

Every NCC ad campaign includes a reference to the number of supporters (virtually all of whom are in Ontario, Alberta, and B.C.) the organization claims to have. However, there is inconsistency in the figures the NCC reports — both 40,000 and 45,000 have been published in different NCC documents for 1996.[53] It reported a membership of exactly the same number from 1979 to 1986, a constancy that is hard to credit given the variation in the popularity of its campaigns. Efforts to find out what membership entails have repeatedly failed, but anecdotal evidence suggests that once you join you are on the NCC's membership list for many years.

The NCC claims, "We do not lobby politicians or bureaucrats — we speak directly to our fellow citizens." This statement, from "Who We Are and What We Do 1996," the most recent organizational pamphlet, is another attempt to cultivate a grassroots image. In fact, the people that run the NCC rarely speak with fellow citizens or even with their own supporters. What the NCC does do (a typical campaign is its right-to-work crusade in Alberta) is commission opinion polls, try to generate public pressure on politicians through opinion pieces and mass-media advertising, cultivate political friends who will push its policies to the forefront, and make submissions to government. These are all the traditional activities of lobbyists.

The NCC has always had privileged backroom access to politicians, starting with its founder Colin Brown, who took Ontario Conservative premiers Bill Davis and John Robarts along with him on annual chartered flights to the Masters Golf Tournament in Georgia. And over the years, well-connected right-wing politicians have been on its advisory board: Sarah Band, who ran for the federal Tory leadership; Eric Kipping, a former Tory MLA from New Brunswick who led a delegation of former Conservatives from the Maritimes to join the Reform Party; Ernest Manning, and the late Robert Thompson, former national Social Credit leader.

The NCC gives $10,000 prizes to politicians who have contributed to "freedom" — as the NCC defines it. Politicians who have made the grade have been Tory cabinet minister John Crosbie, Reform senator Stan Waters, and Tory premiers Ralph Klein and Mike Harris.

The NCC has hired former Reform MP Stephen Harper to take over from David Somerville as president. Harper worked with Stan Waters on the Reform Party's original policy book. Somerville, commenting on the founding convention of the Reform Party in 1987, said, "If NCC supporters notice a remarkable similarity between the political agendas of the RPC [the Reform Party of Canada] and the NCC, it may be because an estimated one third to one half of the delegates were NCC supporters."[54] As guest speaker to the NCC's Colin M. Brown Memorial Dinner at the Hamilton Golf and Country Club in Ancaster, Ontario, in 1994, Harper cited the achievements of the Reform Party and the NCC since the last time he had addressed the same gathering in 1989:

> What has happened in the past five years? Let me start with the positive side . . . Universality has been severely reduced: it is virtually dead as a concept in most areas of public policy. The family allowance programme has been eliminated and unemployment insurance has been seriously cut back . . . These achievements are due in part to the Reform Party of Canada and . . . the National Citizens' Coalition.[55]

In 1994, NCC president David Somerville was invited to speak to the Ontario Conservative Party's Policy Advisory Council. He recommended the government "come out strongly in favour of privatization, contracting-out, repeal of pro-union labour laws and immediate action to eliminate the deficit and reduce the province's debt."[56] All of these recommendations coincide with the current policies of the Conservative government.

THE NCC AND THE MEDIA

By 1987, the NCC could report to its donors: "The NCC has attained a high profile in the major media. Hundreds of articles about the Coalition appear weekly in newspapers and magazines across the country. Television and radio stations follow the activities of the NCC very closely. In 1986, over 1,000 letters to the editor from Colin Brown and David Somerville were printed in newspapers across Canada."[57]

Starting in 1986, the NCC was supplying 160 newspapers with a weekly column. A comparison of NCC news releases on a campaign such as "Tales from the Tax Trough" with the articles major dailies printed reveals how uncritically some Canadian editors deal with NCC material. On issues like election spending limits and MP pensions, Canada's major dailies have adopted NCC terminology — for example, election spending limits are called gag laws, and MPs receive "gold-plated pensions." In its publication *Consensus* the NCC reports on numerous success stories of its influence in the media from prominent columnists and journalists. And many open-line shows use NCC spokesmen on its "Pigs-at-the-Trough Day."[58]

The NCC rewards journalists who have the "right" perspective. Three of the eight Colin M. Brown Freedom Medals and $10,000-cash awards the NCC has given out have gone to journalists: Barbara Amiel Black in 1987, Lubor Zink in 1989, and Diane Francis in 1995.

OTHER PLAYERS

The Fraser Institute and the National Citizens' Coalition are, of course, not the only corporate-funded institutions working overtime to change Canada's communitarian political culture. In 1994, an East Coast clone of the Vancouver-based Fraser Institute was established with $450,000 from the Donner Foundation. The Atlantic Institute for Market Studies was set up as an "economic and social policy think tank . . . with a view to determining whether and to what extent market-based solutions can be successfully applied to the myriad social and economic problems facing Atlantic Canada."[59]

And the C. D. Howe Institute has played a dual role of building elite consensus and of changing public opinion. Linda McQuaig has documented in her book *Shooting the Hippo* the influence the C. D. Howe Institute wields within government circles. One institute study, touting the elimination of inflation as an overarching goal for government policy, was "used by the Bank [of Canada] and by the government to justify John Crow's highly experimental zero inflation policy."[60]

Widely distributed C. D. Howe Institute studies foster panic about government debt, recommend radical cuts to social programs, and undermine confidence in the Canada Pension Plan. While it does not claim to speak for business in the way the BCNI does, the C. D. Howe Institute and the BCNI share corporate sponsors, as detailed in chapter 7. In 1996, the Royal Bank contributed $52,000 of the institute's $2-million budget. A December 1995 *Globe and Mail* survey of Canadian think-tanks quoted McQuaig's concern: "You see them referred to in the press as an independent think tank and that leaves out the fact that they're almost exclusively funded by Bay Street."

The C. D. Howe Institute seems to try to position itself vis-à-vis its larger rival, the Fraser Institute, by emphasizing that it is less committed ideologically and more objective, saying this "means refraining from polemics, keeping an open mind about solutions to difficult problems, encouraging support and input from a broad private sector membership base, and engaging in regular, substantive discussions with federal and provincial government policy makers." How much the institute avoids polemics is open to question. By calling the Canada Pension Plan a "Ponzi" scheme in its promotional material, the institute boasts that it has been able to "electrify" the public debate.

Right-wing foundations in Canada used to be a minor force relative to their counterparts in the U.S. The main player in recent years has been the Donner Canada Foundation, the tenth largest in the country with an endowment of close to $100 million. Established in 1950 by American steel magnate William Henry Donner, who had taken an interest in Canada, the foundation was until 1993 "the epitome of middle-of-the-road Canadian liberalism."[61] But since it was taken over by conservative Donner family members, it has become one of the principal funders of right-wing propaganda in the country. Under the direction (until late 1996) of American Devon Cross, former editor of the libertarian journal *The Idler*, the foundation gave out $2 million a year, almost exclusively to right-wing causes. By giving $400,000 to the Fraser Institute, bestowing large sums to fund the charter school lobby, bankrolling the conservative journals *Next City* and *Gravitas*, funding the market-oriented Energy Probe and its various spin-offs, and coming up with the cash to launch the Atlantic Institute for Market Studies, the Donner is a major actor in the campaign to "change the ideological fabric" of Canadian society. The Donner Foundation has adopted the strategy of its American cousins with a very focussed, deliberate promotion of vehicles for the dissemination of neo-liberal ideas.

MUTUAL SEDUCTION: RIGHT-WING ORGANIZATIONS AND THE MEDIA

The mere fact that the Fraser Institute, the NCC, and other right-wing organizations work so hard to attract media coverage should not guarantee that they will get it. Ideally, the amount of coverage would reflect the representativeness of these organizations and the reliability of their statements. Minimally, the media should be alerting the public to their political agendas, such as when the NCC announced it intended to wipe the Ontario NDP government off the political map.

Instead, as the Fraser Institute's annual reports highlight, there is a cosy relationship between prominent Canadian journalists and the Fraser. The *Financial Post* co-sponsors the institute's Economy in Government prize, which has rewarded such ideas as creating publicly funded private schools. Diane Francis, editor of the *Financial Post*, is pictured in an annual report photo addressing a Fraser Institute fundraising luncheon. *Financial Post* editor-at-large Neville Nankivell and *Globe and Mail* columnist "Terry" Corcoran are shown "sharing a joke" and "taking part in a discussion" with staff at the institute's offices.

The Fraser Institute seems to have a particularly cosy relationship with CTV news. In 1994, chief anchor and senior news editor Lloyd Robertson lent his support to the institute by serving as guest speaker at one of its fundraising luncheons. Mike Duffy, host of CTV's public-affairs program *Sunday Edition*, also helped the institute fundraise by being a guest speaker in 1995.

Some reporters do provide balanced coverage of the Fraser Institute and the NCC. But as right-wing organizations increased their media-influencing capability, forces within the corporate media were making it more open to influence. In 1970, Keith Davey's senate committee on mass media sounded a warning about the increasing concentration of ownership. Eleven years later, with the disappearance of even more newspapers, another federal investigation, this one headed up by Tom Kent, raised the alarm again. Not only were independent newspapers being bought out by such major chains as Southam and Thomson but chains were now swallowing up other chains. Government remained complicit in this steady erosion of democracy by declining to act on the key recommendations coming out of these reviews, a press own-ership review board, and a Canadian newspaper act.

In the 1990s, Conrad Black's Hollinger Inc. has gobbled up the Sifton newspaper chain in Saskatchewan, bought into the company that publishes the *Toronto Star*, taken over seven Thomson dailies in Atlantic Canada and six in Ontario, vied to take over the *Financial*

Post, and attempted to buy out all of the remaining shares that Black does not already own in Southam. Hollinger spent half a billion dollars in 1996 gorging itself on Canadian newspapers. It now owns 60 of Canada's 105 daily newspapers, has monopolies in three provinces, and controls the Canadian Press wire service.

Hollinger's voracious appetite makes statistics on media concentration in Canada continually outdated. The ultimate Black conquest of all of Canadian newspapers, including the last significant holdouts in the Toronto market, seems inevitable. As it is, Black influences all but four Canadian daily newspapers. Through Canadian Press's Broadcast News, Black's influence extends to 425 radio stations, 76 TV outlets, and 142 cable stations — at a time when at least six countries have taken steps to encourage more diversity in newspaper ownership. Hollinger now controls 43 percent of Canadian newspaper circulation. In contrast, Gannett, the largest American chain, controls only 10 percent of that country's circulation.

With successive takeovers, more and more Canadian newspaper staff lost their jobs — 1,550 over three years in the Southam chain after Hollinger took over. Hollinger president David Radler, a.k.a. "The Human Chainsaw," radically cuts staff at small-circulation papers to create cash flow for new acquisitions. With fewer journalists on staff, news editors increasingly turn to the copy provided by organizations like the Fraser Institute to fill the "news holes" between advertisements in their papers.

The preference for right-wing copy starts at the top of Hollinger, with CEO Conrad Black and vice-president of editorial Barbara Amiel, whose neo-conservative views are documented in Maude Barlow and James Winter's *The Big Black Book: The Essential Views of Conrad and Barbara Amiel Black*. As well as running Amiel's weekly column, Black hired his cousin Andrew Coyne and Amiel's ex-husband, George Jonas, to flog their conservative views in Southam papers. David Radler, who has said it is important to have his employees fear him, states flatly that Hollinger papers, on principle, will endorse only free-enterprise parties, explicitly ruling out any paper's support for the NDP.[62]

Even with all the firings at Southam, journalists have been willing to admit that Black's influence is a factor in the newsroom. Karen

Sherlock, national editor at the *Edmonton Journal*, has said, "His shadow is a big shadow and we're feeling it."[63]

The transformation of *Saturday Night* magazine after Black bought it has also been a factor in the prevalence of right-wing opinion in the Canadian print media. With former *Alberta Report* staffer Kenneth Whyte as the magazine's editor, *Saturday Night* has been serving up a steady diet of Whyte's "advice for the right" columns, mean-spirited critiques of such Canadian heroes as anti-child labour activist Craig Kielburger and Farley Mowat, and articles on why women should be in the home rather than the workforce. *Saturday Night* gives yet another platform for Southam columnists Andrew Coyne and George Jonas to air their views, as well as to neo-conservative journalists from the Sun newspaper chain, such as David Frum, Michael Coren, and Peter Worthington.

In his biography of Conrad Black, *The Establishment Man*, published in 1982, Peter C. Newman provided an insight into the fate that would inevitably befall *Saturday Night* once Black took it over. Newman's book contains the following excerpt from a letter Black wrote to American arch-conservative William F. Buckley on how to change a magazine the way Buckley had transformed *National Review*:

> I take the liberty of writing to you on behalf of many members of the journalistic, academic and business communities of this country who wish to convert an existing Canadian magazine into a conveyance for views at some variance with the tired porridge of ideological normalcy in vogue here as in the U.S.A. [during the 1970s]. We are aware of the lack in Canada of serious editorial talent of an appropriate political coloration . . . We are, however, people of some means as well as of some conviction, and unless faced by an insuperable economic barrier, intend to persevere with our plans, to execution.[64]

As though the rightward turn of Canada's self-described "most influential magazine" was not enough, the Donner Foundation financed two new right-wing magazines. *Next City*, established in 1994 with a $1.4-million commitment from the foundation, seems to specialize in eroding compassion for the poor; writers since 1995 have celebrated Latin American shantytowns, portrayed beggars as scam artists, and declared that poverty is a matter of personal choice.

Editor Lawrence Solomon wrote in the summer 1996 issue that "for most people lifestyle choices dictate income levels, not the other way around." *Next City* has carried articles by Andrew Coyne, Fraser Institute senior fellow Filip Palda, and Fraser Institute writer Karen Selick, and has been distributed nationwide as an insert in the *Globe and Mail*.

The Donner Foundation gave a $390,000 grant in 1995 to neo-conservative Ian Garrick Mason to transform his newsletter, "Gravitas," into a quarterly magazine. *Gravitas* serves as a vehicle to distribute output from other Donner-funded organizations, such as the Fraser Institute, the Atlantic Institute for Market Studies, and the Society for Academic Freedom and Scholarship, whose members attempt to use research on brain size to attack anti-discrimination policies at universities.

Beyond the direct control that some of these owners exert over "their" media outlets (a *Vancouver Sun* reporter who asked to remain anonymous claims that David Radler calls the paper at least once a day to monitor content), there is the process of what Noam Chomsky calls "manufactured consent." Reporters, too, are subject to the tidal wave of neo-liberal and social conservative ideology sweeping over Canada from the dozens of sources outside the media. As in academia, those with left-wing or even moderately small-l liberal views feel pressured even by their colleagues to suppress their opinions, which in so many other venues are dismissed as archaic, naive, or flying in the face of the new "common sense." Public broadcasting is no less subject to these pressures, especially when right-wing commentators repeatedly single out the CBC for criticism.

The role of the public relations industry in selling corporate rule deserves a book of its own. The application of extremely sophisticated manipulative techniques in polling and the advertising that results from it are a critical element in the ideological assault on democracy. Some of the corporations engaged in this activity, like the giant Burson-Marsteller, are large transnationals in their own right. The largest, Burson-Marsteller, played a major role in selling NAFTA in the U.S.

Another public relations giant, Hill and Knowlton, gained notoriety for its "sales pitch" for the U.S. war on Iraq. President George Bush faced a disinterested American public not keen to save an obscenely wealthy and authoritarian elite in one country from the ruthless dictator of another. Hill and Knowlton, hired by the Kuwaiti government, put their people to work to come up with an image that would shake Americans out of their peaceful complacency. They came up with the story of Iraqi soldiers "ripping" premature babies from incubators in Kuwaiti hospitals, tossing them on the floor and stealing the incubators. The story was fabricated in a brainstorming session, as Hill and Knowlton later admitted, but it had the desired effect. In a famous documentary by the CBC's *fifth estate*, the young executive who "handled" the Kuwaiti account seemed completely unaffected by the fact that, as a result of his work (the incubator story was widely credited with shifting American public opinion), hundreds of thousands of people would die.

The political public relations industry's lack of morality is legendary; indeed, it almost defines the industry. It is characterized by the placing of powerful weapons of psychological manipulation in the hands of people who, in order to do their jobs, must cleanse themselves of ethical considerations. The most successful firms boast about how many corporate disasters they have managed to smooth over or spin into obscurity; how many deaths have been explained away. Typical services the spin industry provides to corporations are revealed in the brochure for Vancouver-based Verus Group International, which boasts in its list of accomplishments: "450 negative stories prevented, nine chemical spills explained, three mergers supported, six industrial deaths explained, 23 environmental protests handled."[65]

The application of public relations techniques to the political process is now a science. A particular type of polling, which reveals under what conditions people will accept change that their values would otherwise cause them to reject, is now commonplace. First used in the early 1980s in Canada, one of its original practitioners was Decima Research and its chief, Allan Gregg. One of Social Credit leader Bill Bennett's advisers described the service Gregg provided: "Decima believes that you can take [poll results] . . . and we can change your mind. We can move you to do something that you may not have agreed is the logical thing to do . . . We can move you to the other side of the ledger."[66]

Recent federal governments have taken the final step in merging policy making and public relations. They contract out much of the important policy development work to public relations firms that do polling, provide the research, and set the agenda. According to the CCPA's Duncan Cameron, "Even under the [Chrétien] Liberals most of the policy work in finance is done by the Earnscliffe [Research and Communications] Group, run by a Tory and ideologically preoccupied by the deficit."[67]

THE REFORM PARTY AND FRIENDS

The ideological activities of organizations like the Fraser Institute, the National Citizens' Coalition, and the C. D. Howe Institute all combine to undermine communitarian values and Canadians' faith in government. But these organizations focus primarily on neo-liberal economic, social, and fiscal policies. The assault on political culture comes from another source as well, and that is neo-conservatism, the expression of what are often called traditional values, particularly so-called family values.

Conservative ideology is expressed in the formal political arena by the Reform Party and its leader, Preston Manning. Manning's political roots are found in extremely conservative evangelical Christianity and are a significant part of the ideological fight against government. Manning's strategy since founding the Reform Party has been to promote the neo-liberal state by harnessing populist anger. The debates about abortion, gun control, immigration, the death penalty, youth crime, and human rights legislation such as affirmative action and so-called special rights for Quebec, aboriginals, and gays and lesbians have a dual impact on the political culture.

First, if one group is set against the other, any efforts to organize people around economic and social equality issues are made that much more difficult. Second, and perhaps more important, focussing on these volatile issues diverts attention from broader social and economic issues. In part, the appeal of such issues is rooted in the sense that here, at least, there are simple answers. People often feel ill equipped to cope with the larger questions of economic policy, the deficit, interest rates, "jobless" recoveries, and corporate power because all of these issues are put to them as inextricably linked to globalization. But youth crime seems open to obvious solutions — lock up young offenders at younger ages, for longer periods, and punish them with harsher treatment.

Central to this populist message is anger at or contempt for politicians and government, a sentiment that Manning, like his allies in the National Citizens' Coalition, carefully nurtures. This relentless attack serves to legitimize people's cynicism about politics (legitimate for other reasons as well), a feature that showed up dramatically in the 1997 federal election, which had one of the lowest voter turn-outs in sixty years.

In addition to undermining respect for the idea of government, Reform promotes the conservative values of the family, of women once again taking on the responsibility for social ills, of individual self-reliance, and charity. As the neo-liberal state cuts back and eliminates social programs, these "traditional" values are of great utility because they provide the rationale for shifting community and government responsibilities back onto women.

The influence of Reform has helped spawn supportive conservative social movements, which it then draws on for its electoral purposes. The Canadian Taxpayers' Federation has signed up tens of thousands of members at $50 a head in support of its campaign against the egalitarian state. Rather than attack social programs directly, the CTF typically goes after the "high taxes" Canadians pay. Originally organized as a virtual pyramid selling scheme, with most of the money going to its officers, the CTF and its provincial wings are, like the NCC, totally undemocratic. Members have no say in who runs the organizations, who is hired, how money is spent, or what the policies will be. There is considerable overlap between the Taxpayers' Federation and the Reform Party, as there is in the anti-gun control lobby, the anti-abortion movement, and the Ontario-based Alliance for the Preservation of English in Canada. All of these groups and movements have in common a visceral contempt for government, a theme they promote in virtually everything they do.

While Reform carefully nurtures its populist image, it is a party founded with corporate money from the Alberta oil patch. From the time he started the party, Preston Manning has made great efforts to attract corporate money, and in the past two years has been increasingly successful. Conrad Black's Hollinger and Canadian Pacific are two notable contributors in the past few years.

❖

Starting in the mid-1970s, the largest corporations in Canada launched a series of independent projects aimed at establishing a solid elite consensus regarding the long-term strategy of capital and the appropriate political direction of the country. The elite consensus was the job of groups like the Business Council on National Issues, other business organizations, and the C. D. Howe Institute. But the project to fundamentally change the political culture of the country, away from its communitarian tradition and towards a more individualistic bent, would be the job of a different set of agencies: arm's-length groups, funded and directed by corporations or corporate executives, but capable of acting as independent voices. They would be purveyors of ideology, not lobby groups for particular corporate interests.

Yet the massive output of the Fraser Institute, the NCC, and the C. D. Howe, popularized by the Reform Party and its allies, is only as good as the efforts to implement it into public policy. It is the strategic use of the issues these institutes and political organizations raise that determines the outcome for ordinary citizens. The goal of all of these efforts is, after all, the dismantling of the egalitarian state. Exactly how that was accomplished was played out in the broader political world in which governments used the scorched earth provided by the corporate propaganda agencies to implement the corporate counter-revolution.

9

PROPAGANDA WARS: THE REVOLUTION OF FALLING EXPECTATIONS

[A] large part of my message as a politician is to say: we have to put an end to rising expectations. We have to explain to people that we may even have to put an end to our love for our parents or old people in society, even our desire to give more for education or medical research.

— PIERRE TRUDEAU, JANUARY 1977

A campaign to lower our collective and individual expectations as citizens and as income earners has been under way for more than twenty years. That campaign has been waged by the two most powerful organizations in history, transnational corporations and the state. The range of institutions, organizations, and resources dedicated to selling this counter-revolution against civil society is staggering. And the targets are obvious. The notions of equality and fairness, of democracy, of governments acting for the public good, of a public service dedicated to the ideals of community, all of these ideas and values have come under an unprecedented assault by corporations and the institutions of ideological warfare labouring at their behest.

The reason is brutally simple. Corporations and the wealthy elite who run them and benefit from their power are determined to experience democracy never again. The post-war period, particularly the 1960s to early 1970s, was as close as liberal democracy has ever come to achieving equality and security in Canada. That period was an aberration, and the ruling elite intends to keep it that way. To do that, the expectations that citizens here and in other industrialized countries developed in that period must be wiped from the collective memory. Rid the world of those high expectations, pacify those who would otherwise challenge you, and you make it safe for capitalism.

This campaign is reminiscent of the U.S.-backed Contra war against the Nicaraguan revolution. The strategy was not to win a military victory; it was to destroy the dream of social justice. Thus the Contras attacked and destroyed schools, day-care centres, health clinics, workers' co-ops, indeed any government agency or service that was working to make life easier for peasants and workers. The message was unmistakable: forget about things getting any better. If you try to make them better, we will kill you.

In Canada the corporate agenda is the same even if the tactics are considerably less brutal. The goal is to ratchet down the expectations of the majority of Canadians regarding their standard of living and the quality of life of their communities. The campaign, started in earnest in the mid-1980s, has been multifaceted. The strategy is to attack government on a whole series of fronts with the intention of lowering expectations of what the state can or will do. The Fraser Institute, the NCC, the C. D. Howe Institute, the Reform Party, and the corporate media have spent their money with great strategic care on the propaganda machinery that the corporations finance directly.

First came debt terror. Then came the attack on public services; if public services were no good, then the more "efficient" private sector could do it better. When the free market failed to deliver on its promises and people worried about unemployment, the campaign declared regretfully that governments can't create jobs. And now we are entering the final campaign: tax cuts. Governments having been proven no good for anything, we will give customers their money back.

There will be, if these campaigns are successful, nowhere to run. Corporations and governments will have established a permanent state of insecurity whose impact on democracy will be profound.

The campaign to lower expectations was paralleled by the very real decrease in what government and the private sector delivered. First, the huge cuts to government spending reduced the sphere of action in which governments exercise their sovereignty. Second, the multilateral trade and investment deals further restrict what governments can do. In the private sector, the strategy is simple: in the context of a manufactured recession, demand more and more of workers and provide less and less; drive up the amount of work to be done, provide fewer full-time jobs, demand rollbacks or freeze wages. Put the fear of the depression years back into the hearts of workers.

THE DEFICIT SCARE

In the world of government "downsizing" propaganda, no other single idea, no other single aspect of public policy has been so effectively manipulated to turn back the egalitarian state as the debt/deficit issue. Indeed, the debt is so effective precisely because every other issue leads back to it. Try to force a government to defend medicare and the conversation turns to the deficit. If citizens demand that the government do something about unconscionably high unemployment rates, the government shrugs apologetically and says, as a title to a Canadian Centre for Policy Alternatives booklet put it, "The Deficit Made Me Do It." You simply cannot have a discussion about public policy without reference to the debt and deficit. Even with the deficit disappearing, the huge debt looms in the background like some monster the government can set loose whenever it chooses.

The deficit hysteria campaign began in earnest the day after the free-trade election on November 22, 1988. The noon-hour news on CBC Radio announced that the country faced a debt "crisis." It must have developed overnight: there had been no mention of it during the election. And, in what became a consistent pattern, the reporter did not question this declaration, its source, or its suddenness. The love affair between the media and the deficit story had begun.

For the Tories, the debt crisis campaign could not be launched too early. Deficit talk had begun some years earlier and was simply eclipsed by the free-trade debate that raged months before the election was called. But cranking up the deficit volume became a critical strategy precisely because of the free-trade fight. Opponents of the deal had zeroed in on medicare and social programs as Canadian institutions threatened by the deal. The government and its allies had been obliged so many times to deny this claim that their denial became imprinted in the public memory. Any hint that medicare or education were going to be sacrificed to free trade, and the government would have been pilloried.

The Free Trade Agreement was, in any case, just one piece in the restructuring of the country. The free-trade imperative worked inexorably to lower all Canadian government social programs and regulatory regimes to U.S. levels. The use of the debt to justify cuts to social programs was a useful back-door route to implement the implied objectives of deregulated trade and investment. But it had a much wider application. The persistent claim that social programs caused the debt had a dual purpose. By justifying reduced spending on social programs, the state increased the insecurity of most Canadians. And by blaming the debt on social programs, government reduced expectations by implying that we could not afford them and by making people feel greedy for wanting them.

I will show decisively, later in this chapter, that social programs have not contributed significantly to the country's debt, nor to the provincial debts. The neo-conservative ideologues know this; the corporate think-tanks know it, too. But only on rare occasions do any of them admit it publicly. As the Canadian Centre for Policy Alternatives noted, "In the United States . . . David Stockwell and other officials in the Reagan administration now openly admit that, at the behest of their corporate friends, they deliberately increased the deficit so that it would justify later cuts in social programs funding."[1]

In Saskatchewan the Devine government dramatically decreased the royalties on oil and gas and thus added more than $4.5 billion to the provincial debt inherited by the NDP.[2] Next door in Alberta the debt story was almost identical. The Klein government railed on about public spending "skyrocketing" out of control. The truth lay elsewhere. Former civil servant Kevin Taft, himself a Tory, revealed in his exposé *Shredding the Public Interest* that government spending had been declining since the 1980s — long before Klein came to office in 1992. The debt was due exclusively to massive subsidies to corporations and to falling resource revenue.

It was important in the neo-conservative plan that the issue of the debt be presented as a crisis and not just a problem. The word *debt* appeared only attached to the word *crisis*. If it was just a problem, it would be commonplace; if it was a crisis, people would be prepared to make sacrifices. This political wisdom was put forward in 1993 at a colloquium put on by the International Institute for Economics, a Washington-based think-tank, to examine how governments in various countries could sell the policies of structural adjustment. The goal was to produce a "manual for technocrats and technopols involved in implementing structural adjustment programmes."[3]

A key hypothesis tested at the event was formulated by its convenor, economist John Williamson. According to New Zealand analyst Jane Kelsey, Williamson argued that societies tend to become "sclerotic and their flexibility declines. When a major crisis occurs within the existing system, it creates new opportunities for actors who until then have been prevented from taking the initiative. Where a crisis does not occur 'naturally,' it might make sense to provoke one to induce reform."[4] Williamson could have used Canada as a case study.

The campaign to sell the idea of a debt crisis involved dozens of players from nearly every sector of the ruling elite: politicians, corporate think-tanks, media owners, key columnists and broadcasters, academic economists, financial analysts, the Bank of Canada, and even, on occasion, foreign commentators as well as foreign bond-rating agencies. Even the IMF gave the debt warriors a hand. One might be forgiven for suspecting a conspiracy. But this just underlines the strength of the elite when it has reached a consensus, particularly one rooted in an ideology that all can adopt on faith rather than reason.

Corporate think-tanks and alliances took the lead in creating deficit hysteria. The BCNI's key anti-deficit document was entitled "Canada's Looming Debt Crisis." According to Seth Klein, coordinator of the B.C. branch of the Canadian Centre for Policy Alternatives, "During January and February, 1993, a team from the BCNI took the report on the road, visiting the premiers of New Brunswick, Quebec, Saskatchewan, British Columbia, Nova Scotia, and Manitoba, the finance minister of Ontario, Kim Campbell, Jean Charest, and the Liberal shadow cabinet."[5] Sam Boutziouvis, the BCNI's senior economist at the time, was happy with the council's overall efforts. "Did we have an effect there? I believe we did."[6] The C. D. Howe Institute was also pleased with its propaganda efforts, including its major piece, "The Courage to Act: Fixing Canada's Budget and Social Policy Deficits." According to the co-author Tom Kierans, "This has been a time of high visibility . . . In recent months our studies have reverberated in newspaper editorials across the country, on television news, and in parliamentary debates."[7]

The campaign was waged with particular ferocity by columnists such as Peter Cook, Terence Corcoran, and Diane Francis and media commentators like the C. D. Howe's William Robson and right-wing darling David Frum. Andrew Coyne, then writing for the *Globe and Mail*, told Peter Gzowski that "denying the debt problem is akin to denying the holocaust" and implied that writer Linda McQuaig was "out of her mind" for criticizing the Bank of Canada's high interest rate policy. Popular broadcasters also took up the call, with Mike Duffy, Michael Campbell, and Eric Malling all hammering on the issue. Malling produced an inflammatory and extremely influential W5 documentary on New Zealand's alleged "debt crisis" asking the rhetorical question about Canada's chances of hitting the "debt wall."

The debt warriors even managed to get some mercenaries from the U.S. onside. One prominent commentator generously called Canada a "banana republic" because of its debt. The more vigorous of Canada's debt warriors were hard on the mercenaries when they didn't perform up to snuff. In her book *Shooting the Hippo*, Linda McQuaig tells the story of interviewing Vincent Truglia, one of the most feared bond raters in New York, specializing in Canada for Moody's Investors Service. McQuaig expected a lecture about Canada's high debt but instead got a tirade "against members of the Canadian investment community for overblowing Canada's debt problems."[8]

The fact that Canada's debt situation never resulted in a credit downgrade was almost never commented upon. At the height of the ideological assault on the deficit, Moody's Investors Service stated: "We see no significantly negative trends in Canada's debt burden that could justify a change in the (triple-A) ratings of the nation's Canadian dollar and foreign currency debt. Canada's an extraordinarily low risk; that's the message."[9] While such expressions of confidence in Canada's debt management were quietly reported in the business pages, they were studiously avoided in the popular media.

Canada's bonds were always snapped up immediately, and in 1997, when the federal government issued no new bonds for the first time in twenty-five years, investors panicked about a "bond shortage." As economist Jim Stanford pointed out, if Canada's $600-billion debt suddenly vanished, "brokers would be leaping from their skyscrapers over the sudden loss of such a lucrative and risk free investment outlet."[10]

One of the most effective pieces in the debt arsenal was the argument that government was just like a household and no household could survive for long spending more money than it took in. "Putting our fiscal house in order" appeals to people's sense of personal and social responsibility. Just as it would be irresponsible to burden your family with debt by spending beyond your means, so too is it irresponsible to create a "legacy of debt" for future generations.

This argument is simply false. Governments, unlike families, have enormous authority and capacity to determine their revenues. They can increase taxes, lower interest on their own debt, stimulate the economy to create jobs and revenue. As well, no indebted family would slash everything in its budget; it would cut out luxuries first and only then cut back on essentials. Canadian governments, however, have slashed such essentials as health care, education, and social services. There is little talk among the elite of the legacy to our children of gutted social programs and a crumbling education system.

Seth Klein documented the propaganda techniques in his study on the debt, "Good Sense versus Common Sense: Canada's Debt Debate and Competing Hegemonic Projects." The arguments were designed to overwhelm any sceptics, with so many negative consequences of government deficits that no one in the opposition ranks is left standing. "The country will soon hit a 'debt wall,' the debt prevents Canada from lowering interest rates, and the foreign debt threatens Canadian sovereignty; the debt discourages and 'crowds-out' private sector investment; . . . the government has no room to raise taxes; the country cannot escape its debt crisis through increased economic growth; and the private sector, left free of government interference, will undertake productive investment," if the debt is brought down.[11]

The source of the debt was rarely spoken of by neo-conservative players. And in the end it didn't matter. The debt was so serious that only by huge cuts could we solve the problem. The debt took on the character of an infestation that had to be destroyed at any cost.

THE REAL DEBT PROBLEM

Let's be clear here, the debt was and is a problem. Any time we are spending thirty cents out of every tax dollar in interest payments we have a problem. But the debt is not *the* problem. The crisis is not the debt itself but in how and why it was accumulated and the way it is being addressed by current governments and their corporate benefactors. Canada and other Western countries have had very large debts before, but they were never viewed as a "crisis" in the same way the debt is portrayed today in Canada.

Debts were viewed as a problem, and governments set out to solve the problem at the same time as they set out to build a growing and stable economy. In short, the solution was part of a broad economic policy. The debt issue was resolved as the result of economic and industrial policies designed to accomplish other objectives, economic and social.

Jim Stanford, an economist with the Canadian Auto Workers, suggests a number of reasons why the debt is a problem. First, the accumulation of the huge debt means that it must be paid off, and that represents a massive transfer of wealth from poor, working, and middle-class Canadians to the wealthiest Canadians and the largest corporations. Tax money collected from the vast majority of Canadians goes to wealthy and corporate bondholders. Stanford argues that this transfer of tens of billions of dollars is "more regressive than other income redistribution issues (such as the negative distribution effects of consumption taxes)."[12]

The fall-out of debt terrorism on the public can hardly be over-estimated. Even in 1997, when the federal deficit and several provincial deficits are under control and even disappearing, the effect of ten years of bullying and fear-mongering is still ingrained in the public psyche. It is no longer as prominent in the propaganda of the neo-conservative forces, yet it underlies other campaigns and haunts any talk of increased public spending.

It is important to know where the debt came from, so we can

understand where it fits in the whole restructuring package and in the propaganda used to sell it. Deliberately created or not, the debt was the result of a series of interrelated neo-conservative policies, all of which were designed to enhance the corporate bottom line.

The federal debt was accumulated over a period of twenty years starting in 1975, the result of three government actions. The first was a shift to monetarism, which handed the money-creation powers of the Bank of Canada to the private banks. The second was a number of policies, including the deindexing of income tax and a huge increase in the number of tax expenditures (grants provided through the tax system) for the wealthy and Canada's largest corporations, which contributed to a dramatic decline in revenue beginning in the mid-1970s. The third and arguably the most important government policy was the crusade against inflation, a high interest rate/high unemployment policy aimed at bringing inflation to zero, which caused interest payments on the debt to skyrocket.

In 1975, when the Bank of Canada adopted monetarism as its broad policy approach, it abandoned its post-war practice of financing a good part of federal and provincial deficits through what amounted to interest-free or low-interest loans. In 1974 the Bank of Canada held 20.7 percent of the federal debt; in 1994 it held just 5.8 percent.

As the government adopted monetarism, it launched an unprecedented number of tax incentives for business and wealthy investors. The measures failed to create jobs, and the resulting loss of revenues has amounted to tens of billions of dollars over the past two decades. Researcher Kirk Falconer looked at corporate tax breaks and found that untaxed profits had steadily increased from $9.9 billion (from 62,619 corporations) in 1980 to $27 billion (from 93,405 corporations) in 1987. The total exceeded $125 billion for the eight years. This was just for corporations that managed to reduce their taxes to zero; many more billions were lost in reduced taxes.

The majority of this largesse went to the largest corporations, many of them foreign-owned. In 1987, fully 84 percent of those untaxed profits were earned by corporations earning $1 million or more in profits; 57 percent were accounted for by those earning $25 million or more. For this latter group, 145 of the very largest corporations in Canada, the average untaxed profit was $106.4 million.[13]

By 1980 the accumulating debt was getting serious; it was about to go through the roof. Interest rates hit 20 percent and the interest payments on the debt skyrocketed. Following this period of astronomically high rates, the Bank of Canada launched its high interest rate crusade for zero inflation, which lasted through 1995. The combination meant that by 1992 the accumulating interest payments had outstripped the original debt.

In 1991 the extent to which the revenue crisis and the high interest rates had generated the large federal debt, then at $420 billion, was revealed in a Statistics Canada study that looked at the accumulation of the debt between 1975 and 1991. The study revealed that 50 percent of the debt was due to shortfalls in revenue, that is, a decline in revenues relative to the growth in GDP, much of it a result of tax breaks for corporations and wealthy individuals. Interest charges accounted for 44 percent of the debt by 1991, and just 6 percent was from increases in program spending.[14] The study was so damaging to the carefully constructed neo-con view of the debt that the finance department tried to suppress it.

A 1995 report issued by the Dominion Bond Rating Service confirmed the Statscan study and other analysts' contention that interest charges were a key factor in the burgeoning debt. The study pointed out that the entire accumulated program deficit was created between 1975 and 1985. From 1986 to 1995 there was a $12-billion surplus. All the rest was interest charges.[15]

The Bank of Canada's policy of high interest rates was the principal tool in the government's strategy to create, in the words of the Bank of International Settlements, "more satisfactory levels of unemployment." The cost of "disciplining workers" shows up as a staggering cost to the country.

Examining the figures for 1992 and 1993, economists Diane Bellemare and Lise Poulin-Simon calculated that for each 1 percent of unemployment the costs to the government in lost direct taxes exceeds $3 billion, in indirect taxes just over $2 billion, and $1.2 billion in additional social assistance spending. If the $1.2-billion drain on the unemployment insurance system is added in, the total cost to the treasury of each 1 percent in unemployment weighs in at $7.4 billion a year. The total cost to the economy from unemployment — including lost wages, profits, and tax revenue — amounted to $109 billion in 1993.[16]

The Bank of Canada's high interest policy went far beyond that waged by the Federal Reserve Board in the U.S. and accounts in large measure for the difference in unemployment levels between the two countries. But it wasn't just the high interest rates that flattened the economy. According to a CIBC/Wood Gundy study, the government's spending cuts reduced growth by 3.5 percent from 1994 through 1996.[17] Independent economists such as Pierre Fortin put the cost of the cumulative unemployment at "about $400 billion in forgone national income" between 1990 and 1996, equal to 30 percent of the losses of the Great Depression.[18]

Of the G7 countries only Canada recorded a net loss in GDP between 1990 and 1995. An OECD survey of GDP growth from 1989 to 1996 showed that of thirteen developed countries only Canada had a negative growth.[19]

The question is not whether to bring down the debt but how to bring it down. In a democracy there are always alternatives. The Canadian Centre for Policy Alternatives and the Manitoba social justice coalition Choices have since 1995 produced the Alternative Federal Budget (AFB), a comprehensive proposal for government spending and tax measures presented as a clear and progressive alternative to the federal Liberals' annual budget. Produced with the input of dozens of economists and advocacy groups, it is an unprecedented example of democratic budget making and has garnered endorsements from 164 economists and political economists in universities across the country.

On the spending side, the AFB questions government priorities by focussing on unemployment and poverty. It established National Social Investment Funds in the areas of health care, education, income support, child care, retirement income, unemployment insurance, and housing. It also includes specific measures to increase employment. The AFB would see federal spending gradually increase to levels experienced in the 1980s. Seventy percent of the new revenue would come from increased economic growth, but it would also come from fair tax reform, which would raise an additional $5 billion.[20]

The AFB's plan is deliberately modest. Other critics of the Liberals, including tax policy expert Neil Brooks, have called for more radical measures, including eliminating $3 billion in corporate tax breaks, and an $8-billion decrease in personal tax exemptions. Another method by which the government could raise tax revenue and at the same time cool money speculation, particularly in bond markets, would be to impose a domestic financial transactions tax. This tax, applied to every sale of stocks and bonds, is applied already in a dozen OECD countries, including Britain, France, Germany, Italy, and Hong Kong. Even Singapore, a model of corporate libertarianism, has such a tax. A financial transactions tax set as low as 0.1 percent would reduce speculation and encourage productive investment and would, according to economist Jack Biddell, raise about $27 billion in revenue each year, compared to $17.4 billion raised by the regressive GST.[21]

The question, of course, has never been whether or not the money is there. It has always been a question of corporate domination and the power of the ideology supporting that domination.

Governments of all persuasions, infected by this market ideology, took advantage of the propaganda and have been cutting social spending for ten years. But that cutting was still no easy task. The values of Canadians have proven remarkably resilient. The 1994 Ekos poll "Rethinking Government" proved that, as did many other polls. Neo-cons like Andrew Coyne have ridiculed the idea that a country can define itself by its social programs precisely because they know the idea is so popular. It is also dangerous: it is one of the few aspects of government that people can still identify as fundamentally linked to the notion of a collectivity, a community. So the corporate elite and their neo-con allies had to open a second front: trash public services.

THE ATTACK ON PUBLIC SERVICES

The attack on public services has necessarily been more complicated compared to the debt war, which had the advantage of having a clear and simple target. The motivations for social program cuts were also more complex. There had to be deep cuts to social assistance and unemployment programs because these directly supported workers in their fight with employers for a share of output. Medicare and education were the largest expenditures, but cuts here had additional long-term goals. As we will see below, corporations are eager to invest in these areas because the profits are potentially so enormous. As well, the free marketeers recognize that these programs are the main source of public support for government. Breach this defensive wall, the new right reasons, and the rest will crumble. Other programs, particularly in the area of culture and heritage, were to be cut because they provided a strong national identity, which reinforced people's high expectations of government and their sense of social solidarity.

The attack on public services does not address all these particulars openly. While some programs, like EI and welfare, are criticized for "encouraging unemployment," the attack on public services is broad-based. Various arguments are used to undermine support for social spending. Canadian social programs are "too generous"; government service monopolies are inefficient and need competition; public services are dominated by vested interests and bureaucratic "empires" and are "not accountable" to the public; public services are simply not working any more and therefore not worth defending; universality in social programs should be replaced by two-tiered services, that will "free up" public services while the wealthy pay for their own.

One of the main propaganda pieces in the attack on medicare and education is that we are spending too much, with the mantra that health-care costs are spiralling out of control. This is the classic big lie, since this has never been proven anywhere in Canada. In Saskatchewan, for example, health care took up 31.2 percent of the program budget in 1980 and 32.1 percent in 1990. By 1995, public spending on health care in Canada was at its lowest level since the introduction of medicare in the 1960s.

The attacks on the public education system, like those on medicare, claim we are spending far more than other countries and that we are not getting our money's worth in quality. This too is false. The figures used include post-secondary education, and Canada has had one of the highest levels of post-secondary participation of any country in the OECD.

Of course, these attacks go well beyond costs. The Fraser Institute's bogus study regarding waiting times is typical of the fear-mongering, and critics of public education continue to use false and misleading claims to raise parents' fears. The one-two propaganda punch of excessive spending and poor results is intended to weaken public support for the two most important community services.

The notion that Canadian social programs are too generous was a familiar theme throughout the early 1990s in preparation for the Liberals' huge budget cuts from 1994 on. Yet the argument had no basis in fact, unless the country we were being compared with was the U.S. An OECD comparison of seventeen industrial nations in 1990, when the propaganda campaign began, revealed that Canada was one of the most miserly of any of the developed countries. The study revealed that Canada placed fourteenth, tied with New Zealand, for the percentage of GDP going to social spending. In that year Canada spent 18.8 percent of GDP on social programs, lower only than Australia, the U.S., and Japan (11.6 percent). The U.K., Germany, and France spent more, and Sweden 33.9 percent. Far from being generous, the OECD report indicated that Canada would have had to increase its social spending by $18 billion just to meet the average of the OECD countries.[22]

There are a great deal more data showing how inferior Canada's social programs are compared to other industrial nations. Even in 1991, before the UI program was slashed, Canada ranked sixteenth out of nineteen OECD countries in "generosity."[23] At the time Canada had one of the highest unemployment rates of any OECD nation, putting in serious doubt the claim that our "overly generous" UI was causing unemployment. The program now ranks with Japan's as the stingiest of any OECD country, with 46 percent of the unemployed eligible for benefits, below that of the U.S.

As seen in chapter 6, Canada's social assistance programs rank below many of those in the U.S., in spite of popular notions to the contrary. Canada's maternity-leave provisions are equally tightfisted. Of twenty-four countries (the U.S. and Australia provide no benefits), Canada placed fourth last in the number of weeks covered and dead last for rate of benefits as a percentage of salary.

It is clear now that the Liberal government's objective from the beginning has been not deficit reduction but a dramatically reduced government presence in the economy, a systematic shrinking of the egalitarian state. This was stated explicitly in a 1995 speech by Finance Minister Paul Martin at Jackson Hole, Wyoming, in which he boasted that Canada would be spending significantly less than the U.S. within two years. "Looking to 1996–97, the U.S. budget forecasts a reduction to 16.3 percent of GDP while Canada's ratio will have fallen to just over 13 percent, the lowest level since the 1950s."[24] In fact he beat his own target, lowering spending to 1949 levels and to about 12 percent of GDP. This is what gets Martin his greatest accolades on Bay Street and admiration on Wall Street.

The new-right argument that public services are dominated by bureaucratic "empires" unaccountable to the public is propaganda at its most transparent. The bureaucracy that runs the medicare system in the U.S., the paragon of free-market health care, is so sclerotic and byzantine that it is hard to find anyone who can adequately explain just how it works. We do know that the administrative costs of that system, a good indicator of bureaucratic gridlock, are more than double those of the public system in Canada. As for accountability, that depends on how you define it. For the 40 million Americans who cannot get coverage at all, the American system must seem very unaccountable.

The attack on public services is often couched in terms of attacks on those who provide those services. The number of times that service providers, civil servants, and government employees are referred to as "bureaucrats" in the media reveals something of this campaign to discredit those hired by the community who provide services *to* the community. Government workers are portrayed as selfish, lazy, overpaid, incompetent, resistant to reforms, and, through their unions, protective of an overly generous system of privileges.

The objective in this campaign is to portray public servants as alien to the community, rather than as serving it. Portraying civil servants bargaining for a new contract as selfish individuals who should be grateful that they have a job is intended to distance the public from the people who provide it with services. Characterizing workers in this manner undermines public confidence in public services and therefore makes it easier for government to cut them. It is a divide-and-conquer tactic, encouraging one set of victims to resent another set while the victimizer accomplishes his goals with impunity.

This portrayal of public servants is obviously false. Besides providing crucial services, civil servants, like other working people, are family breadwinners. They spend hundreds of millions of dollars in their local communities, they are volunteers, they are people's neighbours, they have kids in local schools, they pay taxes. They are, in short, citizens like everyone else, with the same concerns for the future and, indeed, in need of the same public services as everyone else.

Everyone has an anecdote about bad service or surly treatment from a civil servant somewhere, but neo-con propaganda often magnifies these to mythic proportions. Meanwhile, in the private sector, fraud, overpricing, price fixing, bad service, shoddy and dangerous goods, and outright theft are commonplace. But this is somehow expected of the private sector, which Canadians instinctively know has lower ethical standards. It is ironic that part of the assault on pubic services, of which people demand high standards, is to suggest that the private sector can do the job better.

The notion that civil servants are overpaid, even at the highest level of the public service, is nonsense. Senior policy analysts and administrators would quickly double or triple their salaries if they went to the private sector. Martin Harts, compensation specialist with the forecasting firm KPMG, points out that a deputy minister's salary and benefits package is about $175,000, compared with the $1.3-million average paid to CEOs with similar responsibilities.[25] Unfortunately, with that kind of lure, many have left. While the federal civil service has declined by 20 percent overall, the number of managers has gone down 33 percent. But thousands of civil servants stay in the public service *despite* working conditions that have steadily worsened throughout the 1990s. Federal civil servants have gone six years without a pay increase, an inexcusable way of treating those who serve the country. The media, content to play their role in discrediting government, miss the irony of business voices attacking "bureaucrats" as incompetent and overpaid and then, when they are laid off, hiring them at many times their former pay.

Social workers face ever increasing caseloads yet stay on the job because they are committed to the work. The same is true of nurses, teachers, childcare workers, employees protecting the environment and ensuring safe food as well as the thousands of people who work in administration. Stevie Cameron's book *On the Take*, on Brian Mulroney, documents many examples of senior civil servants who quietly defended the public interest against an assortment of political crooks and opportunists, often at great cost to their careers.

The assault on public services is, in part, designed to reduce the confidence of people in public services and to drive a wedge between them and government. But a related objective is to open up huge new areas of investment for the billions of dollars roaming the world looking for places to make a profit. Thus the attack on the effectiveness and cost of public services has one ultimate purpose: prepare the ground for privatization. The underlying message: we should hand over our services to the lean, efficient, accountable private sector.

Even a cursory examination of the private sector's record of efficiency, performance, and accountability demonstrates that handing our public services over to corporations would be disaster for citizens and communities. This is true even if we just examine the behaviour, since 1980, of the world's largest corporations. In Canada and elsewhere, they have been characterized by unbridled greed, spectacular examples of fraud, and the longest period of unproductive speculation in decades, possibly in this entire century. Throughout the latter half of the 1980s and continuing to today, enormous sums, far outweighing new productive investment, were put into leveraged buy-outs, hostile takeovers, stock and money market manipulations, and real estate speculation.

Business culture in Canada and the U.S. is full of stories about criminal fraud by people who were lauded as brilliant and heroic before they were caught. The Canadian fraud artists and their takes have included Donald Cormie ($491 million), Robert Vesco ($220 million), Leonard Rosenberg ($131.8 million), and Julius Melnitzer ($75 million), to mention just a few.[26] This kind of outrageous and destructive fraud is nonexistent in the history of the public service. Yet we are being asked to put the most important aspects of our community into the hands of this sick subculture of greed and corruption.

Beyond this sorry record, the structure of North American corporations is more bureaucratic than any government department or "state monopoly." According to researcher David Gordon, corporate bureaucracies in the U.S. and Canada distinguish themselves among developed countries by their extremely top-heavy management. In 1993, as many as 16.6 million people were employed in the U.S. as managers or supervisors. This was almost as many people as worked in the entire public service of the U.S., and the cost in salaries was

$1.3 trillion, almost a quarter of the total national income.[27]

This bloated bureaucracy, according to Gordon, is rooted in the ten-year effort to "discipline" labour out of its share of output. The destruction of unions in the U.S., the downward pressure on wages (real wages are now at 1967 levels), and the trend to contingent labour have resulted in the need for more and more supervisors. The strained labour relations that arise out of this strategy require "the threat of job dismissal as a goad to workers." The alternative model used in Europe emphasizes job security, wage incentives, and employee involvement in decision making.

"In such a hierarchy," Gordon writes, "you need supervisors to supervise the supervisors . . . and superiors above them and managers to watch the higher level supervisors and higher level managers to watch the lower-level managers." You also need to maintain a signif-icant wage differential to keep the hierarchy working. As CEOs demand higher compensation, "they find that they have to allow for upward creep in the salaries of their managerial and supervisory sub-ordinates as well," whether they deserve it or not.[28] The money for high wages for nonproductive staff comes out of workers' earnings and what might otherwise have been retained for new investment.

The corporate drive for privatization has a simple motive: the huge areas covered by public services provide the single largest area for investment remaining in developed countries. Health and education alone would absorb hundreds of billions of dollars in capital investment in Canada. So privatization is a key dimension of the new-right agenda. It not only provides enormous new areas for profitable investment. It also eliminates the example of public-purpose enterprises and the challenge they present to private corporations.

The particular way privatization has been implemented has also has been used to shift the political culture from communitarian values to those of possessive individualism. The privatization program of Margaret Thatcher in Britain, subsequently copied in Australia, New Zealand, and Canada, has often set out to build a social base for the new-right counter-revolution. Madsen Pirie, one of Thatcher's prin-cipal consultants on privatization, also advised the Saskatchewan Tory government of Grant Devine.

The strategy is a crude appeal to greed. Make a public share offering to all citizens (offering them the opportunity to "own" shares in an enterprise they already own as citizens) at a cut-rate price. The share price typically rises rapidly to something approaching its real value, whereupon most initial purchasers sell at a tidy profit. The provincially owned potash industry in Saskatchewan was sold off for approximately half its market value. Within a few short years, the majority of the shares were owned by large investors.

But all those "successful" small investors were, or so the theory goes, bitten by the market bug, many for the first time. That would lead, suggested Pirie and others, to more middle-class people getting into the stock market, helping build a base of supporters who would defend later market reforms. The Devine government took the propaganda dimension one step further, setting up a department just for privatization: the Department of Public Participation.

When privatization ideology becomes aggressive, it can simply declare that government should not be in any business, period. This was the case with the Alberta Liquor Control Board. A study by four University of Alberta academics shows that the privatization "was conceived with little thought, and implemented in haste." The study reveals what Albertans already knew: prices were higher, and selection declined The government also lost $400 million in annual revenue, gaining only $40 million from the sale of the board's assets, half what they cost originally. Thirteen hundred full-time jobs, at an average wage of $30,000, were lost. The new system pays workers between 35 and 50 percent less, resulting in less spending in the community and a loss of tax revenue.[29] It was almost as if the Klein government punished itself for ever daring to have a public enterprise.

The experience of privatization in Britain has been a disaster, with the level of services plummeting, CEOs taking home obscene pay packages, companies earning enormous returns on investment, and a failure in most cases to maintain the assets, which in many cases were sold at cut-rate prices. The *Globe and Mail*'s *Report on Business* declared in 1996 that "the British experience with privatization can claim few successes." The article starts out with an account of the newly privatized bus service in North London. "The posted timetable tantalizingly promises a bus every ten minutes . . . But half an hour has elapsed by the time the . . . bus finally trundles into view. There is a near riot when the people realize that they can't get on the crowded vehicle."[30]

The greatest failure of Thatcher's scheme was its inability to make good on the most important free-market promise, that of choice. British citizens, it seems, not only have lost their sovereignty as citizens by losing public assets, but have gained precious little in the way of consumer sovereignty in return. In part, this is because competition, the panacea for everything evil about state services, simply doesn't work for things like water, gas, and electricity. If you get lousy bus service, you don't get to patronize another bus line. There isn't any.

Privatization of water in Britain has become a nightmare. The system breaks down so often that, on average, nearly a third of the water piped into the system leaks out again. Lawsuits abound: there have been 250 successful prosecutions since Thatcher privatized water in 1990; and throughout 1996 there were, on average, successful prosecutions of water companies once every three weeks. The papers are full of stories about people who are forced to make do with a basin of water a day. Low-income people have been cut off for nonpayment. Rate increases have averaged 85 percent and in some areas exceeded 300 percent.[31]

MEDICAL CARE AMERICAN-STYLE

Even if the bloated corporate bureaucracy was pared down, some services just aren't appropriate for the private sector. The record of health care in the U.S. is one dramatic example as horror stories continue to emerge from that profit-driven system.

In the U.S. most people get their medical insurance through their employers as part of their benefits package. In the 1980s medical insurance premiums skyrocketed. Many employers experienced 35 to 40 percent annual premium increases, and they began demanding cost controls. The solution that developed was HMOs, or health maintenance organizations. They are a frightening example of what happens when you apply the ruthlessness of corporate cost control to the health of citizens.

In his book *Health Against Wealth: HMOs and the Breakdown of Medical Trust*, George Anders tells horror story after horror story about the "managed care" system. Like the parents of a baby boy in Georgia who had to race 42 miles to get treatment for their baby's meningo-coccemia because their managed care plan would not pay for care at a more expensive, but closer hospital. The boy survived, but only after having his feet and hands amputated, something doctors said might not have been necessary had he been treated even a few minutes sooner.[32]

Other evidence was provided by Dr. Linda Pino, a former "physician executive" with managed care plans. Pino explains, "The gate-keeper position . . . limits access to other specialists or other tests because he or she is being paid a lump sum to take care of all their patients and if they don't spend their money they get to keep it when it's left over." Dr. Pino is the kind of doctor who terrifies the HMO industry — a whistle blower. When she testified at a congressional hearing, her opening words brought dead silence to the room. "I am here primarily today to make a public confession. As a physician I denied a man a necessary operation that would have saved his life and thus I caused his death. No person and no group has held me accountable for this because in fact what I did saved a company a half a million dollars . . . If I am an expert here today it is because I know how managed care maims and kills patients so I am here to tell you about the dirty work of managed care."[33] Pino's job as a "physician reviewer" was to maintain a denial rate of at least 10 percent or she would be replaced. Her employer offered the physician with the highest denial rate a Christmas bonus.

Managed care is already coming to Canada. The huge American health corporations, which must like all corporations grow just to survive, are eyeing the Canadian system as an investment opportunity. Hospitals are already applying the gate-keeper principles to health care, according to Pat Armstrong, an authority on Canadian health care. "It has a multitude of forms; it's there already . . . private labs, rehab hospitals, the [corporate] management of the more public hospitals. It's happening in ways that are just so hard for Canadians to see that before we know it there will be nothing to defend unless we defend it right now."[34]

The giant health corporations like Columbia/HCA, Tenet Health-care Corp., and Kaiser Permanente have plans to set up for-profit hospitals either alone or in partnership with Canadian corporations like MDS. The insurance companies — Sun Life, Manulife, Liberty

Mutual, and Great-West Life — are already taking advantage of governments' continued "delisting" of services from public health coverage. (Virtually none of the new procedures in medicine are now added to the list of covered items.)

Although Canada does not yet have HMOs and for-profit hospitals, the business-oriented philosophy behind them is seeping in. One example of the intrusion of corporate values into public medicare is the software being purchased by Canadian hospitals that includes patient classifications designed according to cost-cutting criteria. "Some call it an evidence-based approach," says Pat Armstrong, "others call it assembly-line health care." It is an insidious process because there are no announcements that the philosophy is changing, no debates in Parliament, and nothing in the way of visible decisions that patients and their families can document. This is commercialization by stealth.

Two parallel developments are setting up Canadian medicare for incremental privatization. Cuts to health-care budgets are forcing more health-care services out of the public realm and into the private. (Nearly 30 percent of money spent on health care was being spent in the private sector in 1997, compared to 23 percent in 1986.) At the same time, medicare is being commercialized, blurring the differences between private and public health care, differences that form the basis of popular support for the public system. As those differences blur, the rationale for defending the public system gradually disappears.

The Canadian government, despite its statements about the importance of medicare, is complicit in this shift. In 1995 representatives of government and health corporations gathered in Singapore to discuss "corporatizing, commercializing and privatizing opportunities [in the] most rapidly expanding market in the world."[35] As Ottawa's power to maintain national standards erodes, most provinces are moving to regionalization of health care, in effect voluntarily weakening provincial authority and empowering regional authorities to pursue private options.

Ever expanding U.S. health corporations are driving the global health-privatization push. According to health researcher Colleen Fuller, U.S. health corporations are amongst the most fierce opponents of so-called trade barriers erected by countries like Canada to protect public health care. Many of these barriers have already fallen with NAFTA, and more will fall if the MAI is successful. The U.S. giants promise to bring a number of trends to Canada. The American focus on high-tech care has resulted in skyrocketing health costs in that country and, says Fuller, "massive increases in profits of drug, hospital and insurance corporations."[36]

In addition, the trend in the U.S. has been to de-skilling, replacing professional staff with unlicensed, unskilled, inexperienced, and cheaper staff. These trends have made the health "industry" the most profitable sector in the States. Dr. David Himmelstein of Harvard Medical School concluded from his comparison of the Canadian and American systems that private providers are "extraordinarily efficient at extracting money from the health-care system. Other than that, there's not an iota of evidence of greater efficiency in the for-profit sector."[37]

TARGETING EDUCATION

Medicare is a hot issue in Canada, and because of its obvious public popularity, the media have provided some coverage of the threat posed by cuts and the growing portion of the system falling into private hands. Yet the ideological attacks on the education system are much more fierce than those against medicare, and the threat of privatization and commercialization of education is very real.

As with other public services, the groundwork for corporate incursions into education begins with a sustained assault on the effectiveness of public education. Corporate-funded think-tanks have led the way, with the Fraser Institute and the C. D. Howe Institute playing key roles. But nearly every corporate voice in the country, from chambers of commerce, boards of trade, the BCNI, and the corporate media have contributed to the campaign to undermine public confidence in public education.

The myth making is now well established: our schools graduate students who are illiterate; students aren't being prepared for work in the new corporate world; their math and science skills are inferior to those of Asian students; there is a 30 percent drop-out rate; teachers and their unions resist change and make it impossible to fire bad teachers; there is no "choice" in education, and public schools and their students remain "prisoners of mediocrity and educational gridlock."

All of these claims are either outright falsehoods or deliberately misleading. According to Statscan, only 3 percent of Canadian-born 16- to 24-year-olds (the most recent graduates and senior students) have any literacy problems, and achieve by far the highest literacy rate of any age group. Figures from a 1988 OECD study show that Canada had the highest rate of post-secondary participation of any of the developed countries and graduated 50 percent more engineers per capita than Japan.

True, Canada placed ninth in math and science out of fifteen countries, but Asian countries devote enormous energy to preparing students for such tests as a matter of national pride, and often hand-pick the schools that take the international tests. The 30 percent drop-out myth is pervasive despite Statscan figures that show the graduation rate to be at least 82 percent and could prove to be as high as 90 percent if surveys tracked people through age 25 rather than 20.[38]

The efforts of corporations to break into public education have taken two separate but related paths in Canada. The first is through the heavy promotion of education "partnerships" between corporations and school boards, schools, universities, and colleges. As budgets are slashed, "good corporate citizens" arrive on the school doorstep offering assistance that inevitably involves hooking the school into product lines or trading materials or cash for the exclusive right to peddle or advertise their products in the school. (Coke, Pepsi, Burger King, and McDonald's are the prime examples of the latter.)

The second track is corporate support (the Royal Bank, Bank of Montreal, Syncrude, the Donner Foundation) for the campaign to promote charter schools, publicly funded private schools first introduced in Britain, the U.S., and New Zealand. The key promoters of the charter concept in Canada are all in the neo-con camp. Charter advocates use the market language that is familiar to other new-right campaigns — parents are "customers," education the "product," and students the "value-added" result. Advocating "choice" promotes the libertarian value of a private benefit over the public-purpose philosophy of the public system. Charters are seen as a halfway step to school vouchers, the ultimate consumer-driven system wherein parents receive a certificate that they can "spend" at any school they choose. Vouchers go hand in hand with contracting out school administration, which is already happening in the U.S. In 1996, Lehman Brothers investment house prepared a detailed study, "Investment Opportunity in the Education Industry," that declares that there is great potential in education privatization. "The health care sector 20 years ago and the education industry today have several similarities that, given the massive private sector growth in the health care sector, make the education sector extremely attractive to investors."[39]

The analysis is explicit about the positive role education "reformers" are playing in preparing the ground for investment opportunities. "Private companies owe much of their success to the ability of the public sector to open the education system to competition. The [for-profit] Edison Project was granted a [contract] from one of Massachusetts' charter schools to manage one grade school, illustrating how a private company can use a public reform movement to grow and build its own credibility."[40] The study goes on to map out strategies for using various reform movements as gateways to investment.

Yet reports out of the U.S. suggest that privatization experiments have virtually all failed to deliver. Education corporations have doctored performance records and provided no cost savings to the states and boards that hired them. So far, contracting out school administration isn't on the Canadian agenda, but corporations are aggressively preparing the ideological ground for direct involvement. Already, dozens of schools in Canada have named classrooms after corporations in return for financial assistance. According to author Tony Clarke, there are twenty thousand business-school partnerships in Canada "with technology and communications corporations such as AT&T, Bell Canada, General Electric, Hewlett Packard, IBM Canada, Northern Telecom, Unitel and YNN."[41]

The corporate message is being injected into the Canadian curriculum through corporate publications. *What!* magazine is targeted at 13- to 19-year-olds, who, says publisher Elliott Ettenburg, "aren't children so much as what I like to call 'evolving consumers.'" The *Globe and Mail* "Classroom Edition" (twelve times a year) is free and accompanied by a teacher's guide and lesson plans. It is promoted as a vehicle for corporate culture to its potential sponsors (fee: $100,000 a year) with the promise that it is "the ideal vehicle to provide information about your company, products or services." In the U.S.,

THE MYTH OF THE GOOD CORPORATE CITIZEN

curriculum kits and science projects are brazen in their promotion of products. Campbell Soup has a science project designed to prove that its Prego spaghetti sauce is thicker than Unilever's Ragú. McDonald's gives away a kit that shows students how to design a McDonald's restaurant and how to apply for a job at McDonald's.[42]

The direct connection between the control of education and the strategy of transnational corporations to "capture" people at the earliest possible stage is frighteningly apparent in this commercial assault on public education. The transformation of citizens into consumers logically begins with transforming the schools whose original purpose included citizenship training.

The major ingredient missing from the investment picture in Canada is the severe education crisis that has spawned reform movements in the U.S. But business, ever eager to create opportunities where none exist, is working hard on this issue. Hand in hand with such right-wing politicians as former Ontario education minister John Snobelen (famous for talking about the need to "invent a crisis" to kick-start reform), business continues to call for massive cuts to public spending at the same time its think-tanks attack the system for failing.

The unprecedented confrontation between teachers and the Ontario government in 1997 is precisely the "crisis invention" that neo-conservatives require. The government's seizure from school boards and teachers of complete control over education policy making fits the classic mould of taking power away from "vested interests." The billion dollars in cuts to Ontario schools put tremendous pressure on teachers and schools to accept the various freebies and partnerships that are the fifth column in the long-term plan to make profits off education. It also opens the door to a middle-class exodus from the deteriorating public system to the private system, and it increases pressure for charter schools and publicly subsidized private schools.

Universities and colleges have not escaped the encroaching corporate profiteers. Enormous cuts to university budgets are slowly forcing our almost exclusively public system to mimic its private American counterpart. University presidents are being hired on the basis of their ability to get corporate donations. Corporate sponsorships inevitably raise questions about the objectivity of research as well as what research will get done.

In their book *Class Warfare*, Maude Barlow and Heather-jane Robertson state, "Educators who once jealously guarded their autonomy now negotiate curriculum planning with corporate sponsors . . . Professors who once taught are now on company payrolls churning out marketable research while universities pay the cut-rate fee for replacement teaching assistants."[43] Almost every aspect of university funding is commercially tainted. According to Barlow and Robertson, "A professor's ability to attract private investment is now often more important than academic qualifications . . . Provincial and federal funding . . . is also increasingly tied to commercial considerations."[44]

The convergence of corporate and university interests is becoming increasingly formal and explicit. The Corporate-Higher Education Forum is "a national [Canadian] coalition of university presidents and corporate CEOs designed to merge goals and activities . . . [It] promotes corporate-education interaction by placing members on one another's governing bodies."[45] The forum supports lower state funding in order to encourage greater corporate influence.

"GOVERNMENTS CAN'T CREATE JOBS"

By early 1996 the deficit issue was not getting the same play as it had through the first half of the 1990s. Polls consistently showed that unemployment was increasingly the biggest concern of most Canadians, often showing numbers twice as high as those concerned about the deficit and debt. In addition, when asked what the government's priorities should be, Canadians believed that it should be doing something about unemployment and that it *could* do something.

Consequently, the business and neo-con propaganda machine has been working overtime to disabuse citizens of the notion that their governments can do anything useful. The mantra is familiar: "Governments can't create jobs; they can only create the conditions for the private sector to create jobs." The most dramatic example was that given by Jean Chrétien on the famous televised town-hall meeting when he told a Regina woman with three degrees and no job, "Some are lucky, some are not. That's life."

Few areas in public policy demonstrate so clearly the profound shift in the role of the state in society as does job creation. Nothing is more important to an individual or a family than their access to employment, their ability to lead productive lives. Nothing is so central to the health of communities, indeed to their survival, than the employment of their citizens. If democratically elected governments abandon the responsibility of even trying to ensure that people have jobs, they have effectively abandoned everything.

The argument that government can't create jobs rests in part on the assault on public services, and the effort to denigrate public servants and the jobs they do. The Reform Party and the National Citizens' Coalition take this argument the furthest with their declarations that "government jobs are not real jobs." This notion is plain silly. It suggests that someone lobbying on behalf of the tobacco industry has a real job while a nurse attending a cancer patient does not. It also suggests that the person working for the public liquor board in Alberta didn't have a real job until it was privatized and wages cut in half. Indeed, government jobs are so pervasive in the community that a 1996 examination of the résumés of Reform MPs revealed that twenty-three of them used to work at "government jobs."

The work done by teachers, nurses, park-maintenance people, and those providing municipal services and ensuring that our food and water are safe, are real jobs. Without them our communities would collapse. But government job "creation" goes far beyond a direct provision of public services. The government creates hundreds of thousands of jobs in the private sector through government purchases. Road building, the purchasing of supplies by schools and hospitals, the building of coast guard vessels, the purchase of police cars and fire trucks, the provision of electric generators for public utilities, all testify to the fact that most goods and services produced in Canada depend on a complex set of public-sector/private-sector connections. This includes purchases, the salaries of public employees, and transfer payments — family allowance, welfare, and pensions — to individuals.

A study by researcher David Robertson in 1985, before spending cuts started, reveals just how much the private sector relies on government purchases. In the mid-1980s, all levels of government spent some $68 billion on the private sector. Within the service sector, government purchases accounted for 6 percent of the total output; in transportation, communications, and utilities, 14 percent, and in advertising, 18 percent. The percent of purchases consumed by the public sector in publishing and printing was 21.6 percent; ready-mix concrete, 48 percent; pharmaceuticals, 17 percent; shipbuilding and repair, 20.2 percent; petroleum refineries, 17.6 percent.[46]

In total, government purchases of domestically produced goods and services generated or maintained more than one million jobs in Canada, about 12 percent of all private-sector jobs. This was in addition to the half million private-sector jobs created by the spending of $30 billion in government salaries. Transfer payments to individuals accounted for an additional $30 billion spent on private-sector goods and services, creating a further half million private-sector jobs. Robertson's calculations did not even include the multiplier effect of all this spending, nor did they include the expenditure of UI payments.

In 1997 we have chronic unemployment of over 9 percent (add discouraged job hunters and the involuntarily underemployed and it exceeds 17 percent), and it is widely recognized, even in the financial community, that government spending cuts are a major cause. Economist Jeff Rubin of CIBC Wood Gundy stated: "The Canadian economy would be far more closely on a par with the full employment U.S. economy" had governments not tackled their deficits so vigorously.[47]

Government can and does create jobs and has even more tools at its disposal to do more. The government could require that banks, as a condition of their operating licences, devote 0.5 percent of their loans to small community and cooperative enterprises. The banks would then have to encourage and seek out such development, rather than promote leveraged buy-outs.

Government could change labour and tax laws to redistribute work. It could reduce the official work week to thirty-five hours and discourage overtime by raising the ceiling for the maximum insurable earnings under UI/EI. It could increase the annual-leave and educational-leave provisions in labour codes.

The government could implement changes in the tax code that would penalize companies for gratuitous downsizing at times of increasing profitability. It could do the same with respect to the deductibility of interest payments on loans used to engage in mergers, leveraged buy-outs, and currency speculation, thus encouraging productive investment. If companies insist on paying their CEOs outrageous pay packages, the government could limit deductible business expenses to $500,000, or twenty times the average employee's compensation. It could lower the ceiling on the percentage of pension funds and RRSPs that can be invested abroad, making more money available for investment in Canada.

Most important, the government could, as the Alternative Federal Budget and the proposals of other analysts have pointed out, stop the destruction of public services and return to the principle of democratic governance. It could embark on a program to strengthen communities through investments in education, health care, child care, social housing, enhancing the environment, and refurbishing the economic infrastructure in communications and transportation, and it could triple its spending in the area of culture, one of the least expensive and most socially rewarding ways of creating jobs.

The new right's counter-claim that the private sector will create jobs if only the government creates favourable conditions stands thoroughly discredited. The conditions that corporations say are necessary to persuade them to invest are all in place. That is what the FTA and NAFTA were supposed to do; that is what low minimum wages were supposed to do; that is what slashed taxes for high-income Canadians was supposed to do; that was the rationale for wrestling inflation to the ground and for gutting unemployment and social assistance programs.

When critics of the government negatively compare our social programs to those of other Western countries, the answer is always a reference to the U.S., our main trading partner. Yet the notion that the U.S. provides cheaper business costs than Canada has also been thoroughly discredited.

In 1995, a KPMG study, sponsored by the Canadian and U.S. governments, compared business costs in various cities in the two countries. The eight Canadian cities were all found to be less expensive than any of the seven U.S. cities. The study was repeated in 1996 with thirteen Canadian cities. All were cheaper than any of the twelve American cities, on average 6.7 percent cheaper. This was true of every industry examined. Most of the differential was due to Canada's much lower labour costs, in large measure because of our universal medicare. Taxes played a role, too; payroll taxes in Canada were 35 percent lower than in the U.S. Canada would only begin to lose its advantage if the dollar rose to 87 cents U.S.[48]

A further KPMG study, released in 1997, showed that Canada was the least expensive location to invest of seven countries studied, including the U.S., France, Germany, Britain, and Sweden. Most important, given the constant complaint about high business taxes in Canada, the study showed that Canada and Sweden were tied with the lowest corporate taxes of any of the seven countries.[49]

The ten-year decline in real wages and the slashing of social programs was undertaken not to make us more competitive but to re-establish capital's historic "share" of output. The corporate sector has had ten years to show the country that the enormous sacrifices Canadian have made were worth it. Yet the private sector's job creation record is abysmal, despite the best government-created "conditions" in a generation. In 1995, following a pattern set in the late 1980s, net new investment in Canada (after replacement of old plants and equipment costing $100 billion) was $11 billion. In comparison, $78 billion was expended on mergers and acquisitions, and tens of billions more on speculative activity in currency, real estate, the stock market, and other areas, none of which created a single "real" job or any real wealth.[50]

Every few months the headlines in the business press report on the merger mania continuing apace. The *Globe and Mail*'s business section reported in February 1997, "Merger Wave Gathers Momentum"; in July, "Mergers on Target for Record," and in October, "Mergers and Acquisitions Jump in Third Quarter."[51] Every such headline heralds the loss of more jobs and the loss of government revenue — the huge interest charges on the money borrowed for these deals is deductible. In the third quarter of 1997, there were 347 mergers, worth $21.6 billion. Assuming that pace continued, the year-end total was $88 billion, compared to the previous high of $78 billion.[52]

Glenn Bowman, of the investment banking firm Crosbie and Co., expects that the "global drive to consolidation" will continue unabated. Sheer size continues to be seen as an advantage because it allows for efficiency — which means fewer employees. One American example: the merger of Chase Manhattan and Chemical Banking will result in one hundred of the current six hundred branches closing, throwing 12,000 of the 75,000 employees onto the streets.[53]

The corporate record of job creation makes it clear that the conditions demanded by the corporate elite had nothing to do with a commitment to create jobs. It had everything to do with seizing a larger share of output for profits, and of effectively deregulating labour. Indeed, the conditions, both actions and inactions by government, have contributed to the elimination of tens of thousands of the best-paying, highest-skilled jobs in the country. The Canadian Centre for Policy Alternatives, using *Financial Post* figures, has tracked forty-four BCNI corporations since the free-trade deal came into effect. Between 1988 and 1996, thirty-three of those corporations posted a total job destruction of 216,004, on average a cut of 35 percent of their workforces. During this period, these corporations increased their revenues by $40 billion, or 34 percent. Eleven of the companies created 28,073 jobs, with one, Seagram, accounting for half the total.[54]

THE TAX-CUT SCAM

The last piece in the five-part propaganda assault on Canadian expectations of government was tested in the June 1997 federal election. The panacea for economic growth and jobs, everything else having failed to prod business into action, is tax cuts. The argument for tax cuts follows a similar pattern to those for cutting the deficit. Not all proposals are the same, with the Liberals talking about a tax cut for low- and middle-income earners, but only after the deficit is gone; Reform demanding across-the-board tax breaks so that the rich would benefit, and the Tories campaigning on an immediate tax break. The desired effect, as it was with the deficit questions, is a debate about how much and when, not about *whether* to cut taxes.

Because the country is preoccupied with unemployment, the tax cutters must couch their propaganda in terms of job creation. Even Preston Manning, who for the first nine years as leader of the Reform Party never referred to unemployment as a problem, now expresses concern over the issue and promotes a tax cut with the populist rhetorical question: "Who knows better how to spend your money, you or the government?"

Yet most studies demonstrate that tax cuts are a poor way of stimulating job growth. One analysis, done in 1997 by the economic fore-casting firm Informetrica, shows that tax cuts, as a strategy for job creation, compare very poorly to direct and indirect government spending. Informetrica looked at how many jobs could be created with a billion dollars spent in various ways. The most effective way: direct hiring. If the government spent a billion dollars hiring back the teachers, nurses, government employees, and cultural workers it laid off in the 1990s, it could create 56,000 jobs. Increased spending of $1 billion on goods and services in the private sector would create 28,000 jobs; in infrastructure spending, 26,000 jobs.

Tax cuts don't even come close. A billion dollars put back into people's pockets through a cut in the GST would produce 17,000 jobs; in corporate taxes, 14,000; in personal income taxes, 12,000, and in payroll taxes, just 9,000 jobs.[55]

As tax-policy professor Neil Brooks points out, the whole notion of a tax cut is based on the false premise that people want to make choices only in the things they purchase in the private sector. But where is the evidence that people really want more private cars and less public transit, more private roads and fewer public ones, more user-pay vacation spots and fewer public campgrounds?

The pressure for tax cuts will not go away. The entire world cap-italist system depends on ever expanding consumer spending. With incomes in a nearly permanent state of stagnation in North America, one of the only ways left to increase disposable income is through tax cuts. And although they fare badly as a method of job creation, tax cuts are an effective policy tool for corporate governance. They reduce government finances, making return to egalitarian government programs more difficult, and preserve the debt at high levels so that the debt terror campaign can be revived whenever pressure for gov-ernment spending arises. Lastly, tax cuts are yet another ideological appeal to individualism, which is part of the neo-liberal campaign to change the political culture.

Despite the barrage of calls for tax cuts — from the same right-wing coalition of forces that campaigned against the deficit — Canadians are resisting the attempted seduction. A *Globe*/Environics poll conducted at the end of 1996 showed that only 9 percent of respondents supported this option. Thirty-one percent wanted money to go to job creation, 25 percent wanted more money spent on health care, and 13 percent preferred spending on benefits for children in poor families.[56] An Environics poll done for the Alberta government in 1997 showed that, even in the province alleged to be the most suspicious of government, citizens want more spent on public services and reject a tax cut. Thirty-seven percent wanted the government's new-found surplus to focus on education, 29 percent chose health care, and 22 percent picked job creation. Just 11 percent cited the debt, and a mere 5 percent, barely more than the margin of error of the poll, wanted tax cuts.[57]

A Vector poll showed that most Canadians are actually willing to pay more taxes for certain public services. For child poverty the support was 74 percent; for training, 68 percent; for free day care so poor parents could work or get training, 57 percent; for education, 58 percent.[58] This is a remarkable endorsement of public services and the principle of equality, given that we are already paying more and getting less for our tax dollars because of debt-servicing charges.

The battle over tax cuts is just beginning, and the new right will be just as relentless on this issue as they were on the deficit. In late 1997, the elite opinion on the issue, however, had not yet reached a consensus. In November, the *Globe and Mail* headlined an Angus Reid poll that claimed Canadians wanted debt reduction and tax cuts by a large margin over new spending. The federal government responded quickly by releasing a poll by Ekos, the same firm conducting its yearly "Rethinking Government" survey, showing that Canadians back increased spending on social programs strongly but not on other items like helicopters and Internet access.[59] The fight for public opinion on tax cuts will be a key indicator of the future of civil society in Canada, and a measure of how resistant Canadians are to appeals to individualism.

❖

Has the counter-revolution of lowered expectations succeeded? It has had dramatic success in the private sector. That is, for those who depend for their livelihood on selling their labour in the private market, expectations are at their lowest in decades, probably since the

Great Depression.

But in the campaign to lower expectations of government, the campaign has largely failed. Despite a plethora of think-tanks, economists, bond raters, and the corporate media to sell the campaign, the collusion of political parties to implement the program of the corporate agenda, and the failure to date of progressive forces to mount an effective opposition to it, the goal of transforming the political culture has not been accomplished. Polls show that people support medicare, think it should continue to be publicly funded, and call for the reinstatement of monies already cut. They are tenacious in their defence of public education. They hold firm to the conviction that governments should do something about unemployment, that areas of high unemployment should get special attention from the federal government, and that the crisis in child poverty should be addressed.

The relative failure of the propaganda campaign should give citizens and those fighting corporate rule some solace, yet overall the news is clearly not good. Obviously, if the vast majority in a democracy opposes virtually every element of a revolutionary change their government is implementing, and the government is able to carry on regardless, there is a crisis in democracy. People's expectations are still high; they still believe in the power of government to improve their lives and to provide them with security. But they are profoundly disillusioned and disappointed that their government seems unwilling to carry out their wishes, and they have very low expectations that governments will change direction.

The old egalitarian state is rapidly transmogrifying into what has been called the market state, which sees as its role promoting not just the accumulation of capital but the commercialization of the functions of government and the commodification of public services. It is the institutional parallel to the transforming of citizens into customers. The state is rapidly restructuring by adopting the corporate ethic as its own, assessing its role by judging how well it adapts to globalization, and by judging its delivery of services as if they were widgets. This is the state that is emerging from ten years of corporate domination and the downsizing of democracy.

10

THE MARKET STATE

Better telephone service. Telecommunications has become
very competitive. The range of services is now as great
as anywhere in the world. You have to judge [the reforms]
by whether the consumer is served or not.
—SIR ROGER DOUGLAS, CREDITED WITH LAUNCHING NEW ZEALAND'S
FREE-MARKET REFORMS, ASKED TO DESCRIBE THE COUNTER-REVOLUTION'S
GREATEST SUCCESS

The extent to which we have lost democracy in Canada is concealed by the paraphernalia of democracy, its institutions, elections, the sight of politicians from different parties on our TV screens. Yet people obviously take little comfort in these democratic trappings when Ottawa casually dismantles all the things that people say make them proud of the country they have built. The corporate counter-revolution is upon us and our institutions have been hijacked in its service.

Fraser Institute economist Walter Block's musings about a return to the time when only those with property, meaning capital wealth, could vote seem outrageous. Yet formal universal suffrage notwithstanding, this principle has found its way into our "democratic" politics. We now have a political system in which only those with property have "effective" votes, because, when substantive policies and visions for the country are up for debate, only those with property are listened to. The rest of us have been silenced.

Every method of seeking out people's values and desires with regard to government shows that the vast majority believe in a forceful citizen state, that they want more money spent on medicare and education, that they want strong, enforced environmental laws, that they don't trust corporations and don't want them to be involved in social programs, that unemployment should be the main priority for government, that they don't want a tax break, but they do want a well-funded state that can do its work effectively.

Yet none of this matters a whit to the governing elite, and they have made it clear that the majority will not rule; they will not be allowed their vision of their country. Paul Martin meets with those who put together the Alternative Federal Budget (AFB) and says, yes, this is a viable document. Polls and other surveys show that most people support the values reflected in the AFB. So what? Property and the propertied rule.

It isn't just the pro-business "policies" of government that have left so many Canadians reeling. Government itself has simply abandoned the ethical and moral ethos of democratic government. It is now no different from Bell Canada, which casually announces the layoff of 10,000 people and then, a couple of years later, with record profits, announces the layoffs of 2,500 more. The federal government just as casually laid off more than 55,000 people. Our governments are becoming corporations in everything but name.

Governments are now infected with the economic rationalism that drives the market. We have prime ministers and premiers who have forgotten their history, their culture, their own values and good sense, and have lost their ethical centre. How can these "leaders," brought up in Canada, display such a stunning indifference to their own communities? Simple: ideology. It allows them to dismiss all facts, all history, all disbelievers. It is government by faith in dogma, and it is immune to the pain and suffering it causes. It is turning our democratic state from an expression of community into a rationale for the market. Just as this new contractual state cannot integrate history or culture into its decisions, it cannot see long-term social consequences, because everything is based on contracts.

If ideology is meaning in the service of power, then since the mid-1970s, but increasingly since the early 1980s, that ideology has been economic rationalism. Understanding this theory of human behaviour makes the actions of our governments more understandable, if no less acceptable. The theory conveniently promotes the liberation of the forces of transnational corporations and international capital, even though it claims to place the "free market" on a philosophical pedestal. Economic rationalism now dominates the thinking of senior policy advisers in nearly every government in Canada.

This abstracted individual is called "economic man" and its innate sexism is the least of its problems. Economic wo/man is always, and only, maximizing his/her satisfactions as if individuals have no other connection to any other human being. By abstracting the individual to this extent, economic rationalism escapes the consequences of its view of human beings as essentially selfish.

The most famous expression of this abstract human-being-with-no-community is Lady Margaret Thatcher's declaration: "There is no such thing as society, only individuals and families each pursuing their own interests." By focussing so exclusively on the individual, economic rationalism ignores the existence of community and all of the human actions, values, attitudes, and principles on which community depends.

Economics has now taken on the status of a religion by which others are judged. Keynes was wary of economics, proposing that it be a matter for specialists and that economists think of themselves as being on a level with dentists. Instead, it has been inflated to imply an entire philosophy, a way of seeing everything. Now, when we choose an economic theory, we choose a particular kind of society.

Before we examine how economic rationalism has been applied to the functions of the state, here is what economic rationalism says about human behaviour and the economy. Economic rationalism states that our economic resources are better allocated through market forces than by government intervention. This proposition is based not on experience or empirical data but on deductive reasoning. It goes something like this: Markets are efficient. Canadian industry is plagued by inefficiencies. Therefore, markets should be freed from all the restrictions that make them inefficient, such as tariffs, financial regulation, environmental and labour regulation, and investment rules.

Economic rationalism today attempts to incorporate empirical evidence to justify its obsession with efficiency. The new right has raised the spectre of "special interests" putting pressure on government for their own narrow benefit. How can an anti-poverty group be a special interest? Creating policies on the basis of people's social condition is inefficient because it puts on the economic model demands that cannot be accommodated. The state's response "is an undesirably complex and incoherent set of policies which obstruct the achievement of the 'national interest.' The prescription: strip away the policies and all will be better off."[1]

Economic rationalism does not recognize the possibility that the so-called special interests are citizens concerned about the quality of life in their communities. The special interests whose pressure has produced the incoherent policies are citizen groups whose sense of social responsibility has led them to take action on child poverty, the degradation of the environment, the erosion of health care and public education, Canada's relationships with poorer countries, and dozens of other aspects of community life.

But economic rationalism does not permit such motivation. Because all individuals are exclusively engaged in a continuous struggle to maximize their satisfactions, all action is, by the deductive reasoning of the economist, self-interested. We are by definition reduced to the status of consumers, on a lifelong quest to quench unquenchable desires. For the economic rationalist, the only sovereignty that matters is consumer sovereignty.

The whole edifice of the counter-revolution is constructed on the single value of efficiency in the name of economic freedom. If we are to make sense of the nonsensical situation in which the economy is doing well but the people are not, we can only do so by returning to this first principle. Everything, including the well-being of citizens, communities, and nations, is to be judged in the court of the market on the basis of whether or not it contributes to efficiency.

Good sense, as opposed to common sense, tells us that efficiency is just one among many values by which to judge an economy. Indeed, a preoccupation with efficiency would make sense in a context of a society that is extremely poor, where people's basic needs are not being met, and where, as a result, it needs to increase its production and consumption. But it makes no sense to be obsessed with efficiency, to the virtual exclusion of all else, when we live in an affluent economy.

In Canada, our goals can and should be much different. The obvious "rational" goal of economics, in the context of community and organized society, is to provide everybody with the necessities of life. The economic rationalists have a lot of explaining to do, for as we become increasingly affluent and productive, we get further and further from that truly rational objective.

We must carefully examine just what "efficiency" means to mega-corporations and their ideologues. Efficient at what? As Sam Gindin, economist with the Canadian Auto Workers, argues: "Capitalist competitiveness . . . rules out other forms of 'efficiency' — for instance, the efficient production of high quality goods or the efficient provision of services under conditions controlled by workers, not to maximize the profits for capital but to fulfill social needs."[2] The devastating social consequences of corporate efficiency belie the implied universality of the term.

THE MYTH OF THE MARKET'S INVISIBLE HAND

The Fraser Institute sells Adam Smith ties, and the Adam Smith Institute in Britain promotes free-market policies, including privatization, around the world. Much is done in the name of Adam Smith that the man himself would, and did, object to. Smith's notion of the invisible hand of the market (allocating resources efficiently until an equilibrium was reached to the benefit of everyone) could exist only in a society permanently characterized by thousands of small producers. But the market Smith talked about ceased to exist at around the time he was writing about it. According to Allan Engler, "By the time Smith's vision of the individual in the market had become the foundation of economic theory, the rise of machine industry had made economic independence an unattainable dream for most people. How could factory workers freely exchange the products of their own labour in the market when [their labour] belonged to others?"[3]

Yet Smith had already recognized the changing situation and wrote condemning those who exploited labour. The corporate backers of

Michael Walker's Fraser Institute would recognize themselves in Smith's critique of the great manufacturers and merchants of his day. They were, he declared, "an order of men, whose interest is never exactly the same as that of the public, who have generally an interest to deceive and even to oppress the public and who accordingly have, upon many occasions, both deceived and oppressed it."[4]

Adam Smith had something to say that was directly relevant to today's ruling corporate and political elite and their fondness for permanent recession to encourage "market" forces: "Servants, labourers, and workmen . . . make up the far greater part of . . . political society . . . What improves the circumstances of the greater part can never be regarded as inconvenience to the whole."[5]

The notion that the market can do a better job of allocating resources than an economy regulated by the state assumes that there is still a free market. Yet the kinds of policies promoted by the Fraser Institute, the NCC, and other right-wing think-tanks actually destroy the conditions necessary for entrepreneurial risk taking and innovative investment. As pollster Angus Reid points out in his book *Shakedown*, only in a civil society in which people have trust in their institutions and respect for the political process will people take risks. Yet the market liberals and their ideological sidekicks ridicule the very notion of a civil society.

The Fraser Institute, the C. D. Howe Institute, and the corporate media, for all their talk of the market, have for fifteen years been promoting the accumulation of power and control by transnational corporations, which are notorious for crushing their competitors in the drive for ever greater control of the markets. The corporations' control of capital and their use of an enormous percentage of that capital for nonproductive activity reduce the capital pool that might otherwise be available for creative local investment. Robson Street in Vancouver and Elgin Street in Ottawa, just two examples of once vibrant expressions of local culture and entrepreneurial spirit, are now being wiped clean of any local expression, homogenized by a corporate blitzkrieg.

As giant corporations came to dominate economies and businesses, the invisible hand of the market was replaced by the very visible hand of managers. The multiple units of production and distribution of modern large corporations, and particularly TNCs, saw coordinated administration replace the market in the allocation of resources. Indeed, the evolution of the modern TNC was driven by the effort to gain administrative control over materials, labour, markets, technology, and finance. The more control, the fewer risks, the more profit. Far from taking risk, large corporations, as we saw in chapter 3, devote enormous energy and planning to avoid it.

The constant attacks of business leaders, market liberals, economists, and neo-con politicians on the whole notion of planning the economy and regulating demand are based largely on the myth of "the play of market forces." But what else are large corporations if not huge planning institutions? The largest corporations in the world are larger than most countries and have far more capacity to plan than all but the most developed nations. Furthermore, corporations are not restricted by issues of accountability to broad communities of voters and their varied interests. They are accountable only, and only in the narrowest share-price terms, to shareholders.

Corporations and governments are both hierarchical, bureaucratic planning organizations. The difference isn't in the planning but in the goal of the planning. In governments that goal has been, until recently, to exert some influence over the allocation of national resources to achieve social objectives; for corporations it is to achieve profits and maintain growth. With the increasing application of economic rationalism to the principles of governance, though, the differences are blurring. The egalitarian, public purpose of government planning is being transformed, as market objectives and market-inspired performance assessment seeps into the civil service.

It is revealing of both the objectives of the TNCs and the morality of those who labour in their interests that the two countries often identified as preferred models by the corporate elite and economic rationalists are Chile and New Zealand. Both countries are characterized by almost completely deregulated and privatized economies — and the extreme class divisions that such economies naturally produce. In both cases, the structural adjustment regimes were imposed by coups, a military coup in Chile in 1973 (examined in chapter 3) and a political coup in New Zealand in 1984.

GOVERNMENT BY FUNDAMENTALIST FANATICISM

New Zealand in the 1980s became the darling of the neo-con set as the Little Country That Could. Not only did it completely deregulate its economy, from the financial sector to the ending of tariffs, agriculture supports, and labour deregulation, it privatized virtually every public enterprise, to the tune of $16 billion, and devalued the New Zealand dollar by 20 percent to encourage foreign investment. The result was an orgy of foreign purchasing of the country's assets that was symbolized by foreign corporations buying up every major New Zealand bank. No other developed country has passed policies so favourable to transnational corporations and finance capital.[6]

But the neo-cons' admiration for New Zealand extends to how it has transformed the state in the image of corporation, economic rationalism, and market liberalism. In a manner that has some parallels in Britain, successive New Zealand governments, of both the Labour Party and the conservative National Party, have extended the counter-revolution into the civil service and the services provided by the state, such as education and health care.

What has come to be described as the contract state or market state is not just a deregulated state. It is a state that adopts the competitive principles of corporate management as its model and corporate "values" as its national values. Its assumptions are appropriated from economic rationalism and systematically adapted into operational plans for governance on market principles. It is the corporate takeover of the state in all but name.

Not only has the New Zealand government established a regime of corporate libertarianism, it has superimposed on democratic government a model of management identical to that of corporations. The traditional public service, established and trained to reflect the communitarian values intrinsic to the definition of society, has been all but swept away, replaced by corporate executives, planners, and managers immersed in the ideology of the market.

The application of economic rationalism to democratic governance has spawned a number of faith-based theories, all of them rooted in the notion of what Canadian philosopher C. B. Macpherson called possessive individualism. These abstracted theories about human behaviour have a variety of names, each with special application: public choice theory, agency theory, a whole system of management philosophy applied to the public service called new public management, and the "new contractualism," which reduces all relationships to business contracts. These theories have all found their way into the practice of governance in New Zealand. And they all reduce citizens to customers, and governments to enterprises.

As the University of Waikato's Paul Havemann says, these theories have the effect of "hollowing out the state, that is, cutting out its citizens-focussed core. In New Zealand the contract state is explicitly the undemocratic state . . . The idea that the public service should be run in a 'business-like fashion' has been conflated with running it like a business, i.e. for a profit."[7]

Applying the principle of contractualism transforms the citizen into a customer contracting with the state for a service. Public accountability through the normal democratic process is replaced by contractual responsibility — two otherwise socially disconnected entities fulfil a one-time, binding contract. By this model all social relationships are turned into commodities to be exchanged on the market.

Nowhere do these neo-liberal theories permit the notion that any person would choose to work for government because he was committed to the idea of public service, that any politician would run for office to contribute to her community. "Concepts like 'public spirit,' 'public service,' and 'the public interest' have not figured . . . in the public choice literature . . . because they are thought to lack meaning or relevance."[8]

Their application of such theories starkly demonstrates just how impoverished is the new right's view of human nature. It is ideology gone berserk. As John McMurtry, author of *Unequal Freedoms: The Global Market as an Ethical System*, suggests, the market doctrine smacks of "fundamentalist fanaticism." It is immune to the influence of the everyday experience of even those promoting the theories. Every day we engage in and observe dozens of actions that are not self-interested, at home, in the workplace, on the street. Organized society could not possibly exist if economic rationalism had any basis in reality. Yet this fundamentalist ideology now guides the entire governance structure, social services, and health care and education in New Zealand.

According to Jonathon Boston of Victoria University in Wellington, "Government agencies have been seen as businesses; ministers have been likened to board chairpersons and department heads to chief executives . . . and the taxpayers have been seen as shareholders." The health-care system now carefully separates "purchaser" (the state) from "provider" (private and public health organizations) for fear that conflicts of interest and "bureaucratic capture" will undermine efficiency and accountability.[9]

Government departments have been commercialized and corporatized; commercial operations have been separated from noncommercial. Yet TNCs, one of the most successful organizational forms in history, have grown in size, bureaucratic complexity, and hierarchical structure at the same time as large departmental bureaucracies have been radically decentralized in the name of avoiding bureaucratic capture. This is pure political ideology, a rationalization for deconstructing the democratic state.

No empirical evidence whatsoever suggests that bureaucrats are primarily interested in maximizing their budgets. They are influenced by many factors, not least of which is often a strong belief in community values, but also integrity, reputation, and professional standards. It is presumably these qualities that corporations value when they hire these "bureaucrats" after they have left government.

The wholesale application of this orthodoxy also paints politicians as inevitably opportunistic. Yet politicians repeatedly do things that their constituents don't like and risk losing votes. They are also committed to the ideas their parties espouse. We can presume, for example, that the politicians in New Zealand believed in thier counter-revolution. With laws in place to "reduce the scope for political interference," New Zealand has entered the Orwellian world of laws and constitutional amendments that stop elected representatives from "interfering" in the governing of their country.

Much of the restructuring of the New Zealand government was based on the apprehension of "bureaucratic capture," that is, the manipulation of politicians by "special interests" and by empire-building civil servants. "Special interests," of course, include the people actually providing all the public services. As a result, policy making during the counter-revolutionary period (from 1984 on) was made with the explicit exclusion of those who had knowledge of the policy area in question. Educators and health-care experts were mostly excluded on the assumption that they would resist change in defending their "special interests." In their place were CEOs and business administrators.

Within a few years of the reforms, New Zealand's social statistics gave stunning evidence of what "the market" does to a community when it is unleashed from any controls. New Zealand now has the highest youth suicide rate in the world, skyrocketing prostitution among young women, a child poverty rate of nearly 25 percent, food banks proliferating everywhere in a country that had never seen them, the loss of half the manufacturing jobs in the country, chronic high unemployment (especially among the Maori and as high as 100 percent in some rural communities), and the legislative destruction of unions (from 63 percent of workers organized to 26 percent).

There has been a dramatic reversal of the gains women had made in income and security, and new class divisions are now a permanent feature of New Zealand society. Hundreds of children have been forced to leave their schools because their learning disabilities are "too expensive" to deal with; the diseases of poverty, eradicated in the 1940s, are back with a vengeance; lengthy hospital waiting lists are now "normal," and New Zealand boasts one of the highest violent crime rates in the developed world. Tens of thousands of people have emigrated to escape the destruction of their own country.

No area of policy escaped the zeal of the marketeers, but, of all the areas transformed, the effects in education are perhaps the most revealing. Because public education is such a critical area for creating an egalitarian society, neo-cons and market liberals focus a great deal of attention on reforming it. The free-market revolution is not just indifferent to social equality; it is hostile to it, believing it to be a barrier to rewarding those who excel.

The commercialization of education in New Zealand took the form of charter schools, which marry the principles of private schools, with their emphasis on exclusivity and choice, with the state funding of a public system. The government eliminated school boards and replaced them with local school committees of parents who were mandated to run some aspects of their schools. Super-imposed on this site-based management model was the principle of school "choice," a key concept for the economic rationalist and the libertarian.[10]

Within three years, half the schools in the country were losing students and the other half gaining them, a shift based on the notion of good schools and bad schools in which the privileged rushed headlong to ensure that their children got the "best." What became known as the good school syndrome was a self-fulfilling prophecy.

While student fees weren't compulsory, they were expected, and the disparity between poor and wealthy schools grew even wider. The average student fee paid in the former is $48 a year and in the latter $200, producing an average budgetary difference of over $180,000 a year.

The educational and social consequences were almost immediate. What is termed "white flight" leaves schools of mixed class and race impoverished — they lose model parents, state per-pupil funding, and, increasingly, their best teachers. Parents ended up identifying more with their social class than they did with their neighbourhood.

Segregated by social class and denied the opportunity to work and play with those of other races and classes, children become increasingly vulnerable to the unsympathetic stereotypes of the poor and nonwhites that prevail in New Zealand society. The new school system institutionalizes the class divisions created by other free-market policies.

The fruits of consumer sovereignty are hard to find. Popular schools effectively choose students from those who apply, not the other way around, and to keep their grade-average high (to attract funding), the "good" schools have systematically excluded those students who don't perform well. Parents have little say in the substantive issues of education and spend most of their time on administrative details and fundraising.

As Havemann writes, this "model of development requires the deconstruction of the universalized citizen and promotes the construction of the citizen-customer."[11] In this new world of the citizen-customer, those who do not produce, those who have not earned money to qualify as a customer, are automatically defined as noncitizens. The government's deliberate division of the poor into deserving and undeserving is a reflection of this effort at transformation.

None of the major reforms to New Zealand's economy and

government were ever voted upon, an approach that was begun by chance and developed later into a handbook for the rapid restructuring of Western economies. In the 1984 election, both Labour and the governing National Party ran on their traditional platforms, both of which included continuing tariffs, farm subsidies, currency exchanges, and full-employment policies.

But behind the scenes, some very different thinking had been taking place within a small group in the Labour hierarchy. Led by Roger Douglas, these technopols had seized control of Labour's economic policy making and were determined to bring radical changes to the country's stagnant economy. At the same time, a number of officials in the treasury branch (the finance department) and the Reserve Bank, trained at the monetarist schools in the U.S., were preparing comprehensive plans for restructuring. Beginning in 1982, these two groups and some new, aggressive businessmen in the finance sector met regularly to discuss economic and state restructuring. Immediately after the 1984 election, a currency crisis provided the opportunity for the wholesale introduction of nearly the entire neo-liberal program.

Two other benchmarks of the modern pattern of restructuring featured in the New Zealand counter-revolution. First, the core of new-right radicals moved quickly to expand their base by seizing the initiative in the other main political party, the National Party. At the same time, they systematically neutralized centres of opposition in government or government-funded agencies.

Second, the neo-cons recognized the need to ensure that a significant portion of the population substantially gained income and social status from the changes so that, regardless of obvious failures in other areas, there would be a strong base of support for the reforms. In these two efforts they were largely successful. While poverty increased dramatically, much of the middle class has been seduced by access to foreign luxury goods, lower taxes, access to foreign currency and stock markets, investments in privatized state assets, and the resulting higher incomes and greater social status.

Promoting a comprehensive ideology for corporate rule provides an enormous advantage for those committed to restructuring, for it provides converts with a complete package of reforms that purport to have the answers to everything. This package, including guidelines on how to implement it, presents itself as much more than an economic theory or an approach to governance. It is the equivalent of a religion, and its proponents' faith in its tenets is a powerful incentive to continue the "program" regardless of the consequences; to proselytize to anyone who will listen, and to ostracize those who challenge the faith. Faith is a powerful weapon against all doubters.

The New Zealand model has been marketed around the world by Roger Douglas, now Sir Roger, who has been to Canada nearly a dozen times. One of his most high-profile appearances here was at the 1991 federal Reform Party convention, where he was the keynote speaker. He described ten principles for implementing the counter-revolution. The first was, "Consensus for 'quality decisions' does not arise before they are taken; it develops progressively after they are taken." This principle of deliberate electoral deception must be combined with implementing reforms in "quantum leaps using large packages" because otherwise "interest groups will drag you down." And the reforms must be implemented "at maximum speed."[12]

The New Zealand experiment is now virtually a restructuring handbook for other Western nations. At the colloquium on structural adjustment held by the International Institute of Economics in 1993, a number of key requirements were identified, all of them elements of New Zealand's reform program. There had to be a crisis on which to launch the changes, a systematic program and a core of technocrats and technopols strategically placed to carry it out, support from institutional power, a political leader not concerned about his or her popularity, and "beneficiaries likely to fight to protect the reforms."[13]

STRUCTURAL ADJUSTMENT IN CANADA

Restructuring has been uneven in Canada; ruthless and uncompromising in some jurisdictions, gradual in others, effectively blocked in at least one. But the ideology and parts of the program are present across the country, either explicitly applied by governments or seeping into the civil service and the administration of programs.

The federal government under both the Mulroney Tories and the Chrétien Liberals were not and are not as ideologically consistent or committed as the Labour and National governments of New Zealand.

In part this is true simply because Canada is a federation, and even in national parties competing regional influences interfere with purely ideological programs. But Brian Mulroney was prepared to implement major elements of the corporate economic agenda regardless of the political and personal consequences, sacrificing public popularity to his commitment to corporate objectives.

Mulroney did not achieve everything the corporate elite asked. His failed constitutional initiatives meant that property rights and amendments to the Bank of Canada's mandate (to make inflation fighting its exclusive mandate) did not go through. And his cuts to social spending were nowhere near the levels demanded by the corporate elite. Yet he started all the projects that constitute the program of economic rationalists. Mulroney's greatest success was the free-trade deal, still the centrepiece of corporate rule.

The Liberal Party's Red Book for the 1993 election stated: "We do not believe that the only solution to our economic problems is another five years of cutbacks, job losses and diminished expectations." Yet that solution is what Paul Martin and Jean Chrétien believed in before and after they approved the publication of the Red Book of promises. And it summarizes very well what they did between 1993 and 1997. Their course of action had, in fact, been determined at the "thinkers conference" convened at Chrétien's behest, in Aylmer, Quebec, in the fall of 1991. This conference, and Chrétien himself, set the stage for corporate rule.

To achieve their return to power the Liberals followed Sir Roger Douglas's first principle for implementing structural adjustment: electoral deception and the hope that they could build retroactive consensus in time for the next election. There is no evidence that any of the economic facts changed after the election, and the Liberals do not claim that anything had changed. They simply lied, and with a cavalier indifference that betrayed their eagerness to get down to business. And they did just that. As Maude Barlow and Bruce Campbell write:

> Within two years, the party that came to power on a pledge of jobs, social security, and preserving the nation-state would gut Canada's social programs, break the collective agreement with its public sector workers, privatize its transportation system,

commercialize its cultural sector, abandon its environmental obligations, endorse world-wide free trade, sever trade from human rights, promote deregulated foreign investment, yield control of the economy to global investment speculators, and become the apologists for the corporate sector it once vilified.[14]

For a party that had staked its ground on opposing free trade and promising to renegotiate NAFTA, the Liberals did more to establish a level playing field for corporate investment than Mulroney ever found the will to do. Taking Michael Walker's advice, Martin cut social spending back to levels (as a percentage of GDP) not seen since 1949 and now below the spending levels of the U.S. Critics of these massive cuts have rightly focussed on their impact on ordinary Canadians, but it is also true that they directly benefit TNCs.

Cuts to social spending constitute a transfer of power from real citizens to corporate citizens, and the rationale for them is clearly revealed in documents, studies, and position papers of international agencies and corporate think-tanks around the world. Social spending is not simply a redistribution of wealth; it is a redistribution of political power, because it provides security and independence otherwise unattainable by those who have to sell their labour to survive. Every time medicare is weakened, or parents have to pay for school materials that used to be paid for by the school board, or labour standards are reduced, or a municipal service is privatized because of the downloading of cuts by higher governments, ordinary people and their communities lose power to corporations.

As we saw in chapter 6, the capacity of people and communities to resist the ever greater demands corporations make on them is very much connected to the role of governments. The federal Liberals' creation of a level playing field in social spending is explicitly a part of the FTA promise made to the U.S. The Americans had tagged as "unfair subsidies" the social programs now being cut. Market liberals saw them as nontariff barriers, a part of the old protectionist past, a market "rigidity" and a barrier to efficiency. Behind all this jargon: the demands of corporations for greater freedom to act.

In fact, the social spending cuts actually promote the growth of TNCs while they undermine the interests of many Canadian corporations. Universal medicare provides an enormous advantage to Canadian manufacturers because they do not have to pay private medicare premiums for their employees, as American corporations do. As Canadian medicare is eroded, employers, in order to keep employees and keep them healthy, will eventually have to start paying their employees' private insurance premiums. The same is true with education. The result is that corporations in Canada will actually be less competitive with their American counterparts, increasing pressures to produce off-shore, externalize costs, and merge into ever larger entities. Despite this contradiction for Canadian corporations, ideology prevails, even, it would seem, at the expense of the shareholder.

One of the Liberal government's most draconian and shameful initiatives has been its savaging of the unemployment insurance system. The special targeting of UI is more evidence of the rapid development of the market state in Canada, a mark of the government's acceptance of the economic rationalists' arguments about human nature. (Economic rationalists assume that no one would work if other income is provided.)

The Liberals' Green Book, its policy paper on UI, is an exact replica of the position of the OECD, the most free market of the multilateral organizations. The Green Book states that UI "may deter some workers from seeking alternate employment, relocating, developing broader skills, or tapping their creativity and potential for small scale enterprise."[15] There is no evidence that generous UI payments cause unemployment except at extremely low levels of joblessness. If that were the case, the unemployment rate should have been coming down steadily, with the UI cutbacks of the 1990s. And the "logic" of forcing workers to relocate is economic rationalism at its most obvious: sacrificing community for abstract economic efficiency.

Another key indicator of how the Canadian state is transforming its role is the Liberal government's changes to its policy on international human rights. Thus, in May 1997, Canada announced that it was considering a request from Indonesia for "military training assistance, police training, regular exercises with the Canadian navy and a full-time military attaché in Ottawa." The fact that the Suharto regime is one of the most ruthless and violent dictatorships in the world and widely condemned for its genocidal policies in East Timor was reduced to a public relations problem. In the words of an unnamed foreign affairs official, "It has to be finessed at a political level. It's the optics of putting out public dollars to train people who are associated with the ABRI [the Armed Forces of the Republic of Indonesia]. That's what makes it so difficult."[16]

In July, the government announced that it would apply sanctions to companies doing business with Burma, another country guilty of gross human rights violations. The reasons for the different approaches to two equally repressive regimes is not difficult to determine. Trade with Indonesia reached $1.5 billion in 1996, almost one hundred times the $16 million with Burma. A spokesman for foreign affairs told a worried mining investor with assets in Burma that the sanctions were, in any case, "largely symbolic."[17]

The most dramatic demonstration of the new role of the Canadian government vis-à-vis international human rights has been the four Team Canada junkets to Asia and Latin America. The prime minister and assorted premiers became cheerleaders for transnational corporations in a whole raft of countries with horrific human rights records, from China with its forced-labour camps, and India and Pakistan, notorious for their child slave-labour factories.

Bill Saunders was an award-winning television documentary maker in New Zealand before the Labour government "commercialized" the public broadcasting system. In doing so, the government eliminated any requirement that the New Zealand Broadcasting Corporation produce any New Zealand content in its programming. Saunders had a meeting with his superior. "The new mandate, I was told, was to deliver the audience to the advertiser. Full stop. I stayed on for a while but I eventually left. All productions had to be geared to the international market. You had to be able to sell them abroad or forget it."[18]

As *Globe and Mail* reporter Doug Saunders pointed out in "Exporting Canadian Culture," the global product imperative is very much in play in Canada. The four-part TV series based on Peter Newman's history of the Hudson's Bay Company was "carefully tailored to appeal to European and U.S. audiences." According to the series producer, Michael Levine, "We could tell it from a Canadian viewpoint in a way that absolutely *nobody* would have bought it." Said Saunders, "This is how culture is created in Canada today."[19] You must prove you have an international audience or you won't get financed.

When Eggleton, then minister of trade, commented on the WTO ruling in favour of split-run magazine editions, he set off a panic. He suggested that protecting culture was a nonstarter, that we should be producing for the global market. This position wasn't stated again so blatantly and may have been a testing of political waters. Heritage Minister Sheila Copps was given the opportunity to lead a charge in favour of doing *something* about the WTO threat. But the reactions all around suggested that the WTO ruling was completely unconnected with anything Canada had done or could do. Yet Canada signed the WTO agreements and when this ruling came down was involved in secret MAI negotiations that would make things far worse.

The door to the attack on Canadian culture was opened by the signing of the FTA and NAFTA and much of the erosion of Canadian culture results directly or indirectly from those deals. Yet most of the actions taken by the federal government were not forced on it by NAFTA. They were voluntarily taken, demonstrating not just that the government knows exactly what NAFTA requires but that it is fully supportive of the ideology.

While the government would no doubt like to look as though it is defending Canadian magazines, its policy decisions in other areas of cultural activity have devastated Canadian production of films, TV documentaries and dramas, and books. Incentives delivered through the tax system for these areas all but disappeared under the Tories between 1990 and 1992, from $1 billion to nearly zero. More than any other single act, this drove media companies to look for foreign funding. The Liberals have done nothing to reverse this policy.

Consistent with that policy are the Liberals' cuts to the CBC, the flagship of Canadian cultural organizations and the one most identified by Canadians as such. The sheer size of the cuts under the Liberals — 29 percent when the average cut to program spending under the Liberals has been 22 percent — suggests that rather than trying to protect the CBC (as promised in the Red Book) they have targeted it for special treatment.[20]

Most of the support programs for Canadian publishers have been eliminated or cut back. Publishers now routinely reject book proposals that would have been viable just a few years ago. While the Canadian film and TV industry is doing well on the international market, many Canadian themes just don't get addressed. According to the CBC's Mark Starowicz, many Canadian stories aren't being told and are not even being brought forward. Writers censor their own ideas. "In documentaries . . . we don't change our stories, we murder them in the crib."[21]

Ironically, the government still spends a great deal on cultural "industries," giving tax breaks to Hollywood studios to encourage investment and funding private production houses. Documentary producer John Kastner asks, "Are [the CBC], Telefilm, the OFDC [Ontario Film Development Corporation], all of these government-funded agencies really subsidizing independent producers who are making American-directed stories?"[22]

In 1997 the Senate Subcommittee on Communications tabled its interim report on Canada's international competitive position in communications. With the macho title *Wired to Win*, it is a stunning example of the betrayal of Canadian interests and their capture by the globalization hype. The senators recommend that Canada "move away from policies based on *protection* and towards those that seek to more proactively *promote* Canadian products."[23] The attitude of the senators towards industry spokespeople is reflected in their fawning over IBM's John Warner (with his corporate-rule title of director of government programs); he told the senators that "it is essential to link industrial and cultural policy objectives [which] are best met through an increased reliance on market forces."[24]

The senators as good as endorsed IBM's recommendations that would, "within a period of roughly 10 years, see the complete phasing out of all regulations in the area of licensing, foreign ownership, Canadian content and mandatory contributions to Canadian production."[25] It would be hard to outdo the chamber of sober second thought in handing over parliamentary sovereignty.

The new right's call for decentralization is a piece of the restructuring plan that is less obvious to the casual observer. It is often sold, as it has been by the Reform Party, as a more democratic alternative because it brings services closer to the people who are being served. This is nothing more than deliberate deception.

National programs, such as medicare, social assistance, and post-secondary education, provide national citizenship rights and a national identity, and these become a central part of the political culture. If programs are delivered by a national government, they are then universally available, and opposition to their removal can be more effectively focussed. According to the guru of economic rationalism, Milton Friedman, there are two steps to the elimination of democratic governance. The first is limiting the scope of government. The second is the dispersal of government power. "If government is to exercise power, better in the county than in the state, better in the state than in Washington. If I do not like what my local community does, be it in sewage disposal, or zoning, or schools, I can move to another local community . . . If I do not like what Washington imposes, I have few alternatives in this world of jealous nations."[26]

The BCNI has consistently pushed for decentralization. Its latest initiative, in the summer of 1997, used Quebec nationalism as a stalking horse for the devolution of the national government. The Chrétien Liberals have already taken decisive steps towards decentralization. Building on the policies of the Mulroney Tories, the cuts to social program transfers in themselves are a de facto decentralization, as they reduce the impact of the national government. The Tories cut federal spending on health, education, and welfare to 15 percent of provincial spending (from 20 percent), and the Liberals followed by cutting that to 9 percent.[27]

But the Liberals have taken it further. They placed a cap on federal spending for the Canada Assistance Plan, which established national standards for social assistance, and implemented the Canada Health and Social Transfer by which federal transfers to the provinces for health and education were rolled into one, allowing provinces to spend the money as they saw fit. The government is also increasingly leaving environmental regulation to the provinces, and by its massive privatization of the national transportation system has all but abandoned that field as well. In 1996 it handed over to the provinces employment training and housing.

TRANSFORMING THE PUBLIC SERVICE

The state is far more than just the elected representatives, the provincial legislatures, and the House of Commons. Part of the traditional system of checks and balances built into democratic governance is the professional civil service, whose job it is to devise policy for elected governments and to ensure that those policies are carried out. During the post-war period of the social contract they were a critical element in the creation of the egalitarian democratic state.

That role has now changed dramatically in Ottawa and the provinces. Through attrition and the changing ethos of the bureaucracy, the public servants who created the egalitarian state are rapidly disappearing, replaced by those who are chosen because they reflect the new market ethos or by younger professionals trained in new public management theories or in the ideology of public choice theory.

Duncan Cameron is head of the Canadian Centre for Policy Alternatives and a former civil servant in the finance department. He explains that the transformation of the public service was a complex affair. It started out as a result of how successful the mandarins had been at guiding the policy process. "They had too much success. The mandarins by the time Trudeau came in were dominating the government's agenda. Trudeau wanted the elected ministers to lead the policy debate. It was Trudeau who actually dismantled the mandarin system. As a result, with the growth of government and its complexity, the culture of the policy adviser changed from mandarin as policy thinker to mandarin as manager. Once you're into that management mode you're into the business ethic."[28]

It was in the mid-1970s that the ethos of serving the public began to seriously erode. Cameron compares two deputy finance ministers. Robert Bryce who had studied with Keynes, refused on principle to work for the private sector when he retired. Mickey Cohen, deputy minister through most of the 1980s, after making a tax ruling that put $600 million in the pockets of the Reichmann family, joined the company six months after quitting the department.

Another major change is shown in the way people were recruited. The Public Service Commission used to hire for the entire government, and based its decisions on tests and interviews. But under Simon Reisman's reign as deputy finance minister, the government began hiring straight from university economics departments, dominated by the late seventies by monetarists and economic rationalists. The result was that "they were recruiting the people who had gone through the brainwashing process of academic economics."[29]

Two other trends contributed to the remaking of the public service, completing its transformation into a market-oriented bureaucracy disconnected from the country's history and its social reality. Trudeau undermined the public service ethos, and Mulroney completely politicized the bureaucracy by appointing political operatives like Stanley Hartt into deputy minister positions.

For Cameron, the changes that have taken place since the late 1960s are further symbolized by who in the finance department is in charge of social policy. "When I arrived in 1966 the person on the social policy desk in finance was [the NDP's] Stanley Knowles's son, David. Today the assistant deputy minister for social policy is Tom d'Aquino's wife. She was the one who took over Lloyd Axworthy's social policy review and turned it into a 40 percent funding cut."

The federal public service has by no means been completely purged of those who believe in the idea of government. But the departments that now dominate government, principally finance but also trade and foreign affairs, are captives of this ideology. Treasury Board has studied New Zealand extensively and the economic rationalist theories such as new public management are already being incorporated into the civil service ethos.

In addition, recent years have seen a huge exodus of senior policy people from the federal government. The generous compensation packages in the private sector, combined with a six-year salary freeze for senior public servants, contributed to more than a third of the top officials quitting in 1996. These were mostly people who had joined the service in the 1960s and 1970s and had designed the social programs that are now being slashed. The slow destruction of their accomplishments is also a major factor in their decisions to quit. Many have gone to jobs as lobbyists for large corporations or are with consulting firms.

The transformation of the public service ethic was captured in a 1996 meeting between public-interest groups and officials of the foreign affairs department. The meeting was to discuss funding for the People's Summit on APEC, a forum for representatives of community groups from all the APEC countries, coinciding with the APEC summit in Vancouver in November 1997. In the past these meetings have been friendly affairs, with officials and community representatives sharing a human rights perspective on international relations. The change this time was stunning. Maude Barlow of the Council of Canadians attended.

> We sat down — this was all the big groups, Amnesty International, the CLC, NAC, Canadian Federation of Students, Greenpeace, the churches — and basically it turned into a screaming match. We were coming from different planets. They were coming from a place where they had accepted every single piece of the dogma about trade liberalization . . . At one point MP Raymond Chan, the undersecretary to Lloyd Axworthy, talked about how human rights are improving in China because he had had a meeting with a reporter. The bad news, he said, was that the reporter was arrested a week after this meeting.[30]

It was as if three decades of a democratic ethos had simply never been. When the delegates asked why there had been no consultations on the environmental impact of APEC, an official replied that there had been. Recalls Barlow, "We asked what environmental groups were involved, and he said, 'Well, none.' When we asked why not, he said that the leaders of the economies and the Canadian business people did not want the environment groups involved. He was completely disingenuous when he said this. People were open-mouthed, but he had absolutely no idea what we would be upset about."

The offer on the table to the organizations that have been playing a major role in such consultations for a generation was $100,000, none of which could be used to bring in foreign delegates. Until 1997, CIDA had always insisted that some of the money provided be used for this purpose. And while it was clear that the traditional players were to be cut out of the picture, the government was spending large sums to create its own pro-market, popular sector.

The government spent $700,000 to involve "youth" in the APEC summit. The youth were identified from the subscription list of *Teen Generation* magazine. Similarly, the government sponsored a major women's event called "Stepping Out" for which they hand-picked some Canadian businesswomen and some from the other APEC "economies." Just as the new right ensures that it has a base of support by sharing wealth with a significant section of the middle class, the market state is creating a political base that will support its new approach to international relations.

THE PROVINCES

There is not space in this book to document the commercialization of government at the provincial level. But anyone even casually observing their own provincial government knows well enough that market principles are being expressed in policies affecting everything from medicare and education to municipal services and the arts. The process is uneven, but the influence of monetarist economics, economic rationalism, and the aggressive lobbying of market liberals is everywhere apparent.

Ontario's Mike Harris has followed the restructuring handbook almost to the letter. He has surrounded himself with a core of like-minded ideological true believers whose view of politics really is different from past Tories'. They are prepared to transform the democratic state as a matter of principle, as part of their crusade against equality, regardless of the personal or political consequences. Like Roger Douglas, Margaret Thatcher, and Ronald Reagan, they continue their program with few retreats, and implement it as fast as possible, confident that once the edifice of the egalitarian state is deconstructed it will be impossible to rebuild.

All the elements are there: cuts to health and education; privatization; user fees; slashing of agencies mandated to regulate labour, the environment, and health; elimination of conservation programs; halving of grants to municipalities (seen by many as a direct assault on democracy at the local level); a 22 percent cut to social assistance, the introduction of workfare, and other punitive measures against the poor, and draconian labour legislation that takes workers' rights back to where they were in the 1950s.[31]

In the name of not competing with the private sector, and to advance another ideological principle of the new right, the government eliminated all job creation programs in its first two years. As with the federal Liberals, many of these cuts have no explanation, other than ideology. The government is simply getting out of the business of governing. It is also getting other people out of the business of governing.

The Ontario government's omnibus bill of forty-four pieces of legislation breaks the record previously held by B.C.'s Bill Bennett, whose 1983 Fraser Institute blueprint saw twenty-six pieces of legislation introduced on the first day. Harris's 211-page bill, among other things, gave the government enormous administrative powers to take actions without reference to the legislature, rolled back laws, and gave power to privatize medicare, abolish local governments, raid its employee pension fund, eliminate hospital boards, and amend the Freedom of Information Act to make it harder for citizens to get information about their government.[32]

Later in its mandate, the government cut the number of school boards in half. The resulting Toronto School Board will have 300,000 students, making a mockery of democratic governance. Harris's stubborn confrontation with teachers is classic new-right politics, but it had the effect of identifying teachers as the bulwark for a public education system that is the centrepiece of a democratic society. The government also imposed a megacity structure on the Metro Toronto area, wiping out the democratic governments of half a dozen communities. There was little effort to give these actions a public relations spin. It was being done because there was "too much government." Local politicians were portrayed almost as the enemies of the communities they governed, so self-interested and untrustworthy that Harris put six municipalities under trusteeship until his amalgamation plan was in place.

The Harris Tories reflect another aspect of the state in the new corporate order. The development of the market state necessitates the parallel construction of the security state. As the legitimacy of government breaks down, an inevitable result of the contraction of the egalitarian policies, the coercive function of the state must increase.

To date the opposition to the assault on democracy has been peaceful, with few examples of civil disobedience. Yet ultimately it is only through widespread civil disobedience that the current neo-liberal regimes in Canada will be obliged to change course. And there are already very strong signs that governments will act ruthlessly when civil disobedience begins in earnest. In Ontario the Harris government, early in its mandate, unleashed riot police on a peaceful demonstration at the legislature, producing a scene of unrestrained and highly political police brutality not witnessed in Canada for decades.

In a peaceful demonstration in Ontario, six women were arrested, taken to a high-security prison, and strip-searched. In Harris's own North Bay riding, fifty police were mobilized to break up a demonstration of a thousand teachers, unionists, students, and parents at a fundraising dinner for the Conservative Party at which Harris was speaking. In the background were another sixty tactical police officers in case there was serious resistance.

In Vancouver, during the APEC summit in 1997, the political cleansing of the territory close to the summit site and along the routes leading to it from downtown hotels was reminiscent of the "eyesore free zone" created in Manila for the 1996 summit. A human rights activist, Craig Jones, was held in jail for fourteen hours simply for placing signs reading "Democracy" and "Free Speech" on a roadway where they would be visible to passing APEC motorcades. RCMP spokesmen were aggressive in their defence of these flagrant abuses of democratic rights. Later, students at the University of British Columbia, protesting against the APEC summit being held on their campus, and against the presence of Indonesian dictator Suharto and Chinese president Jiang Zemin, were gratuitously pepper-sprayed in a further demonstration of intimidation. One woman was grabbed from behind by the RCMP, thrown to the ground, and sprayed in the face.

For his part, Prime Minister Chrétien, already infamous for his choking assault on another peaceful demonstrator, and fresh from consorting with dictators, replied to a reporter's question about the police assault with, "For me, pepper, I only put it on my plate. Next [question]." Whether simply a grossly insensitive remark or a signal to police that their actions are approved at the highest level, the meaning for political rights was obvious. Clear, too, was Chrétien's eagerness to comply with Jiang Zemin's request that demonstrators be kept out of earshot and out of sight, a request that became an order to police forces. Several commentators mused about the irony in the federal government's position that dictators like Suharto and Jiang Zemin will moderate their attitudes towards human rights. It seemed as though the result of engagement has been a hardening of attitudes towards human rights in Canada.

These and other recent examples of overwhelming police presence, brutality in the name of security, deliberate intimidation and humiliation are an ominous sign of things to come. So, too, was a memo leaked in November 1997 about a planned $350,000 training program for Atlantic fisheries employees in anticipation of possible "life threatening violence" on the part of fishers at the ending of the TAGS program in May 1998. The message is clear. Accept the downsizing of democracy and the end of social rights or you will get assaulted, or arrested, or both.

❖

Twenty years ago Samuel P. Huntington declared in a Trilateral Commission study that the United States, and by extension other Western countries, was suffering from a crisis of democracy. That crisis was described as an "excess of democracy," a situation in which too many people were engaged in the political process. "Apathy and non-involvement" on the part of a large portion of the population are required for a liberal democracy to be governable, said Huntington. And so we see governments systematically putting in place institutions, bureaucratic regimes, social policies, and a whole new governing ethos, hoping to institutionalize public apathy.

There would seem to be little argument that from the perspective of the ruled in Western societies there is now a severe shortage of democracy. The challenge for those determined to stop the neo-liberal counter-revolution is to renew the struggle for a radical democracy, and to do that we must become intentional citizens.

11

DEMOCRACY IN THE NEW MILLENNIUM

An alternative conception of democracy is that the public must be barred from managing their own affairs, and the means of information must be kept narrowly and rigidly controlled.

— NOAM CHOMSKY

I perceive the divine patience of your people, but where is their divine anger?

— BERTOLT BRECHT

Things are going to get worse before they get better; it doesn't have to be this way. Those two sentiments pretty much sum up the territory on which the struggle for democracy in the new millennium will take place. The so-called new world order is not inevitable, like the weather. It is no more inevitable or "natural" than any other way that we might choose to organize ourselves as human beings. Indeed, it can be forcefully argued that our current path is perhaps the most *unnatural* order of things. For what, if not unnatural, is a way of organizing human existence that virtually guarantees that we will destroy the very basis for that existence? We are now behaving in such a way that an outside observer would conclude that we are a species doomed to die out, incapable of rationally mapping out a sustainable ecological or social future; determined to destroy the means of life.

The demoralization and powerlessness that grip so many Canadians facing the right-wing counter-revolution is its greatest strength. For those who believe that it cannot be stopped, we need to revisit our own fairly recent history. In the Great Depression people faced the ruthless power of corporations and their hired thugs; they experienced incredible deprivation; the organizations they formed to defend their rights were infiltrated by the police, some were declared illegal and their leaders jailed. The unemployed were forced into camps in order to qualify for relief. Activists were murdered. Yet citizens fought back. Indeed, they fought back so effectively, armed with ideas ranging from social democracy to communism, that the most farsighted corporate defenders saw the possibility of a social revolution. And so we got reform.

If people do not resist the onslaught of corporate rule, it not only will get worse; it has to get worse. The logic of the system, driven by a rigid ideology and an elite of true believers, means that there are no natural barriers, no limits to the destructive power of transnational corporations and the international system of finance and mass consumerism they are putting in place. Market liberalism, by its nature unable to value anything but economic efficiency, cannot take into account human suffering, human history, the value of culture or community or the value of the environment.

This system will take everything; it cannot stop. We know what it is capable of because we see it already, in child slave labour abroad, in worsening environmental degradation, in people working in poisonous factories, in advertising aimed at getting children to start smoking cigarettes.

Canadian philosopher John McMurtry suggests that we have entered the "cancer stage" of capitalism. Our social institutions, he argues, acted as an immune system, "recognizing and responding to the vital life needs of social bodies as a whole [which] shielded members from disease, starvation, and disabling morbidities." It is a compelling analogy. The signs of immune system breakdown are unmistakable, says McMurtry, "when money capital lacks any commitment to any life-organization . . . but is free to move in and out of . . . social and environmental life hosts." Our institutional immune system fails to recognize it as a threat and the cancer grows apace, invading every aspect of the host body until it "eventually destroys the life-host in the absence of an effective immune-system recognition and response."[1]

In the absence of effective institutions to protect society and community, the only immune system remaining is the millions of individual citizens who face increasing insecurity and falling standards of living. The challenge will take us back to the roots of democracy, and that is to the struggle of classes over rule by the majority. If we assess our democracy, it is clear that the "problem" identified by the Trilateral Commission more than twenty years ago has been resolved in favour of the corporations that it spoke for.

The "excess" of democracy has been eliminated. For the most part the public no longer questions "the legitimacy of hierarchy, coercion, discipline, secrecy, and deception."[2] We are back to a time when governments can govern simply with the cooperation of a few bankers and Bay Street lawyers, or the modern equivalent, the BCNI. As for the media, the elite no longer has to fear that it is, in Walter Cronkite's words, "inclined to side with humanity rather than with authority and institutions."[3]

Canadians oppose by large majorities nearly every aspect of the new-right agenda and the role of corporations in implementing that agenda. On medicare, education, the environment, job creation, poverty, and the role of government, polls show that Canadian citizens want more money, not less, directed at these issues. Indeed, in most cases we are even prepared to pay more taxes to that end. But the almost universal response of the neo-liberal state is profoundly undemocratic. It is summed up by Brian Mulroney's words, aped by Saskatchewan premier Roy Romanow: When faced with doing the right thing or the popular thing, they always choose the right thing. The willingness to thwart the will of the people has become a sign of the highest level of responsibility that a political leader can aspire to. It is a sign of his or her sense of responsibility to corporations.

The challenge to re-establish majority rule must take place at both the level of ideas and the level of power. At the level of ideas it is really no contest. It would be difficult to imagine a more impoverished set of ideas, principles, assumptions about human nature, and goals for society than those promoted by the new right. They would have us believe that the end point of thousands of years of civilization is a globally homogeneous marketplace of customers (not citizens) whose vision can be summed up in a single value, economic efficiency, and whose ultimate expression of human achievement is the universal availability of Coke and Nike running shoes.

Who are the heroes of this brave new world with whom ordinary citizens have to compete for moral, ethical, and intellectual superiority? Barrick CEO Peter Munk, whose own hero is a fascist general who oversaw the slaughter of thirty thousand unarmed civilians? Conrad Black, who is so contemptuous of his own country that he can't bear to live here? Or does the ultimate challenge come from Bill Gates, a man who with even a minimum of imagination could make fabulous contributions to his community and to humanity with his $54 billion, but instead is satisfied with designing second rate computer software?

Or is the real challenge from the gaggle of new-right columnists and other hangers-on like Andrew Coyne, David Frum, Diane Francis, Barbara Amiel, and *Saturday Night* editor Kenneth Whyte whose generation of new ideas consists of digging through the dust-bins of history to find inspiration in "free markets" that ceased to exist more than a century ago? The collective intellectual leadership of the triumphant new right is the political equivalent of the idiot savant, clever purveyors of ideology but socially retarded, culturally vacuous, and morally indifferent, promoting a world of obscene wealth for the few and insecurity for the many. Is this the vision that is too com-pelling to challenge?

Clearly it is the sheer power of the corporations and not the ideas of their ideological prostitutes that makes the fight for democracy in the new millennium so formidable. The current institutions of democracy, including the political parties, cannot be expected to lead a radical democratic movement against these forces. That does not mean that we must ignore these institutions or, for example, dismiss the role of the NDP, which is the only voice in Parliament that speaks for social justice and will fight against corporate domination. The rejuvenation of a democratic politics will involve engaging the adversary at every level and in every forum, and supporting others who do so.

But to win against the juggernaut of global corporate rule will require a virtual revolution in citizen consciousness, in people's understanding of what it means to be a citizen. That involves a decision to become deliberate, self-aware citizens who make a commitment of time and resources to rescuing their community from its continued destruction. If those who despair at what is happening to our country are not willing to make sacrifices, and change their lives, it is a certainty that we will lose and end up as observers of ever greater corporate domination.

It means that hundreds of thousands of people who normally pay little attention to politics will have to consciously devote time to learn what is happening, talk with neighbours, join social and political action groups, and stop trading in their rights and obligations as citizens for the right to be a customer in the global marketplace. We cannot be both global customers and global citizens, for to be the former explicitly means the demise of the latter.

Of course, increasing numbers of Canadians don't even get to make that trade. The 4.4 million working Canadians who now slip repeatedly in and out of poverty are disenfranchised in both of the competing democracies, the one person, one vote and the one dollar, one vote varieties. They have no access to the "global products." Imagining a revolution in citizen consciousness has to address the issue of class inequalities.

Citizen participation must be directed at seizing back from corporations power that our "own" governments have ceded. In the vacuum of government deregulation corporations have become the organizational form that is now "regulating" society. It is corporations that increasingly determine what kind of work there will be, who will get it, how much damage will be done to the environment and where, what human needs will be addressed and which will go unfulfilled.

Yet refocussing democratic action on corporations does not mean that we can abandon the state. While the state is now being transformed into the market state from the egalitarian state, it is still the only human organization ultimately powerful enough to challenge corporate rule, whether alone or as part of international institutions for world governance. The struggle for democracy has throughout this century been a struggle for control of the state. That will not change. Creating a genuine democracy means, in the words of political scientist Leo Panitch, building "a different kind of state."

Ironically, we can trace the devolution of the current state and the ease with which corporations are dismantling it in part to the powerful democratic movements of the past. Although they enhanced political democracy by increasing the participation of citizens in the process, they failed to apply that democracy and participation to the social programs and the state itself.

But, says Panitch, "the old welfare state reforms . . . actually had very little to do with reforming the state itself; that is, with reforming the mode of administration in which social policy became embedded. It is a mode of administration that is structured in a fundamentally undemocratic fashion, along strict principles of secrecy and hierarchy that owe much to the principles of organization of the 19th-century British Colonial Office."[4]

The state, even though it responded to the democratic movements of workers and other social groups, was not suddenly transformed into an agency of majority rule. It was still an agency of the market economic system, and the reforms were intended precisely to head off majority rule. The state was still "managing" capitalism for corporations. "It was engaged in the regulation of the people who were its clients, establishing rules that governed their behaviour in many large and small, intimate and public, spheres of life."

The "participatory democracy" programs of the Trudeau Liberals were both a strategy for co-opting radical movements and partly a genuine response to previously marginal groups seeking input into policy making. In both cases, the state was trying to make itself legitimate in the eyes of citizens, both those who were active and those who were influenced by them.

Once movement organizations were recognized by the government, much of their time was spent "dealing" with the state about what sorts of programs would be implemented. Gradually, they moved away from building the grass roots of their own movements in part because they no longer needed active memberships to secure access to government and to policy consultation. In fact, in some cases having an active membership making radical demands was a threat to that access.

One of the reasons that the right has so successfully attacked social programs is that those programs are not integrated into the community but are seen as "delivered" by government agencies that have no real connection with citizens and that citizens had no say in creating. Many poor people are sympathetic to attacks on welfare because their experience with welfare has been punitive, humiliating, and simply inadequate. And it is getting worse. As governments adopt market principles as "performance indicators" to assess public services, there is less and less distinction between those services provided to enhance the well-being of the community and those for sale in the marketplace.

Social reformers of the next millennium will have to take account of the fact that an essential part of democratic reform is the reform of how state services are provided as well as what services are provided. A truly democratic social assistance system would be one in which the front-line workers are mandated to act as advocates for their fellow citizens instead of being obliged by the social control ethic to act as gate-keepers for "clients."

At a 1991 conference on social welfare policy, both policy makers and front-line workers imagined what a democratic policy would look like: "Why could not employees and clients of the ministry elect [assistant deputy ministers] from a panel of choices put forward by the minister? Perhaps there could be referenda among clients on policy — such as among the elderly in extended care institutions who might be encouraged to discuss and vote on a series of policy options being considered inside the ministry . . . Public employees [are] well placed to be facilitators of the collective organization of the poor so they would no longer face the state or the market as powerless and passive individuals."[5]

To have any chance of being successful, social reform must inspire hope. The exciting prospect of creating a whole new democratic ethos involving community and government (they should be the same anyway) could inspire hope. And it integrates both the process of democracy and the outcome of the process, involving an alliance of public servants (we should start to refer to them as community employees) and citizens in political decision making and the service itself. The division between government employee and client would be broken down and reconstructed as a relationship between citizens.

Unless the fight for democracy entails such a radical conception it will fail. Not just because the current relationship between citizen and state has been shown to be vulnerable to attack from the right, but because we are otherwise doomed to remain in our current protective mode, defending an eroding system that we never wanted in the first place. How can we expect to inspire hope by defending a system of social services that we never believed in anyway?

As we keep digging trenches in our rear-guard actions against the encroachment of corporate rule, we find ourselves defending things that are increasingly indefensible. What will we be defending next, a bad two-tier health system against the advent of a terrible one? Will activists ten years from now be demanding better conditions in the camps for the unemployed? There is nothing to suggest that the corporate elite is incapable of such measures.

FIGHTING THE MAI, ABROGATING NAFTA

The most powerful political weapons at the disposal of transnational corporations are the trade and investment agreements that have transformed the powers of the state in the interests of corporate rule. Much of the struggle to regain genuine democracy will of necessity be against these agreements.

There is now in Canada and around the world a vigorous fight against the Multilateral Agreement on Investment (MAI) and against APEC, the Asia Pacific Economic Co-operation regime. This is a common struggle of nations and people who are now alerted to the dangers of such agreements, alerted in part by what has happened in Canada but, even more important, by what has happened in Mexico. The World Trade Organization, which reaches it decisions through the democratic consensus of its member countries, faces serious conflict between the dominant developed countries and a growing number of less developed countries not only over the MAI but over the other agreements coming down the pipe.

NAFTA and the agreements it has helped spawn make the achievement of an economically just world impossible. Those who suggest that we abandon any hope of abrogating NAFTA have, unwittingly, already given up the fight. That is not to say that we should never renegotiate any aspects of NAFTA. We should, but as steps along the road to abrogation. We should start with those sections that prevent us from demanding that investment be productive, not speculative; that take away our sovereignty over energy development; that prevent us from demanding the use of local inputs in exported goods, and that threaten our culture.

The context for abrogating NAFTA is not the current political balance of forces, but that doesn't mean abrogation is unimaginable. The truth is, we have not seriously tried to imagine and plan for the day when it will be possible. When we achieve enough political strength in our social movements to force a Canadian government to renegotiate this deal, then we will be on the way to having the power to abrogate it.

Insisting that NAFTA be abrogated is a statement of faith in the future. Yet any disagreement over whether to maintain the option of cancelling NAFTA may in the end be a question of semantics. For in the longer term creating international institutions for social justice will be necessary to challenge the power of transnationals, and such institutions would change NAFTA and other such agreements so fundamentally that the deals would simply fade away.

INTERNATIONAL DEMOCRACY

There are nation-states who have rejected free trade, rejected structural adjustment, rejected corporate rule and the impoverished ideology that drives it. Norway and Sweden, even after some backward steps, are still egalitarian states and they put the lie to the propaganda that globalization is inevitable and that resistance is futile. Norwegian and Swedish citizens just said no; they made a democratic choice to maintain civilized societies. Their governments remained loyal to the principles of democracy.

But for other countries, like Canada, recapturing that democratic reality will be much more difficult than if we had managed to keep it in the first place. We cannot possibly do it alone. The struggle for economic and social justice will, over the next decade and more, become increasingly international because the nature of the adversary demands it. Transnational corporations and the multilateral deals they are brokering are forcing the labour movement and popular organizations in all countries to cooperate in ways they never have before.

This international movement uniting peoples of the developed nations and the less developed nations was pioneered by the cooperation between activists in Mexico, Canada, and the U.S. in their opposition to NAFTA. It continues to develop in opposition to APEC, as was demonstrated dramatically by the People's Summit against APEC, held in Vancouver in 1997.

As ordinary citizens face the daily crises of insecurity, falling standards of living, and eroding public services it is easy to forget that the TNCs who created the new order will face a crisis, too. If a worldwide financial crisis does not arrive first — and in all likelihood it will — the next big capitalist crisis will be the saturation of the global middle-class market. At that point there will be no more growth strategies and the crisis that capitalism has been avoiding for a century will arrive once more.

No matter what the scenario, the result of the crisis will be a need, as John Dillon points out in his book *Turning the Tide*, for a new United Nations Conference on Money and Finance. It will have to address two main issues, hot money speculation and massive indebtedness of the less developed world, because the world system of finance and production simply cannot continue on these paths forever. Everyone knows this, but it will take a crisis to force a solution. A new U.N. conference would have to return to the intent of the agencies established at Bretton Woods.

A World Bank reformed — or more likely replaced — along the lines of its original goals would make credit available to developing countries with balance-of-payments deficits from deposits by developed countries with balance-of-payments surpluses. An aid program, operating out of the democratically run U.N. and not the financially driven IMF or World Bank, would provide grants and low-cost loans to developing countries without the conditions that now require many countries to destroy their social infrastructure. A World Trade Organization designed to actually work for nations rather than provide guarantees for TNCs would work to stabilize commodity prices and promote the production of key consumer goods, from food to housing, in each member country.

The world has changed dramatically since Keynes lost the battle for the design of international governance in 1944. The principles remain the same, but the mechanisms for such governance will have to address the power of transnational corporations and the ocean of hot money that now drives the global economy. One viable solution to the hot money system is the Tobin tax, a measure even Jean Chrétien briefly flirted with until he was quickly re-educated. The tax, designed by Nobel laureate economist James Tobin, would impose a very low tax, say 0.5 percent or even 0.25 percent, on every currency transaction in the market, worldwide. It would be a universal tax; every country would have to pay it. The money raised, about $500 billion a year at 0.25 percent, would be funnelled into the International Monetary Fund or the World Bank to assist the less developed countries. It would also serve to severely dampen currency speculation because even at such low levels it eliminates the tiny margins on which speculators now make their money.[6]

Besides the Tobin tax, an international agreement setting parameters for corporate taxes could ensure that corporations paid sufficient national taxes to cover the costs of infrastructure and social services (such as the health and education of the workforce) they benefit from in the course of doing business.

International regimes would regulate the flow of capital and control speculative versus productive investment. And instead of the vague and largely unenforceable labour, social, and environmental "side deals," new United Nations charters would make these areas of human concern paramount, or at least equal to concerns about trade and investment. Any country wanting access to loans, grants, or debt restructuring or the benefits of trade regulation through U.N. agencies would be obliged to live up to these charters or face punitive sanctions. In effect, the new institutions, or reformed old ones, would have their functions and their ethos transformed from their current role as agencies for corporate domination to agencies for democratic rule.

CHALLENGING CORPORATE RULE

In 1849, Louis Riel Sr., the father of the great Métis leader, led three hundred armed Métis and surrounded the temporary courthouse in which the Hudson's Bay Company was trying three Métis, independent traders, for violating company laws. The Métis did not fire a shot. They just sat, mounted on their horses, their rifles cradled in their arms. Minutes later the company released the three men. Corporate rule by an occupying power ruling in the interests of Britain and hostile to those it governed had come to an end on the prairies. It's impossible to know at what point the Métis, exploited for decades by the HBC, "imagined" ending its economic monopoly.

Part of the challenge of confronting corporate domination is in overcoming the demoralization of seeing "our leaders" willingly and even eagerly ceding power and sovereignty to transnational corporations. Ursula Franklin captures the appropriate awareness and a useful analogy when she describes us as now being under the rule of an occupying power. Current governments govern with no reference to our needs and desires as citizens, without reference to our history and culture, in complete contradiction of our well-being. Like the Vichy government of wartime France, they have seized the governing structures of our society in the interests of a foreign power. They are dismantling them and setting up new structures of authority that reflect the interests of that foreign power, transnational corporations.

Many groups are still involved in consulting with the government even while the government has absolutely no intention of listening. We should not be engaged in the pretend democracy of consulting with an occupying power, otherwise, as Franklin puts it, we are behaving as "collaborators." By agreeing to take part in a consultation process completely corrupted by the government and without any prospect of success, we provide the occupying power with undeserved legitimacy and ultimately betray the people we are struggling to represent. These are not our governments.

The principal adversaries in our struggle for social and economic justice around the world are the transnational corporations, who are merging their way to ever greater concentrations of power. The task of creating a revolution in citizen consciousness begins here, with building a recognition of the role of corporations and the role of the state in ceding our national sovereignty to them. That entails a shift in focus for every citizen organization in the country away from trying to "influence" currently constituted governments and towards exposing every detail of how corporations rule, who are the people behind the CEO titles, and how they control government and those political parties that are governing in their interests.

There are those challenging corporate power who attempt to force corporations back into what is often called a stakeholder model of corporate management. This model encourages corporations to manage their affairs in the interest of not just shareholders but also employees, communities, consumers, and the environment. Yet this model is outdated. The global economy has passed it by. Transnational corporations dominate the world and their decisions determine the fate and the decisions of lesser corporations. The planners of these corporate behemoths do not think in terms of stakeholders because it is irrelevant to their purpose: profits and global expansion.

This does not mean that we should stop organizing against corporations like Nike for employing labour at slave-level wages or stop boycotting Shell Oil for its complicity in the murder of Ogoni activists in Nigeria. Indeed, we need to multiply those actions across the country as a way of reinforcing people's understanding of the role of corporations. But there are simply too many corporations to expose one by one as bad corporate citizens. By trying to change corporate rule this way, in the words of Henry Demarest Lloyd, an anti-corporate activist of the last century, "we are asking them not to be what we have made them to be. We have put power into their hands and ask them not to use it as power."

Exposing the antisocial and anti-democratic behaviour of corporations like Shell, Nike, Barrick, Bell Canada, the big five banks, and the many other destructive corporate citizens, we can educate and mobilize citizens to take power away from them. We can turn the tables on those who would transform us from citizens into customers and use our power as consumers to act as citizens. But this use of consumer/citizen activism must be aimed at undercutting corporate power. In removing the power we have put in their hands, we put it back into the hands of citizens and begin to create the conditions for a genuinely democratic state.

Removing that corporate power is straightforward when it comes to reforming the democratic institutions they now control or influence. Corporations must be prevented from funding political parties. Legislation severely limiting third-party spending in elections must be forced back on the political agenda. Political lobbying by corporations and by professional lobbyists in their hire must be even more restricted than it is, and the tax deduction allowed for this activity, essentially taxpayers funding the perversion of their own government, must be ended. All contacts between corporate representatives and government officials must be made transparent so that every attempted intervention by corporate interests is out in the open for citizens to see and assess. The growing practice of contracting out policy making to the private sector must be banned.

On the broader political front, we must begin to put faces on the faceless corporations by publicly identifying the people who make the decisions that harm our communities. People need to know the connections between millionaire tax-avoider Paul Martin and the other multimillionaires who make public policy in Canada. How is it in a democracy that the vast majority of citizens do not know the faces or even the names of the people who rule them? How is it that millions of Canadians believe that the Fraser Institute is an independent educational institute when it is nothing more than a front for the largest corporations in the country, pimping "free-market" ideology in the cause of eliminating majority rule?

Some unions and citizen organizations are already shifting their focus to exposing corporate domination of the country. The Canadian Union of Public Employees has a whole research team investigating the large corporations who have targeted our health care, municipal services, and educational institutions. A series of cards, for example, profiles the eight most dangerous corporate vultures currently circling the wounded Canadian medicare system. As we examine below, the labour movement in Ontario confronted corporate rule in its Days of Action city shutdowns. The Ontario teachers' strike raised the question of future privatization of education.

The Council of Canadians has targeted the corporate ownership of the media and the concentration of that ownership in the hands of a very few companies. For several years the council (with its 100,000 members) has been shifting focus from pressuring government to exposing the role of corporations. One of its main themes is the development of a citizens' agenda as a counterpoint to the corporate agenda. Its campaign to expose the Bay Street takeover of the Canada Pension Plan has reached hundreds of thousands of people; in addition, the council has led the way in the fight against the MAI.

The International Forum on Globalization, based in San Francisco but with strong Canadian representation, held a conference on corporate rule in late 1996 and brought ninety anti-corporate activists from twenty-two countries together to develop global strategies against corporate rule. Every APEC summit so far has also featured a People's Summit of social activists from all the APEC countries.

THE CULTURAL REVOLUTION: FROM CONSUMER TO CITIZEN

The long-term struggle for democracy and a democratic state entails not just a power struggle against corporate rule. If that democratic dream is global, then the fight has to be against the very logic of capitalism. To defeat transnational corporations, we clearly have to deny them the source of their power over us, and that power is the promotion of mass consumerism. If we do not resist that global strategy, we cannot win. The only way to defeat the global marketing monster is to starve it into a state of submission and weakness that allows another vision to emerge. The crisis in overproduction hinted at in Asia will be an opportunity for citizens to establish production for human need, not for profit.

The need to choose between dollar-democracy or citizen-democracy, between being customers in the global marketplace or citizens of civil society, entails more than simply devoting more time to being informed and active citizens. "Average" Canadians, who consume hundreds of times their allotted, equal share of the world's resources, are already complicit in the corporate plan for a global consumer society.

International capitalism cannot survive unless it continues to grow, and with the added hot money dimension of finance capitalism it now has to grow even faster. That means that it has to use up the limited resources of the planet even faster, exploit the world's working people even more, and put ever greater pressure on the resources of communities as they try to cope with the erosion of the egalitarian state.

And every time we purchase something we don't really need we feed that process. In the fight against corporate greed we need to do more than organize against Nike because it exploits its workers. We need to organize a culture that refuses to pay $190 for a pair of running shoes.

Out of our growing understanding of the need to consume less has come one key tool for changing our thinking about the economy. It is called the Genuine Progress Indicator and it is intended to replace the use of the Gross Domestic Product, a concept that rationalizes and perpetuates the notion of unlimited growth as a social good.

The Genuine Progress Indicator judges economic activity, products, and the distribution of economic benefits by whether they contribute to the community's well-being. It subtracts the costs of pollution, the depletion of natural resources, air and water degradation, and the costs associated with crime and places a negative on unequal distribution of income. It treats as a plus household and volunteer work, which the group Redefining Progress estimates at $1.3 trillion per year in the U.S., increasing total output by almost a quarter. The GPI also counts other aspects of the quality of life, treating loss of leisure time, for example, as a negative. The GPI counts new productive assets as a plus but consumption through borrowing as a negative. Since 1973 the GPI in the U.S. has seen a steady decline, dropping most rapidly between 1991 and 1995 to 34 percent below its 1950 level.[7]

THE POPULAR SECTOR: CHALLENGING THE POWER OF CAPITAL

The use of consumer power by politically conscious citizens has enormous potential for exposing the role of corporations in society. This can and should go far beyond just the specifically organized boycotts against particularly offensive corporations. It should, as suggested earlier, extend to boycotting mass consumer culture in general and reducing consumption to more closely reflect actual needs. We should, simply as individual citizens, initiate our own ethical boycotts. No union or social activist should have their money in the Toronto Dominion Bank, which in 1997 co-sponsored a Fraser Institute right-to-work conference. Nor should they patronize the Royal Bank, which gave the Fraser Institute $20,100 in 1996. These actions alone should cancel the privileges of these banks to use union members' money. Likewise, we should boycott any corporation that moves jobs out of Canada.

But there is also great potential for challenging capital from the other end of the economic process, production itself. Most public attention on economic issues is focussed on two sectors in the economy, the private and the public. With the private-sector ethos creeping into even what remains of the public sector, we are facing an economy that will be increasingly guided by the principles of private investment. And as the state exits many of the public services we still have, corporations are poised to take them over completely. And that means that many needs for millions of citizens will not be met.

A key area in the fight for a new democracy is the expansion of the third area of the economy largely ignored by the media and government. The popular sector, called the social sector in France, in fact has great potential as the social base for building a genuine democracy. The popular sector, comprising thousands of nonprofit groups that provide countless services to their members and the community at large, is more reflective of genuine democracy and citizen consciousness than the formal political system.

It is precisely people's identification as women, environmentalists, health advocates, educators, cultural workers, peace activists, and aboriginal people in their organizations that makes them intentional, aware citizens. These organizations are not only engaged in democratic political representation; they employ people, meet needs, purchase goods and services, and involve millions of people in activity that is generally seen as noneconomic because it doesn't make a profit. Promoting the popular sector through expanded access to capital has the dual effect of creating economic activity that serves real needs and potentially seizing some of the economic and social territory from the realm of the corporate sector.

One enormous source of capital that could be used to expand the popular sector is the money in union pension funds, now sitting at something over $190 billion in Canada. That is the deferred income of employees, but it is also a huge pool of capital that, if it was controlled by those employees, could break down the distinction between owners and employees in the private sector, a distinction that is at the root of the power imbalance between citizens and corporations.

Unions in Canada have played an important role in opposing corporate rule and are moving even more in that direction as the state devolves into corporate governance. As Duncan Cameron of the Canadian Centre for Policy Alternatives argues, "Broadening the role of unions to include the direct stewardship of investment capital could be the most important step since the right to strike."[8]

At the moment few unions have much say in how their funds are invested because legislated control over that money is in the hands of pension trustees whose singular legislated mandate is to maximize fund income with limited risk. But unions could make it a priority to bargain for greater control over those funds and where they get invested. Resistance from union members should be addressed as part of the unions' efforts to educate and mobilize their members in the fight against corporate rule.

The power of union pension funds has already been demonstrated by the largest pension fund in the U.S., the California Public Employees Retirement System. By 2000 the fund will have $200 billion, and though not directly controlled by the unions, its sympathetic president, Bill Crist, has repeatedly used the fund to pressure corporations to change their behaviour. They hold huge portfolios in some of America's largest corporations and engineered a boardroom coup at General Motors, removing senior management who had refused even to meet with Crist. Crist's approach is to pressure against short-term layoffs and to demand that companies the fund invests in have long-term strategic plans rather than short-term share-price goals.[9]

The American labour movement is now beginning to coordinate the holdings of union pension funds, which now amount to $1.4 trillion, fully 14 percent of outstanding shares in the U.S. In September 1997, the AFL-CIO established the Center for Working Capital. The founders envision many possible actions, from influencing bargaining disputes to demanding that fund managers invest in companies demonstrating a commitment to long-term growth.

The International Association of Machinists and Aerospace Workers is using pension money to help convert a former Cruise missile factory in Seattle into a plant assembling high-speed passenger trains. The first forty employees of the union's company, Pacifica, will be skilled union members who were laid off from the Naval Undersea Warfare Center. The company will use an innovative method of work organization that maximizes worker participation and leadership.[10]

These funds have even more potential for giving greater power to subordinate groups that have a more democratic vision of the economy. Using even a half of 1 percent of the $190 billion in funds to finance cost-recovery projects, social housing, or environmental projects would give the popular sector more clout to force governments to legislate in favour of such groups. One possibility would be to bring together unions, popular groups, and allies in opposition parties to change the Bank Act to force banks to lend a certain minimum percentage of their assets to third-sector community development projects.

There is another potential benefit to such projects. Many popular-sector groups now function in isolation from both the private-sector economy and the popular and union-based political movements against corporate domination. Bringing together popular sector groups and unions in projects that are both political and economic in nature creates the basis for a powerful alternative vision of community. More than any amount of political education or lobbying, such models would be compelling evidence of how society could be organized. Tangible, functioning models of a democratic economy will be increasingly important in a political atmosphere dominated by corporate media, right-wing think-tanks, and the market state.

Equally important, these "real-life" projects create community in ways that anti-corporate organizing simply can't do. Involvement in social movements can be isolating in the sense that the political activity is rarely integrated into people's lives. Engaging in boycotts, getting involved in community groups, demonstrating against corporate headquarters, while inspiring and providing a sense of citizen power, are often transitory events and can seem disconnected from the daily reality of work, family, and popular culture. We still go home to joblessness, debt, or insecurity, and the late-night TV news still assaults us with its right-wing bias. Creating community out of citizen consciousness is a key part of the movement for a new democracy.

The Canadian Auto Workers is one union that has put considerable energy into anti-corporate strategies and social justice unionism. The union's principal economist, Sam Gindin, argues that unions must integrate themselves and their democratic politics into the community. "Consider, for example, the creation of new local union committees that are open to workers' spouses, and teenage sons and daughters . . . Such an initiative . . . organizes workers around other aspects of their lives: air [quality], the safety of the neighborhood, the schools our kids attend."[11]

Gindin further suggests that unions could begin to influence jobs and job security by working at the municipal level to press for elected job development boards. These boards would guarantee everyone either a paid job or training to meet community needs. The board could identify a community's needs and then invite the community's proposals to meet them.

SIGNS OF CRISIS, OPPORTUNITIES FOR CHANGE

The struggle against corporate rule and for democracy is a long-term fight. It is hard to exaggerate the importance of seeing the fight in this way. Popular forces seem to lose battle after battle, and the forces aligned against them are indeed formidable. Developing a long-term view gives three advantages to those who would take on corporate rule. First, it reduces the terrible burden of having to win the next battle when there is a very strong likelihood that it won't be won. We know that things will get worse before they get better, but if the next battle is just one on the road to an imaginable victory it is not so demoralizing.

Taking the long view also allows us, indeed compels us, to take the time to revisit our vision of what a truly democratic, equal, fair, and ecologically sustainable society would look like. This means imagining the future. But it also means imagining the actual struggle for democracy by developing medium-term and long-term strategies of where we want to be, when we want to be there, and how we can get there.

Last, and perhaps most important, the long-term view has the potential to transform the day-to-day fight to save the nation from a perpetually defensive fight to one in which progressive forces begin to take the initiative. A good defence won't win the fight. Until we take back the initiative to change society, we simply cannot win.

There are real signs that the triumphalism of the new right is showing some tarnish. Some of the most famous gurus of unrestrained corporate greed and power are looking over their shoulders and warning their brethren to beware the angry workers. Take the UPS strike of 1997, in which 185,000 members of the supposedly quiescent American working class not only won their struggle but captured the imagination of the American public. By a two-to-one margin

Americans supported the strikers and in particular their demand for more full-time jobs. American pollster Daniel Yankelovich stated that the solid sympathy for the UPS workers could well be a turning point in American political culture. The strike, he said, was "a consciousness-raising event."[12]

Stephen Roach, one of the decamped gurus of downsizing, was quick to offer some advice to the myth makers who talk about the amazing American economy. The great American recovery, scolds Roach, does not come from increased productivity but is built exclusively on the backs of workers squeezed to the breaking point. "The labour crunch recovery is not sustainable. It is a recipe for mounting tensions, in which a raw power struggle occurs between capital and labour. Investors are initially rewarded beyond their wildest dreams but those rewards could eventually be wiped out by a worker backlash."[13] Americans don't talk much about class war, but that is clearly what Roach is talking about.

There are other encouraging signs of resistance to the new world corporate order, ranging from the election of many social democratic and socialist mayors throughout Latin America, to governments backing off their radical market agendas, to hundreds of thousands of citizens demonstrating against the destruction of social programs throughout Europe.

The major reversal of the Alberta government of Ralph Klein, under steady public pressure to reinstate previous levels of funding for medicare and education, is a victory for democracy, coming as it does in a province noted for its individualism and free-market politics. The Chrétien government's pledge to return to its social liberal tradition may well prove to be a ruse, but just that it felt compelled to make the declaration is more evidence that the government fears a loss of legitimacy.

The breakthrough of the NDP in Atlantic Canada in the 1997 federal election is also significant, and not only for what it says about people's attachment to Canada's communitarian tradition and their rejection of the Liberal Party. Although the NDP's social democracy is moderate, it retains commitments to social justice lost in other social democratic parties around the world. The party is prepared to confront corporate rule explicitly and is clearly the parliamentary wing of the anti-corporate fight. It represents a version of majoritarian democracy, and the act of voting for the NDP in the Atlantic provinces was a declaration of citizen consciousness.

The Days of Action organized since 1996 by labour and community groups in Ontario have brought out historically unprecedented numbers of people protesting the Harris government's implementation of the corporate agenda. The way the demonstrations were conceived and organized directly addressed the issue of corporate power and the erosion of the egalitarian state. According to the CAW's Sam Gindin, "The emphasis on workplace shutdowns . . . highlighted — successfully — the employer base behind the government's attacks on working people. The public sector shutdowns of transit, schools and post offices were directed at reminding people of the importance of social services they had taken for granted."[14]

The 1997 strike by 126,000 Ontario teachers is another example of resistance whose impact will be measured over the next decade and longer. Never before have Ontario teachers, historically divided into five often fractious unions, been so united. There is a special irony here. Teachers are the favourite ideological target of neo-cons because public education is seen as a key source of "excess democracy." Yet the Ontario fight actually heightened public consciousness about the issue of democracy because it was in part fought over the issue of who controls education. And teachers will inevitably take their own heightened awareness of democracy back into the classroom, just where the neo-cons don't want it.

Of critical importance to the long-term struggle for democracy is the fact that the teachers' strike and the Days of Action were acts of civil disobedience. The change of political consciousness required to mobilize hundreds of thousands of people in civil disobedience should never be underestimated; neither should the strength of the social solidarity built by engaging in such actions. These are events that, in the words of Michael Walker, "change the ideological fabric of society."

In creating a revolution of intentional citizenship, no other political act is more significant. Each such act builds increasing understanding of the original, radical meaning of democracy — that is, a struggle between social classes over the issue of majority rule. The history of the twentieth century is full of evidence for the claim that fundamental social change cannot be achieved without massive civil disobedience. In fact, of course, much of that evidence is found in our own history, in the class warfare of the 1930s that resulted in the only period in capitalist history during which working people achieved any measure of equality.

There are some other signs that some key projects of corporate rule are in difficulty. In both education and health care the shine is off the great predictions of endless and easy profits. The evidence is pouring in that the business "ethic" and these two fundamental aspects of community just don't mix. Columbia/HCA, the largest U.S. for-profit hospital chain, is facing massive lawsuits and criminal fraud charges arising out of its insatiable greed. The indictments against the firm came down just as the number-two giant, Tenet Healthcare Corp., agreed to pay defrauded former patients $100 million.

In education the story is the same. A 1996 report on public school privatization, by researchers at New York University, demonstrated that privatized schools failed to produce either better academic results or savings for the state government. In Baltimore, students' test scores rose by 11.2 percent in the regular school system while they were falling in the privatized ones. The corporation, Education Alternatives, had its contract terminated.

These are minor skirmishes in the corporate drive to expand its investment territory. More troubling for the transnationals' strategy of ever expanding mass consumerism is word from Asia that the expansion is not going as planned. In August 1997 the World Bank issued two reports raising the alarm about increasing poverty through-out Asia. The reports estimated that "as many as 900 million Asians, from Mongolia to South India, live in dire poverty despite the region's surging economic growth in recent years." It seems the obsessive attention on the region's "four tigers" has obscured the desperation in other countries.

The financial crisis in Asia is just a symptom of more trouble to come. There are also signs that the global middle-class growth strategy for Asia is running into problems, too. The volatility in Asian currency markets is, according to Jeff Uscher, Tokyo-based editor of *Grant's Asia Observer*, easy to explain. "After more than a decade of aggressive investment in new production capacity to make all manner of manufactured goods, the region is saturated. Much of this new capacity was funded with foreign capital with the intention of serving the rapidly growing Asian market. The only problem is that the Asian market is not growing rapidly."[15]

The late-1997 Asian currency and stock market meltdown helped expose the overcapacity/overproduction crisis. Analyst Louis Uchitelle reported on the "worries" amongst the biggest players in the global economy about "the tendency of the unfettered global economy to produce more cars, toys, shoes, airplanes, steel, paper, appliances . . . than people will buy at high enough prices."[16] Quoting GE chair Jack Welch as saying "There is excess capacity in almost every industry," Uchitelle's analysis suggests that the global version of the problem Henry Ford faced in the 1920s is already upon us. If the global middle class doesn't have the money to buy the goods produced by the global working class, the system becomes unsustainable.

In short, stock markets and growth cannot be permanently sustained on the basis of a planned recession, of squeezing more and more out of workers by reducing their wages and reducing the number who receive wages. In Asia, the currency crisis and stock market collapses have caused middle-class customers to pull back. That has left Asia's enormous productive capacity (accounting for half the growth in world output since 1991) intact but in desperate need of other markets. Ironically, the corporate owners of this overcapacity are now looking back to the developed world to sell those goods. These goods are now cheaper. But the developed world's domestic economies and the purchasing power of their consumers have been systematically savaged by corporations and governments in the interests of global markets. Every dollar of additional spending in these economies will require ever greater marketing and advertising costs.

The Asian situation may be just a temporary setback, although the care and feeding of the Asian consumer market was supposed to keep transnational growth going for at least another decade and beyond. What this crisis demonstrates is that the supposedly unstoppable investment and growth juggernaut can very quickly look shaky. And there are signs that mass consumerism in the U.S. and Canada may be in for some fundamental changes. Many middle-class families, forced to cut back their spending because of stagnant or falling incomes, may well have decided that they can live on less. Journalist Alanna Mitchell argues that "there are signs that the punishing shocks they have endured during the nineties have fundamentally changed patterns of consumer behaviour." And according to economist Ruth Berry, "The whole cultural environment guiding the economy is shifting."[17]

The backlash against employers who trash their workers is growing in Canada and the U.S. A 1996 Angus Reid/Southam poll revealed that Canadians are becoming increasingly aware of and critical of corporate behaviour and the close relationship between corporations and government. Forty-five percent of those polled said that they thought corporations had become "less responsible" over the past few years compared with 19 percent saying "more responsible." According to 75 percent, corporations that lay people off should be required to provide them with job search assistance or job training; 77 percent said it was "not acceptable" for large corporations to lay people off while making high profits, and 54 percent said they should be forced to pay a penalty, such as higher taxes, for doing so. And 54 percent believed governments listen to corporations "too much."[18]

Attitudes towards corporations are even more critical in the U.S., where there is an upsurge of support for more "government intervention." Between 70 and 80 percent of all Americans see "serious problems" in how corporations sacrifice the interests of employees and communities for those of CEOs and shareholders, and "69 percent favour government action to promote more responsible citizenship and to penalize bad corporate citizenship."[19]

The seemingly unstoppable transnational corporations may be facing a major contradiction they had not anticipated. On the one hand, the devolution of the welfare state and the pattern of excluding huge numbers of people from the TNCs' economic growth strategy suggests the development of the security state in which the use of coercion increasingly replaces efforts at building legitimacy as an overall strategy. But there is strong evidence that a repressive response to social inequality may not be compatible with the new economic order. The fierce competition unleashed by the growth of TNCs creates demands for stable regimes with no surprises for investors. As we saw in chapter 6, the first democratic election in seventy years in Mexico was, ironically, partly due to the entrenchment of NAFTA.

This need for stability goes beyond the requirement for predictable governance. A French report, "The Enterprise of the XXI Century," prepared by an organization of young managers, warns that the drive for labour flexibility has reached its limits and could backfire by destroying "the autonomy of the workforce necessary in a modern organization." The temptation to "enslave man to the economy" could bring about the collapse of the whole system: "Business is in the process of breaking the social links that it used to build. We are convinced that unregulated capitalism will explode just as communism exploded, if we do not seize the chance to put man back at the centre of society."[20]

That explosion may be closer than anyone could have imagined. Witness the pressures building in Europe as popular opposition grows to the European Community's single currency, the conditions for which require significant cuts in social spending and restrictive monetary policies. The financial crisis in Asia threatens to create social unrest and political instability in two of the largest countries and economies in the region, South Korea and Japan. The IMF deal with South Korea requires, at a minimum, adding 1.5 million to the unemployment rolls and inevitably huge cuts to social spending.

In Japan pressure is building to fundamentally change the historic social contract, one that went far beyond anything Canada or Europe ever established. The profound sense of responsibility to community that has characterized the relationship between Japanese political leaders, industrialists, and senior public servants has its roots in centuries of Japanese culture. Japan Inc. is proving no more immune to the forces of global finance and liberalization than any other developed nation. But the "restructuring" of its economy implies nothing short of a revolution imposed from above. The social unrest it unleashes may well be catastrophic. The supporters of corporate libertarianism insist that stable societies are a necessary condition for investment. Yet it is precisely the ability of governments to control investment decisions through industrial policies that leads to an equitable allocation of wealth and, consequently, political stability.

As Martin Khor of the Third World Network points out, "The MAI will make developing countries politically unstable. But all these industrialists, if you ask them why do you choose a particular country in which to invest, their number-one answer is 'political stability.' So companies that promote the MAI are undermining the conditions under which they can actually function."[21] All the corporations that have made billions in Malaysia would never have been able to do so, says Khor, had there been an MAI in place twenty years ago. What made their profits possible were Malaysian policies that regulated investment in such a way as to foster political stability.

❖

Nothing stays the same for long. That lesson of history gives those committed to a radical new democracy a foothold in their struggle against corporate rule. Not only do things change but they can change with breathtaking speed. It is the apparent speed with which we have lost so much that stuns many people and creates the sense that all of this change is irresistible. Yet in fact it has taken the forces of the New Right and the transnational corporations twenty years of determined effort to accomplish what they have.

Not only are there alternatives to the current trends but there is the real possibility of a genuinely democratic society. There has to be. And the alternative to a world completely dominated by TNCs is not a return to the days of the impoverished notion of the welfare state. It is a fundamentally different kind of society, based on equality, ecological sustainability, and a redefinition of work that serves human society and that actually allows us to create socially and culturally liberating communities.

But just because things change doesn't mean they necessarily change for the better. Twenty years from now we will either be straining our imaginations and efforts creating democratic and sustainable communities or we will be witnessing worldwide social chaos and environmental catastrophe. If we are not well prepared to take advantage of the coming global crisis with imagination, energy, and a willingness to change, and begin creating a truly democratic society, we will almost certainly end up with a truly authoritarian one.

APPENDIX
WHAT YOU CAN DO

A major hazard of becoming aware of how things work is a feeling of powerlessness. The more we learn about the forces behind the status quo, the more omnipotent they can seem. However, socially conscious citizens of other eras have achieved major victories for human progress in the face of seemingly impossible odds, and you can, too.

One of the first things you can do is recognize and act on the fact that we are subjected daily to a barrage of propaganda aimed at trashing our values and making us apathetic and accepting of the new corporate reality. To believe that we personally are not affected by what we read is like thinking a steady diet of junk food will not affect our health. Cancel your newspaper subscription. With rare exceptions there isn't a paper in the country that is on balance worth reading. The corporate biases, deliberate censorship of stories and contrary points of view, and aggressive neo-liberal editorial policies of newspapers far outweigh the benefits of the information they provide. While you are at it, cancel your cable. Television, perhaps more than any other single factor, is responsible for the dumbing down of Canadian political culture.

The other side of ridding your life of right-wing propaganda is seeking information and analysis that empowers you as a citizen. I can't overstate the positive effect of having solid information to back up the values you hold. People who have put to memory data about how corporations evade and avoid billions in taxes each year and who know the Statscan study showing the real source of the debt are transformed from being passive victims of propaganda into being activists against debt terror.

An excellent source of information and analysis is the publication of the Canadian Centre for Policy Alternatives (CCPA), *The Monitor*, which is published ten times a year. (The CCPA can be reached at 251 Laurier Ave. West, Suite 804, Ottawa, ON K1P 5J6, ph (613) 563-1341, or in Vancouver (604) 801-5121 and Winnipeg (204) 943-9962.)

Many other publications are also helpful. In Canada, *Canadian Forum*, *Canadian Dimension*, *This Magazine*, *Briarpatch*, and *Our Times* are all excellent. In the U.S., *The New Internationalist*, *The Utne Reader*, and *'Z' Magazine* are first-rate. The Internet has a number of very good WEB sites on corporations, progressive organizations, on-line magazines, and much else. You can access these sites by visiting the CCPA WEB site (www. policyalternatives.ca) and clicking on "links."

As suggested in the final chapter of this book, individuals can begin to change their status from global customer to global citizen in a myriad of ways. Besides reducing television and refusing to consume unnecessarily, those who have savings can invest them as ethically as possible. Ethical companies and mutual funds have lots of problems, given the hazards any company faces by pursuing ethical policies, but they are certainly an improvement over those for whom ethics is irrelevant.

Yet even well-informed citizens are extremely limited in what they can do on their own. In terms of working with others, you have three options: join an existing group fighting on social justice/anti-corporate issues; work to address social issues in other organizations you already belong to; or form new groups specifically to address the issue of corporate rule and democracy. There are dozens of advocacy groups defending democracy and becoming involved in fighting corporations. Any grassroots organization worth its salt will welcome the energy and creativity of new members and find ways for you to contribute your own skills.

Advocacy groups are not the only organizations that can address these issues. Whether it is a parent advisory council, a community health clinic, or even a church, the issue of corporate rule will have an impact on their activity. It could be budget cuts, privatization, or corporate incursions into the classroom. The influence of corporations is so pervasive you would have to look hard to find an organization where it was not relevant. Work with others to learn about and deal with the threat of corporations in the sector you are already involved in.

There are a number of organizations that are now explicitly taking on the issue of corporate domination:

* The Council of Canadians has local action groups across the country and focuses on corporate influence in the media and social programs, fighting the Multilateral Agreement on Investment (MAI), and building a Citizens' Agenda. Their address is 251 Laurier Ave. West, Suite 904, Ottawa, ON K1P 5J6; ph 1-800-387-7177 or in Vancouver (604) 688-8846.
* The Canadian Auto Workers, 205 Placer Court, Willowdale, ON M2H 3H9; ph (416) 497-4110.
* Canadian Union of Public Employees (CUPE), 21 Florence St., Ottawa, ON; K2P 0W6 ph (613) 237-1590. Contact: Jim Turk.
* The Social Justice Centre, formerly the Jesuit Centre for Social Faith and Justice, provides resources for social movements on corporate and other issues. 836 Bloor St., Toronto, ON M6G 1M2; ph (416) 516-0009. Contact: David Langille.
* The Sierra Legal Defence Fund takes legal action against corporations, including a major focus on fighting SLAPP suits. 131 Water St., Suite 214, Vancouver, B.C. V6B 4M3; ph (604) 685-6518. Contact: David Boyd. In Toronto, ph (416) 368-7533.
* The Polaris Institute focuses on enhancing citizens' ability to challenge corporations. 4 Jeffrey Ave., Ottawa, ON K1K 0E2; ph (613) 746-8374. Contact: Tony Clarke.
* CODEV targets mining companies. 2929 Commercial Drive, Suite 205, Vancouver, B.C. V5N 4C8; ph (604) 708-1495. Contact: Jim Raider.
* The Task Force on Churches and Corporate Responsibility engages in shareholder campaigns. 129 St. Clair Ave. West, Toronto, ON M4J 4Z2; ph (416) 923-1758.
* Democracy Watch promotes democratic reforms that empower citizens. It has explicitly targeted corporate lobbying and the outrageous profits of the major banks. 1 Nicholas St., Suite 420, Ottawa, ON K1P 5P9; ph (613) 241-5179. Contact: Duff Conacher.
* Greenpeace focuses on corporate assaults on the environment. 185 Spadina Ave., Toronto, ON M5T 2C6; ph (416) 597-8408.

Of course, taking on corporate domination directly is not sufficient to rebuild community and revive democracy. There are groups in virtually every community — involved in connecting market gardeners with urban consumers, creating housing co-ops, running barter systems — that create real examples of democratic "economies." Many of the good things that happen remain hidden from us because of media bias and because many of the groups are small and local. A great source of examples of how people are using their imaginations as citizens is *Get a Life! (How to Make a Good Buck, Dance Around the Dinosaurs and Save the World While You're at It)* by Wayne Roberts and Susan Brandum.

The shape of democracy in the next decade and beyond is impossible to predict and except for broad principles we probably shouldn't try. It will be determined by what intentional citizens, informed, organized, and making social change, do in that time. We need to create hundreds of new organizations beyond the ones mentioned above, organizations that will not only challenge corporate domination directly but will also create the nuclei of democratic politics and democratic economic activity.

If there are no organizations in your area or none that appeal to you, create your own. Set up a study/action group with like-minded friends or colleagues. Fighting the MAI is a good start (contact the Council of Canadians for a kit). Or focus on identifying a corporation in your area that demonstrates corporate irresponsibility and research it (contact CUPE for a booklet on researching corporations). Then develop a public action plan based on your group's newly developed competence and confidence.

Good intentions alone won't make it possible for everyone to get this involved. Many people find it extremely difficult to make time for such commitments given the incredible pressures in their lives. However, the organizations that are fighting for social change are always desperately in need of money, outspent ten or twenty to one by their corporate adversaries. Give until it hurts.

Becoming a conscious citizen requires a different way of thinking and behaving. It means challenging political ignorance whenever you encounter it, incorporating your political convictions into your daily life, and most important, simply seeing the world as a citizen with the responsibilities and the rights that this implies. As we begin to see and interpret the world as citizens the question of what we can do will begin to answer itself.

NOTES

CHAPTER 1
GLOBALIZATION AND THE RISE OF THE
TRANSNATIONAL CORPORATION

1 In David Korten, *When Corporations Rule the World*, Kumarian Press, West Hartford, Conn., 1995, p.123.
2 Sarah Anderson and John Cavanagh, *The Top 200: The Rise of Global Corporate Power*. Report of the Institute for Policy Studies, Washington, D.C., 1996.
3 Tony Clarke, "The Corporate Rule Treaty," Canadian Centre for Policy Alternatives, Ottawa, 1997.
4 "Index on Globalization," *Canadian Forum*, February 1997.
5 Korten, p.223.
6 Allan Engler, *Apostles of Greed*, Fernwood Publishing, Halifax, 1995, p.43.
7 Engler, p.31.
8 Maude Barlow, *Parcel of Rogues*, Key Porter Books, Toronto, 1990, p.21.
9 Korten, p.225.
10 Ibid.
11 Engler, p.37.
12 Korten, p.221.
13 Peter F. Drucker, *Concept of the Corporation*, Mentor, N.Y., 1983, p.49.
14 Korten, p. 224.
15 "A Survey of Multinationals: Every-body's Favorite Monster," *Economist*, March 27, 1993.
16 Richard Barnet, *The Lean Years*, Touchstone Press, N.Y., 1980, p.240.
17 Korten, p.125.
18 Ibid.
19 Ibid., p.121.
20 Ibid., p.131.
21 Canadian Auto Workers, "Parliamentary submission regarding the future Canadian manufacturing operations of Northern Telecom Ltd.," 1995.
22 Ibid.
23 *Globe and Mail*, September 9, 1997.
24 CAW, "Parliamentary submission."
25 *Globe and Mail*, September 9, 1997.
26 *Globe and Mail*, September 9, 1997.
27 Ibid.
28 CAW, "Parliamentary submission."
29 Ontario Federation of Labour, "Unfair Shares," 1997, p.33.
30 Canadian Institute for Environmental Law and Policy, brief to the Commons Standing Committee on Natural Resources Regarding Mining and Canada's Environment (#287), April 16, 1996.
31 Project Underground, Corporate Watch, January 21, 1997.
32 Ibid.

33 *Multinational Monitor*, Vol. 17, No. 3 (1996).

34 Mineral Policy Institute, Bondi Junction, Australia, news release.

35 *Globe and Mail*, August 30, 1997.

36 Canadian Environmental Law Association, brief to the House of Commons Standing Committee on Natural Resources Regarding Mining and Canada's Environment, April 16, 1996.

Chapter 2
Democracy, the State, and the Corporate Citizen

1 Gil Yaron, "The Corporation as a Person," research paper, 1997, p.13.

2 Ibid., p.14.

3 In Murray Dobbin, "Democracy and the Politics of Human Rights," CBC *Ideas*, November 30, 1995.

4 Michael Mandel, "Rights, Freedoms, and Market Power," in *The New Era of Global Competition*, ed. D. Drache, McGill-Queen's University Press, Montreal, 1991, pp.130–32.

5 Dobbin, *Ideas*.

6 W. P. M. Kennedy, *Documents of the Canadian Constitution: 1759–1915*, Toronto, 1918, p.34.

7 Donald Creighton, *The Empire of the St. Lawrence*, Toronto, Macmillan, 1956, p.38.

8 Gil Yaron, "The Legal Evolution of the Corporation in Canada," research paper, Vancouver, 1997.

9 Gerry Van Houten, *Corporate Canada: An Historical Outline*, Progress Books, Toronto, 1991, p.52.

10 Richard Grossman and Frank Adams, "Taking Care of Business: Citizenship and Charter of Incorporation," Charter, Inc., Cambridge, Mass., 1933, p.8.

11 Ibid. p.13.

12 Ibid., p.18.

13 Ibid., p.20.

14 Ibid., p.21.

15 Alvin Finkel, "Origins of the Welfare State in Canada," in *The Canadian State:*

Political Power and Political Economy, ed. Leo Panitch, University of Toronto Press, Toronto, 1977, p.348.

16 Ibid.

17 Ibid., p.63.

18 Robert Chodos, Rae Murphy, and Eric Hamovitch, *The Unmaking of Canada*, Lorimer, Toronto, 1991, p.15.

19 Quoted in David Lewis, *Louder Voices: The Corporate Welfare Bums*, 1972, p.iv.

20 C.B. Macpherson, *The Real World of Democracy*, House of Anansi, Toronto, 1992, p.5.

21 Ibid., p.6.

22 Ibid., p.10.

23 Stephen McBride and John Shields, *Dismantling a Nation*, Fernwood Publishing, Halifax, 1993, p.17.

24 Interview with the author, August 16, 1997.

25 McBride and Shields, p.47.

26 William Greider, *Who Will Tell the People*, Simon and Schuster, N.Y., 1992, p.332.

27 Ibid.

28 Ibid., p.336.

29 Nick Fillmore, "The Big Oink," *This Magazine*, March/April 1989.

30 Ibid.

31 Barlow, *Parcel of Rogues*, p.8.

32 Fillmore, "The Big Oink."

33 Ibid.

Chapter 3
From Citizen to Customer

1 William Leach, *Land of Desire: Merchants, Power and the Rise of a New American Culture*, Pantheon Books, New York, 1993, p.xv.

2 Richard J. Barnet and John Cavanagh, *Global Dreams; Imperial Corporations and the New World Order*, Simon and Schuster, New York, 1994, p.376.

3 Ibid., p.377.

4 Ibid., p.34.

5 Ibid., p.35.

6 Ibid., p.168.

7 Ibid., p.169.

8 Ibid., pp.171–72.

9 David Korten, *When Corporations Rule the World*, Kumarian Press, West Hartford, Conn., 1995, p.127.

10 Akio Morita, "Toward a New World Economic Order," *Atlantic Monthly*, June 1993.

11 Barnet and Cavanagh, p.178.

12 Ibid., p.174.

13 David Leonhardt, "Hey, Kid, Buy This!" *Business Week*, June 30, 1997.

14 Ibid.

15 Barnet and Cavanagh, p.174.

CHAPTER 4
THE TRANSNATIONAL CORPORATE CITIZEN

1 Allan Engler, *Apostles of Greed*, Fernwood Publishing, Halifax, pp.81-82.

2 J. Patrick Wright, *On a Clear Day You Can See General Motors*, 1979, Avon, New York, 1979, p.61.

3 Engler, p.82.

4 Bruce Livesey, "Provide and Conquer," *Globe and Mail Report on Business*, March 1997.

5 Bernard Lietaer, speech to the International Forum on Globalization, Washington, D.C., May 10, 1996.

6 Ibid.

7 David Korten, *When Corporations Rule the World*, Kumarian Press, West Hartford, Conn., 1995, p.193.

8 Lietaer speech.

9 John Dillon, "Turning the Tide: Confronting the Money Changers," Canadian Centre for Policy Alternatives, Ottawa, 1997, p.26.

10 Ibid.

11 Ibid.

12 Korten, p.188.

13 Ibid., p.203.

14 Dillon, p.30.

15 Ibid., p.33.

16 *Globe and Mail*, November 25, 1997.

17 Canadian Press, Web page, November 30, 1997.

18 Korten, p.210.

19 Ibid., p.211.

20 *Globe and Mail Report on Business*, December 1996.

21 Ibid.

22 *Globe and Mail*, November 13, 1996.

23 Korten, pp.213-14.

24 Ibid., p.214.

25 *Globe and Mail*, November 26, 1996.

26 *Ottawa Citizen*, March 29, 1996.

27 Marc Mentzer, Human Resources Management in Canada, 1997.

28 *Saskatoon Star Phoenix*, October 26, 1996.

29 *New York Times*, February 16, 1992.

30 *Wall Street Journal*, in *Globe and Mail*, November 13, 1997.

31 *Calgary Herald*, November 12, 1994.

32 *Globe and Mail*, January 9, 1996.

33 Ibid.

34 *Globe and Mail*, April 12, 1997.

35 Peter F. Drucker, *Concept of the Corporation*, Mentor, N.Y., 1983, pp.35-36.

36 *Globe and Mail*, April 12, 1997.

37 James Petras and Morris Morley, "The United States and Chile: Imperialism and the Overthrow of the Allende Government," Monthly Review Press, New York, 1975, p.31.

38 Ibid., p.33.

39 Ibid., pp.33-34.

40 *Guardian*, January 26, 1997.

41 George Pring and Penelope Canan, "Slapps: Getting Sued for Speaking Out," *Maclean's*, August 26, 1996.

42 Karen Wristen, Sierra Legal Defence Fund, interview with the author, Vancouver, August 1997.

43 Ibid.

44 Mark Margalli and Andy Friedman, *Masks of Deception: Corporate Front Groups in America*, Essential Information, Washington, D.C., 1991.

45 William Groder, *Who Will Tell the People: One Betrayal of American Democracy*, Simon and Shuster, New York, 1992, pp.36-37.

CHAPTER 5
HOW CORPORATIONS RULE THE WORLD

1 John Dillon, "Turning the Tide: Confronting the Money Changers,"

NOTES

Canadian Centre for Policy Alternatives, Ottawa, 1997, p.94.

2 Jamie Swift, "The Debt Crisis: A Case of Global Usury," in *Conflicts of Interest*, ed. Jamie Swift and Brian Tomlinson, Between the Lines, Toronto, 1991, p.81.

3 In David Korten, *When Corporations Rule the World*, Kumarian Press, West Hartford, Conn., 1995, p.160.

4 Ibid., p.162.

5 Swift, "The Debt Crisis," p.85.

6 Jonathon Cahn, "Challenging the New Imperial Authority: The World Bank and the Democratization of Development," *Harvard Human Rights Journal*, Vol. 6 (1993).

7 Joyce Kolko, *Restructuring the World Economy*, Pantheon Books, New York, 1988, p.225.

8 Duncan Cameron, introduction to *Canada Under Free Trade*, ed. Duncan Cameron and Mel Watkins, Lorimer, Toronto, 1993, p.xi.

9 *The Monitor*, Canadian Centre for Policy Alternatives, October 1997.

10 "Challenging 'Free Trade' in Canada: The Real Story," Canadian Centre for Policy Alternatives, Ottawa, 1996, p.1.

11 Ibid., p.16.

12 Ibid., p.17.

13 Ibid., p.18.

14 Mel Clark, "Canadian State Powers: Comparing the FTA and GATT," in *Canada Under Free Trade*, ed. Cameron and Watkins, p.43.

15 "An Enviromental Guide to the World Trade Organization," Common Front on the World Trade Organization, c/o The Sierra Club, Ottawa, 1997, p.2.

16 Korten, p.174.

17 Ibid., p.178.

18 Elizabeth Smythe, "Your Place or Mine? States, International Organizations and the Negotiation of Investment Rules: The OECD versus the WTO," paper presented at the annual meeting of the International Studies Association, Toronto, March 1997, p.14.

19 Ibid.

20 Ibid., p.19.

21 Bernard Lietaer, speech to the International Forum on Globalization, Washington, D.C., May 10, 1996.

22 Martin Khor, speech to the International Forum on Globalization, Washington, D.C., May 10, 1996.

23 Ibid.

24 Tony Clarke, "The Corporate Rule Treaty," Canadian Centre for Policy Alternatives, Ottawa, 1997.

25 "Multilateral Agreement on Investment, Consolidated Texts and Commentary," OECD, 1997, p.27.

26 Ibid., p.40.

27 Ibid., p.53.

28 Ibid., p.63.

29 Clarke, p.7.

30 Marjorie Griffin Cohen, chair, CCPA-B.C., presentation to Commons Sub-committee on International Trade and the MAI, November 26, 1997.

31 International Chamber of Commerce, Commission on International Trade and Investment Policy, "Multilateral Rules for Investment," 1996.

32 Ibid.

33 *Vancouver Sun*, May 23, 1997.

34 Gary Campbell and Timothy Reid to Art Eggleton, January 26, 1996.

35 "Trading Insults," *Maclean's*, April 28, 1997.

36 Ibid.

37 Jane Kelsey, "APEC Created Solely to Serve Big Business," *The Monitor*, Canadian Centre for Policy Alternatives, July/August 1997.

38 "Canada's Individual Action Plan," 1996.

39 Ibid., p.73.

40 Gord McIntosh, *Calgary Herald*, November 16, 1997.

41 John Dillon, "The Enterprise for the Americas," in *Canada Under Free Trade*, ed. Cameron and Watkins, p.260.

42 Clarke, p.9.

43 Appleton and Associates, "Reservations to the proposed Multilateral Agreement on Investment," November 14, 1997, p.1.

44 Ibid., p.5.
45 Ibid.
46 Ibid., p.23.
47 Ibid., p.16.

CHAPTER 6
RULERS AND RULED IN THE NEW WORLD ORDER

1   John Cavanagh, "The Challenge of Global Rule," keynote speech at the People's Forum on APEC, Manila, November 1996.
2   Ted Wheelwright, "Economic Controls for Social Ends," in *Beyond the Market: Alternatives to Economic Rationalism*, ed. R. Rees, G. Rodley, and F. Stilwell, Pluto, Sydney, 1993, p.21.
3   *The Monitor*, Canadian Centre for Policy Alternatives, March 1997.
4   *The Monitor*, Canadian Centre for Policy Alternatives, March 1995.
5   *Globe and Mail*, November 11, 1997.
6   Study by Irwin Gillespie, Frank Vermaeten, and Arndt Vermaeten, cited in *The Monitor*, Canadian Centre for Policy Alternatives, September 1994.
7   Robert Reich, "Secession of the Successful," *New York Times Magazine*, January 6, 1991.
8   Ibid.
9   Ibid.
10 Ibid.
11 *The Monitor*, Canadian Centre for Policy Alternatives, September 1996.
12 "Challenging 'Free Trade' in Canada: The Real Story," Canadian Centre for Policy Alternatives, Ottawa, 1996, p.4.
13 Ekos Research Associates, "Rethinking Government, '94," 1995, p.12.
14 Ibid., p.13.
15 *Taipan*, cited in *The Monitor*, Canadian Centre for Policy Alternatives, November 1995.
16 *The Monitor*, Canadian Centre for Policy Alternatives, May 1996.
17 In David Korten, *When Corporations Rule the World*, Kumarian Press, West Hartford, Conn., 1995, p.210.
18 Jack Warnock, letter to the author, July 29, 1997.
19 Jack Warnock, *The Other Mexico*, Black Rose Books, Montreal, 1995, pp.176–77.
20 Ibid., pp.181–83.
21 *The Monitor*, Canadian Centre for Policy Alternatives, November 1995.
22 "Toy Industry Conditions Exposed," in *Together for Human Rights*, Number 1, January 1996. Edited by Kathleen Puff.
23 *The Georgia Straight*, October 16, 1997.
24 *Together for Human Rights*, Number 4, July 1996.
25 Korten, pp.216–17.
26 *Globe and Mail Report on Business*, February 1997.
27 Canadian Press, September 21, 1996. Web page.
28 David Crane, *Toronto Star*, November 11, 1997.
29 Armine Yalnizyan, *Shifting Time: Social Policy and the Future of Work*, Between the Lines, Toronto, 1994, p.47.
30 Jane Jenson, "Some Consequences of Political Restructuring and Readjustment," in *Social Politics*, spring 1996.
31 *The Monitor*, Canadian Centre for Policy Alternatives, November 1996.
32 *Globe and Mail*, January 11, 1997.
33 Ibid.
34 National Council of Welfare statistics. 1995.
35 *The Monitor*, Canadian Centre for Policy Alternatives, September 1996.
36 Jim Stanford, "The Economics of the Debt and the Remaking of Canada," *Studies in Political Economy*, No. 48 (1995).
37 Joyce Kolko, *Restructuring the World Economy*, Pantheon Books, New York, 1988, p.234
38 Peter Gottschalk and Timothy Smeeding, "Cross-national Comparisons of Levels and Trends in Inequality," Luxembourg Income Study Working Paper 126, 1995.
39 World Economic Forum, *World Competitiveness Report*, 1994.
40 Ibid.

41 CBC Radio news, July 18, 1997.

42 Kate Bronfenbrenner, "We'll Close! Plant Closings, Plant Closing Threats, Union Organizing, and NAFTA," *The Multinational Monitor*, January 30, 1997.

43 *Vancouver Sun*, January 30, 1997.

44 Clarence Lochhead and Vivian Shalla, "Delivering the Goods: Income Distribution and the Precarious Middle Class," *Perceptions*, Canadian Council on Social Development, spring 1997.

45 *Globe and Mail*, November 9, 1996.

46 *Toronto Star*, July 29, 1997.

CHAPTER 7
CREATING THE ELITE CONSENSUS

1 Peter Thompson, "Bilderberg and the West," in *Trilateralism: The Trilateral Commission and Elite Planning for World Management*, ed. Holly Sklar, Black Rose Books, Montreal, 1980, p.161.

2 Ibid., p.171.

3 Ibid., p.177.

4 *Globe and Mail*, May 14, 1997.

5 World Economic Forum Web page, www.weforum.org.

6 Ibid.

7 *Globe and Mail*, February 1, 1997.

8 Elizabeth Smythe, "Your Place or Mine? States, International Organizations and the Negotiation of Investment Rules: The OECD versus the WTO," paper presented at the annual meeting of the International Studies Association, Toronto, March 1997, p.14.

9 Holly Sklar, "Founding the Trilateral Commission, Chronology 1970–77," in *Trilateralism: The Trilateral Commission and Elite Planning for World Management*, ed. Holly Sklar, Black Rose Books, Montreal, 1980, pp.76–83.

10 Ibid., p.69.

11 Richard Falk, "A New Paradigm for International Legal Studies," *Yale Law Review*, Vol. 84, No.5 (1975).

12 Sklar, p.27.

13 Ibid.

14 Ibid., p.87.

15 Joyce Nelson, "The Trilateral Commission," *Canadian Forum*, December 1993.

16 Trilateral Commission, "Membership — Canadian Group of the Trilateral Commission, 1996," Ottawa.

17 Samuel P. Huntington, in M. J. Crozier, S. P. Huntington, and J. Watanuki, *The Crisis of Democracy: Report of the Governability of Democracies to the Trilateral Commission*, New York University Press, 1975, p.113.

18 Ibid., p.98.

19 Ibid., p.93.

20 Ibid., p.75.

21 Ibid., pp.61–62.

22 Ibid., pp.6–7.

23 Ibid., p.106.

24 Daniel Boorstin, "Welcome to the Consumption Community," *Fortune*, September 1, 1967.

25 Huntington, in *The Crisis of Democracy*, pp.203–9.

26 Jim Stanford, "Policy Alternatives for the New World Order," paper presented to the Federal NDP Renewal Conference, Ottawa, September 1994.

27 David Langille, "The Business Council on National Issues and the Canadian State," *Studies in Political Economy*, autumn 1987.

28 Ibid., p.48.

29 Ibid., p.50.

30 Interview with the author, in "Taxes: The Second Certainty," CBC *Ideas*, 1991.

31 Langille, p.59.

32 Ibid., p.56.

33 Ibid., p.65.

34 Murray Dobbin, "Thomas d'Aquino: The De Facto PM," *Canadian Forum*, November 1992.

35 Canadian Institute of Strategic Studies, "Guns and Butter: Defence and the Canadian Economy," Toronto, 1984, p.50.

36 Duncan Cameron, interview with the author, August 1997.

37 Maude Barlow and Bruce Campbell, *Straight Through the Heart*, HarperCollins, Toronto, 1995, p.49.

38 Ibid., p.94.

39 Ibid., p.93.

40 Jamie Swift, "The Debt Crisis: A Case of Global Usury," in *Conflicts of Interest*, ed Jamie Swift and Brian Tomlinson, Between the Lines, Toronto, 1991, p.97.

41 Business Council on National Issues, "Policy Committee," 1997.

42 A. L. Flood and Tom d'Aquino, "Memorandum for the Right Honourable Jean Chrétien, P.C., M.P., Prime Minister of Canada," June 20, 1997, p.6.

43 Executive Committee, BCNI, "Memorandum for the Honourable Frank McKenna, Premier of New Brunswick and Chairman-Designate, Council of Premiers," July 15, 1997.

44 Ibid., p.4.

45 Ibid., p.6.

46 Cameron interview.

47 Barlow and Campbell, *Straight Through the Heart*, p.52.

48 Cameron interview.

49 Ibid.

CHAPTER 8
CHANGING THE IDEOLOGICAL FABRIC OF CANADA

1 Tony Clarke, *Silent Coup*, Lorimer, Toronto, 1997, p.12.

2 Stephen McBride and John Shields, *Dismantling a Nation: Canada and the New World Order*, Fernwood Publishing, Halifax, 1993, p.37.

3 Beverly Scott, "Against Social Programs: The Campaigns of the Fraser Institute," in *Directions for Social Welfare in Canada: The Public's View*, School of Social Work, University of B.C., p.121.

4 The Fraser Institute, 1996 Annual Report.

5 "Fraser Currents: Special Anniversary Edition 1974–1989" and *Globe and Mail Report on Business*, July 1997.

6 Krishna Rau, "A Million for Your Thoughts," *Canadian Forum*, August 1996.

7 Walter Stewart, *The Charity Game: Greed, Waste and Fraud in Canada's $86-Billion-a-Year Compassion Industry*, Douglas & McIntyre, Vancouver, 1996. p.102.

8 In Allan Garr, *Tough Guy: Bill Bennett and the Taking of British Columbia*, Key Porter Books, Toronto, 1985, pp.91–93.

9 The Fraser Institute, 1996 Annual Report

10 Fraser Institute, "Freedom, Democracy and Economic Welfare," 1988, p.136.

11 In Scott, "Against Social Programs," p.116.

12 Fraser Institute, *Freedom, Democracy and Economic Welfare*, p.140.

13 Ibid., p.76.

14 Ibid., p.44.

15 In Allan Engler, *Apostles of Greed*, Fernwood Publishing, Halifax, 1995, p.101.

16 Ibid., p.xi.

17 Michael Walker, submission to the Standing Committee on Finance, September 17, 1991.

18 Michael Walker, "The Political Problem," notes for a speech to the Fraser Institute Seminar for Members of Parliament, Ottawa, February 1, 1994, p.9.

19 Kathleen Cross, "Off Balance: How the Fraser Institute Slants Its New-Monitoring Studies," *Canadian Forum*, October 1997.

20 Paul Havemann, "Marketing the New Establishment Ideology in Canada", in *Crime and Social Justice*, No. 26 (1986), p.30.

21 Fraser Institute, "Toward the New Millennium: A Five Year Plan for the Fraser Institute."

22 Fraser Institute, 1996 Annual Report, p.4.

23 *Edmonton Journal*, January 16, 1997.

24 Fraser Institute, "Toward the New Millennium."

25 Walter Block and Michael Walker, *On Employment Equity: A Critique of the Abella Royal Commission Report*, Fraser Institute, 1985, note 46, cited in Michelle Valiquette, unpublished paper.

26 Block and Walker, *On Employment Equity*, note 50.

27 "Beloved Regulations Squeeze Us Badly," *Vancouver Sun*, September 25, 1996.

28 "Bad Work: A Review of Papers from a Fraser Institute Conference on 'Right-to-Work' Laws," Working Paper No. 16, Centre for Research on Work and Society, York University, 1997.

29 "Beloved Regulations Squeeze Us Badly," *Vancouver Sun*, September 25, 1996.

30 David Somerville, address to conference of the International Society for Individual Liberty, Whistler, B.C., August 1996.

31 "The Legacy of Colin M. Brown," in program for the NCC's Tenth Annual Colin M. Brown Freedom Medal Presentation, Toronto, 1996.

32 *Vancouver Sun*, March 5, 1987

33 *Chronicle Herald*, Halifax, December 17, 1985.

34 Program, NCC's Tenth Annual Colin M. Brown Freedom Medal presentation, Toronto, 1996.

35 The NCC's advisory council is not mentioned in its bylaws so it is difficult to know what role advisory council members play. Leitch appears to play a very active role since he was given the responsibility of heading a search committee for Somerville's replacement. Other current members are: John Dobson, Robert Foret, Ian Gray, Neil Harvie, James Kenny, Eric Kipping, William Magyar, Kenneth McDonald, Jack Pirie, Donald Thain, Roger Thompson, and staff members Peter Coleman, Colin T. Brown, and David Somerville.

36 Nick Fillmore, "The Right Stuff: An Inside Look at the National Citizens' Coalition," *This Magazine*, June/July 1986.

37 In Fillmore, "The Right Stuff."

38 *Ottawa Citizen*, June 23, 1997.

39 *Financial Post*, June 25, 1995.

40 National Citizens' Coalition, *Overview*, May 1994.

41 In Fillmore, "The Right Stuff."

42 National Citizens' Coalition, *Consensus*, February 1994.

43 National Citizens' Coalition, "Campaign '87."

44 *Consensus*, June 1994.

45 *Consensus*, December 1985.

46 National Citizens' Coalition, "Who We Are and What We Do 1996"; Ontarians for Responsible Government, news release, May 1, 1995.

47 *Consensus*, June 1991.

48 National Citizens' Coalition, news release, May 13, 1996.

49 Fillmore, "The Right Stuff."

50 Rick Salutin, *Waiting for Democracy*, Viking, Markham, Ont., 1989, p.268.

51 *Financial Post*, February 14, 1993.

52 *This Magazine*, July 1986.

53 National Citizens' Coalition, "Who We Are and What We Do 1996" and a May 30, 1996, *Vancouver Sun* story contain NCC claims that it has 45,000 supporters. The February 1996 issue of *Consensus* and the NCC program for the Tenth Annual Colin M. Brown Freedom Medal Presentation in 1996 claim the NCC has 40,000 supporters.

54 *Consensus*, June 1987. Somerville expressed initial reservations about the Reform Party because he thought it might not be conservative enough.

55 *Consensus*, special edition, June 1994.

56 Ibid.

57 NCC, "Campaign '87."

58 *Consensus*, October 1994.

59 Atlantic Institute for Market Studies, Internet site.

60 Linda McQuaig, *Shooting the Hippo*, Penguin, Markham, Ont., 1995, p.133.

61 Rau, "A Million for Your Thoughts."

62 *Globe and Mail*, December 6, 1996.

63 "Journalists Voice Ownership Concerns," *Edmonton Journal*, May 26, 1997.

64 In Peter C. Newman, *The Establishment Man*, McClelland and Stewart, Toronto, 1982, p.183.

65 Verus Group brochure.

66 In Garr, *Tough Guy*, p.42.

67 Interview with the author, August 1997.

CHAPTER 9
PROPAGANDA WARS: THE REVOLUTION OF FALLING EXPECTATIONS

1 Ed Finn, ed., "The Deficit Made Me Do It," Canadian Centre for Policy Alternatives, Ottawa, 1992.

2 Leslie Biggs and Mark Stobbe, eds., *Devine Rule in Saskatchewan: A Decade of Hope and Hardship*, Fifth House, Saskatoon, 1992, Table 1.2, p.298.

3 Jane Kelsey, *The New Zealand Experiment*, Auckland University Press, 1995, p.28.

4 Ibid.

5 Seth Klein, "Good Sense versus Common Sense: Canada's Debt Debate and Competing Hegemonic Projects," master's thesis, Department of Political Science, Simon Fraser University, 1996, p.71.

6 Ibid.

7 Ibid., p.70.

8 Linda McQuaig, *Shooting the Hippo*, Penguin, Markham, Ont., 1995, pp.41–42.

9 *Globe and Mail*, November 10, 1993.

10 *Globe and Mail*, July 25, 1997.

11 Klein, p.60.

12 Jim Stanford, "Rebuilding a Left Economic Alternative," paper presented to Federal NDP Renewal Conference, Ottawa, September 1994.

13 Kirk Falconer, "Corporate Taxation in Canada," *Canadian Review of Social Policy*, No. 26 (November 1990).

14 Murray McIlveen and Hideo Mimoto, "The Federal Government Deficit, 1975–1988–89," Statistics Canada, unpublished paper, 1990.

15 Dominion Bond Rating Service, "The Massive Federal Debt: How Did It Happen?" February 1995.

16 *The Monitor*, Canadian Centre for Policy Alternatives, May 1994.

17 *Globe and Mail*, August 27, 1996.

18 *Globe and Mail*, September 26, 1997.

19 *Globe and Mail*, September 22, 1997.

20 Canadian Centre for Policy Alternatives/Choices Coalition, Alternative Federal Budget, 1997.

21 John Dillon, "Turning the Tide: Confronting the Money Changers," Canadian Centre for Policy Alternatives, 1997, p.101.

22 OECD, Paris, 1990.

23 OECD, "Unemployment Benefit Replacement Rates in 1991," 1992.

24 Paul Martin, "The Canadian Experience in Reducing Budget Deficits and Debt," notes for a speech to the Federal Reserve Bank of Kansas City, Jackson Hole, Wyoming, September 1, 1995.

25 Martin Harts, compensation specialist with KPMG, interview with the author, December 1, 1997.

26 *The Monitor*, Canadian Centre for Policy Alternatives, May 1996.

27 David Gordon, "Workers Overmanaged by Business Bureaucrats," *The Monitor*, Canadian Centre for Policy Alternatives, October 1996.

28 Ibid.

29 *The Monitor*, Canadian Centre for Policy Alternatives, September 1994.

30 *Globe and Mail Report on Business*, May 1996.

31 Lyndon McIntyre, "The Best Thing Since Water," *the fifth estate*, CBC, January 7, 1997.

32 George Anders, *Health Against Wealth: HMOs and the Breakdown of Medical Trust*, Houghton Mifflin, New York, 1997.

33 *Sunday Morning*, CBC, February 9, 1997.

34 Ibid.

35 Colleen Fuller, "Restructuring Health Care: A Global Enterprise," Council of Canadians discussion paper, 1995.

36 Ibid.

37 Ian Austen, "Relax: This Won't Hurt a Bit," *Elm Street*, September 1997.

38 Nadene Rehnby, "Inventing Crisis: The Erosion of Public Confidence in Canadian Public Education," B.C.

NOTES

Teachers' Federation, 1996.

39 Lehman Brothers, "Investment Opportunity in the Education Industry," 1996, p.7.

40 Ibid., p.38.

41 Tony Clarke, *Silent Coup*, Lorimer, Toronto, 1997, p.159.

42 *Business Week*, June 30, 1997.

43 Maude Barlow and Heather-jane Robertson, *Class Warfare: The Assault on Canada's Schools*, Key Porter Books, Toronto, 1994, p.105.

44 Ibid.

45 Ibid., p.106.

46 David Robertson, "The Facts," Canadian Union of Public Employees, July-August 1985.

47 *Globe and Mail*, August 27, 1996.

48 KPMG, "A Comparison of Business Costs in Canada and the United States," 1995; *Globe and Mail*, November 13, 1996.

49 *Ottawa Citizen*, October 10, 1997.

50 Jim Stanford, interview with the author.

51 *Globe and Mail*, February 26, July 8, and October 8, 1997.

52 "Mergers and Acquisitions Jump in Third Quarter," *Globe and Mail*, October 8, 1997.

53 "Merger Wave Gathers Momentum," *Globe and Mail*, February 26, 1997.

54 *The Monitor*, Canadian Centre for Policy Alternatives, October 1997.

55 Alternative Federal Budget (short version), p.12.

56 *Globe and Mail*, January 23, 1997.

57 *Edmonton Journal*, July 25, 1997.

58 *The Monitor*, Canadian Centre for Policy Alternatives, May 1995.

59 *Globe and Mail*, November 10, 1997.

CHAPTER 10
THE MARKET STATE

1 Frank Stilwell, "Economic Rationalism: Sound Foundations for Policy?" in *Beyond the Market: Alternatives to Economic Rationalism*, ed. R. Rees, G. Rodley, and F. Stilwell, Pluto Press, Sydney, p.33.

2 Sam Gindin, "Notes on Labour at the End of the Century: Starting Over?" *Monthly Review*, July-August 1997.

3 Allan Engler, *Apostles of Greed*, Fernwood Publishing, Halifax, 1995, p.17.

4 Adam Smith, *Wealth of Nations*, Modern Library, New York, 1937, p.250.

5 Ibid., pp.78-79.

6 Analysis and data on New Zealand from Murray Dobbin, "The Remaking of New Zealand," CBC *Ideas*, October 12 and 19, 1994.

7 Paul Havemann, letter to the author, August 21, 1997.

8 Jonathon Boston, "The Ideas and Theories Underpinning the New Zealand Model," in *The Revolution in Public Management*, Oxford University Press, 1996, pp.29-30.

9 Ibid., p.28.

10 For a more detailed description of the charter experience in New Zealand, see Murray Dobbin, "Charter Schools: Charting a Course to Social Division," Canadian Centre for Policy Alternatives, Ottawa, 1997.

11 Havemann letter.

12 Roger Douglas, keynote address to the Reform Party of Canada convention, Saskatoon, 1991, in Murray Dobbin, *Preston Manning and the Reform Party*, Lorimer, Toronto, 1991, p.113.

13 Jane Kelsey, *The New Zealand Experiment*, Auckland University Press, 1995, p.29.

14 Maude Barlow and Bruce Campbell, *Straight Through the Heart*, Harper-Collins, Toronto, 1995, p.97.

15 In "The Liberals' Labour Strategy," Canadian Centre for Policy Alternatives, Ottawa, 1995, p.14.

16 *Globe and Mail*, May 3, 1997.

17 *Globe and Mail*, July 31, 1997.

18 Interview with the author, 1992.

19 "Exporting Canadian Culture," *Globe and Mail*, January 25, 1997.

20 Canadian Conference of the Arts, "Reductions in Departmental Spending, 1994-95 - 1998-99," in 1996 Federal

Budget, p.39.

21 "Exporting Canadian Culture," *Globe and Mail.*

22 Ibid.

23 Senate Standing Committee on Transport and Communications, Subcommittee on Communications, *Wired to Win: Canada's International Competitive Position in Communications,* interim report, April 1997, p.26.

24 Ibid., p.51.

25 Ibid.

26 In Michael Walker, ed., "Freedom, Democracy and Economic Welfare," Fraser Institute, 1988, p.48.

27 Barlow and Campbell, *Straight Through the Heart,* p.151.

28 Interview with the author, August 1997.

29 Ibid.

30 Interview with the author, September 1997.

31 Ontario Federation of Labour, "The Common Sense Revolution: 210 Days of Destruction," 1996.

32 Ibid.

CHAPTER 11
DEMOCRACY IN THE NEW MILLENNIUM

1 In *The Monitor,* Canadian Centre for Policy Alternatives, July–August 1997.

2 Samuel P. Huntington, in M. J. Crozier, S. P. Huntington, and J. Watanuki, eds., *The Crisis of Democracy: Report of the Governability of Democracies to the Trilateral Commission,* New York University Press, 1975, p.93.

3 Ibid., p.99.

4 Leo Panitch, "Changing Gears: Democratizing the Welfare State," pre-sentation to Fifth Conference on Social Welfare Policy, Bishop's University, Lennoxville, Que., August 1991.

5 Ibid.

6 James Tobin, "The Tobin Tax on International Monetary Transactions," Canadian Centre for Policy Alternatives, Ottawa, 1995.

7 The Genuine Progress Indicator, Redefining Progress, 1995.

8 *The Monitor,* Canadian Centre for Policy Alternatives, February 1996.

9 *The Monitor,* Canadian Centre for Policy Alternatives, November 1996.

10 *The Monitor,* Canadian Centre for Policy Alternatives, December 1996/January 1998.

11 Samuel Gindin, "Notes on Labour at the End of the Century: Starting Over?" *Monthly Review,* July–August 1997.

12 *Toronto Star,* August 12, 1997.

13 *Globe and Mail,* August 27, 1997.

14 Gindin, "Notes on Labour."

15 *Financial Post,* August 23, 1997.

16 "Global Good Times, Meet the Global Glut," *New York Times,* November 16, 1996.

17 *Globe and Mail,* November 9, 1996.

18 Angus Reid home page, March 29, 1996.

19 News release, undates, Preamble Center for Public Policy, home page.

20 Kees van der Pijl, "The History of Class Struggle," *Monthly Review,* May 1997.

21 Martin Khor, keynote address to the Council of Canadians annual general meeting, October 1997.

INDEX

INDEX